BAD TIME STORIES

Government-Union Conflicts and the Rhetoric
of Legitimation Strategies

YONATAN RESHEF AND CHARLES KEIM

Bad Time Stories

Government-Union Conflicts and the Rhetoric of Legitimation Strategies

UNIVERSITY OF TORONTO PRESS
Toronto Buffalo London

© University of Toronto Press 2014
University of Toronto Press
Toronto Buffalo London
www.utppublishing.com
Printed in the U.S.A.

ISBN 978-1-4426-4882-1

Printed on acid-free, 100% post-consumer recycled paper with vegetable-based inks.

Library and Archives Canada Cataloguing in Publication

Reshef, Yonatan, author
Bad time stories : government-union conflicts and the rhetoric of legitimation strategies / Yonatan Reshef and Charles Keim.

Includes bibliographical references and index.
ISBN 978-1-4426-4882-1 (bound)

1. Collective bargaining – Government employees – Canada – Cases.
2. Employee-management relations in government – Canada – Cases.
3. Communication in industrial relations – Canada – Case studies.
I. Keim, Charles, 1968–, author   II. Title.

HD8005.6.C3R48 2014   331.89'04135171   C2014-900791-4

This book has been published with the help of a grant from the Canadian Federation for the Humanities and Social Sciences, through the Awards to Scholarly publications Program, using funds provided by the Social Sciences and Humanities Research Council of Canada.

University of Toronto Press acknowledges the financial assistance to its publishing program of the Canada Council for the Arts and the Ontario Arts Council.

University of Toronto Press acknowledges the financial support of the Government of Canada through the Canada Book for its publishing activities.

Human conflict begins and ends via talk and text. We generate, shape, implement, remember and forget violent behavior between individuals, communities or states through specific discourse. It is discourse that prepares for sacrifice, justifies inhumanity, absolves from guilt, and demonizes the enemy.

(Nelson, 2003: 449)

Contents

Preface ix

Abbreviations xiii

1 Public-Sector Labour Conflicts: A Different Perspective   3

2 Key Concepts and a Note about the Data   8

3 Government Intervention in Industrial Relations   20

4 The Case Studies   43

5 Authorization-Legitimation Strategy   72

6 Rationalization-Legitimation Strategy   94

7 Moralization-Legitimation Strategy   119

8 Mythopoesis-Legitimation Strategy   151

9 It Is Not All the Same (Stories from Another Book?)   179

10 Findings and Conclusions   187

References   203

Index   215

Preface

In this book we explore how, in the late 1990s and the first decade of the new millennium, Canadian governments and unions mobilized language to frame and justify their viewpoints and conduct during labour conflicts in the public sector. The 1990s have been recognized as "the most stressful decade for public-sector industrial relations since the inception, 25 years earlier, of collective bargaining for public-sector workers" (Swimmer, 2001a: 1). A combination of high deficit and debt had prompted provincial governments to trim budgets, restructure the public sector, and redefine their roles as service providers. One result was a number of notable clashes between governments and unions protesting unprecedented wage rollbacks and layoffs.

The new millennium did not bring much relief. Still hobbled by deficits, debts, the rising costs of services, and a slowdown in consumer spending and overall growth, governments kept administering the unsavoury concoction of wage restraints and layoffs. Recently, Ontario's Premier Dalton McGuinty said that "we can protect our class size, we can protect full-day kindergarten and we can also protect jobs. But it does require that we put in place the kind of salary freeze that we have proposed to teachers" (Bradshaw and Stuec, 2012). These words were conciliatory relative to what many public-sector workers across Canada had experienced during the first decade of the 2000s, and what they would come to experience over the next few years (Fekete, 2011). Not surprisingly, according to the Conference Board of Canada (Shepherdson, 2011), workers deemed it unfair that governments were attempting to balance the books by cutting public-sector jobs and compensation. With frustrated workers expecting unions to deliver more and little left to bargain over, tension between public sector unions and governments was not abating (ibid.: 14-15).

Our study charts new ground by examining how the union-government conflicts were presented and justified through the use of language or, put differently, through a discourse of legitimation. As far as we know, this is the first attempt to explore how governments and unions have marshalled language to win support for their agendas and actions during conflict. We consider the resulting textual dynamics "discursive struggles," or language struggles, and argue that they are no less important than the economic and political dimensions of labour strife. Human beings "generate, shape, implement, remember and forget violent behavior between individuals, communities or states through a specific discourse. It is the mobilization of language that prepares for sacrifice, justifies inhumanity, absolves from guilt, and demonizes the enemy" (Nelson, 2003: 449). Discourses are socially influential, and in this sense labour disputes are also about achieving discursive dominance, which may translate into social, economic, and political supremacy. Hence discourses are worth struggling over and, for that very reason, deserve academic attention.

We draw on materials from seven case studies. Each one occurred in a different province – Saskatchewan, New Brunswick, Newfoundland, Nova Scotia, British Columbia, Alberta, and Quebec. We ask the following questions: How did the parties use language to advance their positions vis-à-vis each other and stakeholders? How did they mobilize language to discredit each other? How similar are the arguments, stories, and images applied by each side across all the cases? Are there themes that are common within government and union and also between them? What can we learn from a comparison of union and government legitimation efforts?

Newspapers are our main source of data. Speakers widely used this mode of communication to converse with the other party, their own constituents, and the public. This is not surprising since the written media play an influential role in the formation of public opinion and the transmission and promotion of particular beliefs and ideologies (Amer, 2009). Besides newspapers, we also drew upon newsletters, Hansard, budget addresses, speeches from the throne, and legal awards to understand the parties' legitimation efforts.

In chapters 5 to 9, we use a series of quotes to illustrate legitimation strategies or certain characteristics of a specific case. Each of these quotes receives a number that indicates the chapter where it appears and its place in the series of quotes belonging in that chapter (e.g., 5.1, 5.2, etc.). To enhance the text's readability and to facilitate the checking of these quotations, sources for the latter are generally presented in the body of the manuscript rather than being consigned to endnotes; however, in a few instances – government documents and the like, and some noteworthy statements published in newspapers – the sources appear both in the text and in the References section at the end of the book. Within the data, text enclosed in square brackets represents our own clarifications and comments.

The structure of the book is as follows. First, in the initial three chapters we sketch out the theme of the book, its intended contribution and conceptual framework, and the nature and extent of government intervention in industrial relations in Canada. Second, in chapter 4 we present the seven case studies. Third, in each of the next four chapters, 5–8, we examine closely the various legitimation strategies used. The discussion compares how each party employed language across the cases in the context of one specific legitimation strategy, while also providing a between-party comparison. Chapter 9 includes a brief discussion of four cases that produced discourses markedly different from the ones we focused on. Finally, chapter 10 sets out our major findings and conclusions.

Writing a book is a journey that may not be accomplished without support from others. We would like to thank the University of Alberta School of Business for its unwavering commitment to research. Reshef would also like to thank Nurit, Amir, and Maya for all the stories they keep crafting and sharing. Do not stop! Keim wishes to thank Hannah, Aden, Levi, Elli, and Rachel, who have provided a lifetime of stories. We would also like to thank two anonymous reviewers who spent a great deal of time and effort on reading, commenting on, and improving the manuscript. Needless to say, any errors, of commission or omission, are ours and ours only.

Abbreviations

ASBA	Alberta School Boards Association
ATA	Alberta Teachers' Association
BCPSEA	BC Public School Employers' Association
BCTF	BC Teachers' Federation
CDA	Critical Discourse Analysis
CSN	Confédération des syndicats nationaux
CSQ	Centrale des syndicats du Québec
CUPE	Canadian Union of Public Employees
FIQ	Fédération Interprofessionnelle de la santé du Québec
HEABC	Health Employers Association of British Columbia
HEU	Hospital Employees' Union
HRM	Human Resources Management
ILO	International Labour Organization
LPN	Licensed Practical Nurse
MLA	Member of the Legislative Assembly
MNA	Member of the National Assembly
NAPE	Newfoundland and Labrador Association of Public and Private Employees
NDP	New Democratic Party
NPM	New Public Management
NSGEU	Nova Scotia Government and General Employees' Union
NSNU	Nova Scotia Nurses's Union
NUPGE	National Union of Public and General Employees
PC	Progressive Conservative
PISA	Program for International Student Assessment
PQ	Parti Québécois
QFL	Quebec Federation of Labour

RN	Registered Nurse
SAHO	Saskatchewan Association of Health Organizations
SFPQ	Syndicat de la fonction publique du Québec
SPGQ	Syndicat de professionnelles et de professionnels du Québec
SUN	Saskatchewan Union of Nurses
TFA	Tentative Framework Agreement
UNA	United Nurses of Alberta

BAD TIME STORIES

Government-Union Conflicts and the Rhetoric
of Legitimation Strategies

Chapter One

Public-Sector Labour Conflicts: A Different Perspective

Since laws permitting public-sector workers in Canada to unionize were first enacted, collective bargaining has been the primary mechanism for determining wages, hours, and working conditions of workers in the public sector. (Here, public sector includes the civil service and the para-public sector, as well as such services as education and health care.) However, notwithstanding the enabling legislation, the past several decades have witnessed frequent unilateral actions by federal and provincial governments that undercut organized labour's ability to exercise its legal right to strike and negotiate collective agreements (Swimmer, 2001b; Thompson, 1986; Lewin and Goldenberg, 1980; Boivin, 1975). Specifically, governments have not hesitated to legislate public-sector workers back to work after the commencement of legal strike action, impose collective agreements, suspend worker rights to bargain and strike, restructure bargaining units, restrict bargaining agendas, and impose wage schemes.

Government unilateral actions have become so widespread that, in some experts' eyes, they render the notion of free collective bargaining a thing of the past (Adams, 2006: 139; Panitch and Swartz, 1988). The National Union of Public and General Employees (NUPGE), a federation of eleven public-sector unions, has deplored these developments: "The slow but progressive development of Canada's collective bargaining laws came to an abrupt end as we entered the 1980's, [with] the dramatic increase in the use of legislative interference by the federal and provincial governments to restrict and/or deny the collective bargaining rights of Canadian workers" (quoted in Adams, 2006: 98–9). Public-sector unions and employees were an easy target for government actions.

Public-sector employees are especially vulnerable because the government is their employer. Governments have access to a power no other employer has, the power to change the law to suit themselves. This power has been much abused in Canada. Legislatures have given the right to collective bargaining and governments have taken it away (Fudge, 2005: 2). Therefore, NUPGE urges its component unions to expect, and actively resist, intrusive government actions:

> Every Component should prepare for every round of bargaining with the view that one of the factors they might encounter may be the imposition of a contract, and the Component should prepare to confront this imposition as one of its key strategies. The confrontation may well involve a refusal to be bound by the legislation and require the continuation of strikes after they have been officially declared illegal. The right to strike was achieved in the first place by a combination of political lobbying and technically illegal activity. Governments that use the law to break the rules should have no right to expect us to obey the law. NUPGE (2006: 4)

Indeed, public-sector unions were not quiet bystanders and did not pull any punches in the face of government attempts to undercut their rights to strike and negotiate agreements (Reshef and Rastin, 2003; Camfield, 2007). Province-wide strikes, mass rallies, demonstrations, and days of action were but some of the efforts unions applied to express their frustration and rage with government assaults on labour rights.

Labour conflicts, especially strikes, are one of the most extensively researched industrial-relations phenomena and have been studied from various angles. Earlier writers such as Marx, Commons, Perlman, and the Webbs had explored the theme. Since then, more contemporary research has advanced our knowledge of how labour conflict may be commenced, perpetuated, and resolved. Understanding the determinants of strikes' duration, number, and volume has been a most popular research topic (Rees, 1952; Kaufman, 1982; Stern, 1978). Comparative analysis of strike patterns across nations has provided another fertile avenue for researchers using statistical methods to explore this expression of labour conflict (Poole, 1984; Hibbs, 1976). Politically oriented researchers have focused on the relationship between politics (e.g., the nature of the government party) and labour conflicts, thus adding a further dimension to the discussion (Shorter and Tilly, 1974; Korpi and Shalev, 1979; Reshef, 1986). More recently, Reshef and Rastin (2003) have studied the different reactions of public-sector unions to the challenges created by the Common Sense Revolution and the Klein Revolution in Ontario and

Alberta respectively. They argue that governments provided the stimuli that spurred union leaders to consider using collective action to foil government behaviour and policy that threatened their existence. Ultimately, their analysis concludes, union leaders' decision about whether or not to mobilize for collective action is a result of a cost-benefit analysis of the merit and viability of such action. The latter process, in turn, is a product of the leaders' perceived degree of the government threat, relevant beliefs, and interpretation of contextual cues.

These research efforts have improved significantly our understanding of labour conflicts. Generally, they focus on the more visible, and perhaps academically attractive, aspect of conflict behaviour, that is, the point where labour is mobilized to act collectively in defiance of employers and governments. Collective action, however, is but one expression of labour conflict, though highly observable and measurable. And indeed a focus on collective action may blind us to other important themes. We may fail to appreciate the bitterness of the dispute, and, as well, we may miss the efforts the parties have made to avoid a conflict, how the initial interaction between the parties has escalated to a full-fledged confrontation, and how the parties have attempted to convince stakeholders to endorse their positions. In short, a focus on the *statistics* of collective action has meant that unique aspects of labour disputes are ignored because they exist apart from the disputes' numerical characteristics. We wish to address such aspects and add to the extant knowledge by shifting the focus away from labour collective action and its numerical manifestations, determinants, goals, and outcomes. We bring to the discussion a hitherto unexplored question – how do public-sector unions and governments mobilize language to legitimate their own, and delegitimate their opponent's, behaviour during conflicts? Thus, language is at the centre of this book.

In the preface to *At War with Words*, Billing (2003: xv) states that "the words of war are central to the activity of war." Language plays a vital role before, during, and after wars and conflicts. As Nelson notes in the epigraph at the beginning of this book, conflicts and wars begin and end with words. In our context, before workers take to the streets and prior to government orders and legislation, words commit the first act of conflict. They also likely end every labour conflict, and probably set the conditions for further conflict. And so we should not neglect the role of language in labour conflicts.

Here, we explore the ways in which language is used to present and justify one's behaviour and discredit that of the opponent. Using various communication outlets, politicians can demonstrate that they are not cold, heavy-handed bureaucrats, hoping that their agendas and actions will not provoke the public to turn against them in the next elections. Union leaders may try to avoid the appearance of a greedy interest group pursuing self-serving interests at the expense of the public. With the public on their side, they may be in a better position to pressure the government to give in to their demands. Through the use of language, each party tries to gain public support, unite its ranks, prepare stakeholders and the public at large for its next move, and undermine its opponent.

This study thus adds a new interpretive lens to the canonical study of labour conflict, one that emphasizes language. We endeavour to glimpse anew the dynamics of union-government conflicts. However, we are not linguists attempting to raise social awareness by studying union-government conflicts. Rather, we are students of industrial relations looking at an intensively researched phenomenon from a different angle. We assume that in politics the most visible playing field for contests is the media. Of course, opposing opinions and agendas also clash in other venues, such as legislature assemblies and courts. However, the media provide the core conduit connecting the protagonists with the public, and sometimes even with each other.

The discussion of our seven case studies is informed by the following general assumptions. First, governments and unions are political entities with elected leaders who have vested interests in remaining in power. As such, they are compelled to publicly justify, or legitimate, behaviour that opposing stakeholders may consider irresponsible, unfair, opportunistic, and even illegal. Second, naturally, both parties seek favourable outcomes from their legitimation efforts. To influence attitudes, policies, and actions, such efforts should resonate with stakeholders' definitions of acceptable behaviour and social values, and touch upon their wishes and desires. Third, the production of legitimation texts should enable the parties to impart a sense of correctness, justify themselves, and discredit the other side. In other words, the parties use language to construct a reality that is congruent with their behaviour and interests.

In this book, then, we study an aspect of labour disputes that has not been on the forefront of industrial-relations research, namely, how the parties use language to build up a popular base for their positions, agendas, and actions. Overt manifestations of union-management disputes, such as strikes, demonstrations, designation of essential employees, and legislation, might have more immediate perceptible effects on stakeholders. Yet, in the long term, the party that achieves dominance through discursive struggles by shaping attitudes and sentiments might be more likely to shape future relationships, power structures, agendas, and perhaps even the contours of the next dispute.

It is also important to state what this book is not. Although we refer to collective bargaining and strikes throughout the manuscript, our book is not an analysis of these two venerable industrial-relations institutions. Nor does it attempt to explore how the advent of neo-liberalism has influenced governments' abilities to impose their will on labour through legislation, and unions' capacity to carry out collective action. Similarly, the book does not deal with the important question of the relationship between the nature of the political, legal, and economic environment and the likelihood of strikes. We touch on some of these issues when the discussion calls for it, but only in passing. To remind the reader, language is at the centre of our research, because we are explicitly concerned with how the parties used language to justify their behaviour, agenda, and position during conflicts.

Chapter Two

Key Concepts and a Note about the Data

The importance of language, written and spoken, in organizational research has long been recognized. Language, symbols, images, and metaphors are the principal mechanism that people use to create a coherent reality that frames their sense of who they are as members of a specific organization. Through talking and writing, visual representations, and the use of cultural artefacts, organization members can reproduce or transform core assumptions regarding how the organization should be run both economically and socially.

Like business organizations, governments and unions use language to reaffirm their raison d'être, enhance organizational solidarity (unions perhaps more than governments), and gain popularity. Our study is concerned with how government and union personnel, in the case studies under investigation, used language to convince members, stakeholders, and the general public that their actions were desirable and proper within a socially constructed system of norms, values, beliefs, and definitions. In other words, we are engaged in a discursive analysis of government and union legitimation efforts. In the following, we discuss the key concepts of our study, ending with a note on our data.

Discourse and Critical Discourse Analysis

Over a decade ago, Mumby and Clair (1997: 181) declared that "organizations exist only in so much as their members create them through discourse." More recently, in their introduction to *The Sage Handbook of Organizational Discourse*, Grant, Hardy, Oswick, and Putnam (2004: 1) have added that "a growing disillusionment with many of the mainstream theories and methodologies that underpin organizational studies has encouraged scholars to seek alternative ways in which to describe, analyse and theorize the increasingly complex processes and practices that constitute 'organization.' One outcome of this search has been that 'organization discourse' has emerged as an increasingly significant focus of interest." Perhaps this is why discourse analysis has increasingly been used as a method for understanding organizational phenomena (Suddaby and Greenwood, 2005: 39).

What is discourse? What gives it the extensive analytical appeal it commands? Broadly speaking, discourse covers "all forms of spoken interaction, formal and informal, and written texts of all kinds. So when we talk of 'discourse analysis' we mean analysis of any of these forms of discourse" (Potter and Wetherell, 1987: 7). Similarly, for Watson (2003: 46), "discourse is a set of concepts, statements, terms and expressions which constitute a way of talking or writing about a particular aspect of life, thus framing the way people understand and act with respect to that area of existence." These definitions imply that discourse occurs whenever human beings communicate regardless of the institutional setting or situation. Discourse analysis, in turn, is the systematic analysis of various modes of communication. Seen this way, discourse is the product of people who interact with each other in various ways, such as chatting, reporting, or negotiating.

Organizations can be conceived as a "particular aspect of life," one that is given substance and brought to life through the discourses its members develop. Within this realm, Grant, Keenoy, and Oswick (1998: 1) define discourse as "the languages and symbolic media we employ to describe, represent, interpret and theorize what we take to be the facticity of organizational life." Equally for Fairclough (2005: 925), an organizational discourse is "a particular way of representing certain parts or aspects of the (physical, social, psychological) [organizational] world." Mumby and Clair (1997: 181) echo this sentiment, maintaining that organizational discourse is "the principal means by which organization members create a coherent social reality that frames their sense of who they are" and "is both an expression and a creation of organizational structure." This is not to argue that organizations are nothing but discourse, but rather to point out the important role that discourse plays in the social construction of reality within organizations (see also Hardy, Palmer, and Phillips, 2000; Lessa, 2006). Through discourse, realities are constructed, made factual, and justified. When discursive practices manage to break away from the hegemony of dominant discourses, a new organizational reality may emerge.

The above quotes constitute a view of discourse as a powerful force which can create a coherent social reality in organizations by shaping relationships, power structures, and roles. Discourse is constructed by people for people. It provides the frames within which people make sense of particular issues and situations. Framing is the assigning of meaning to an interpretation of events. As we will demonstrate, by manipulating language, framing amplifies certain voices and mutes others; magnifies some perspectives and downplays others (Snow and Benford, 1988; Snow, Rochford, Worden, and Benford, 1986). To be effective, to eventually mobilize attitudes and actions, framing should resonate or fit with the life situation, ideology, and experience of constituents.

This study is framed within the scope of critical discourse analysis (CDA). CDA scholars examine discourse practices to decode relationships between language and ideology, language and power, language and control. They pay attention to the way in which power is used and enshrined within the political arena. They are concerned with the way political leaders use language to inscribe their political agendas on the public consciousness, convincing their citizenry to take a certain action, like going to war. CDA grew out of European linguistic analyses of war rhetoric. It was developed by Norman Fairclough and his colleagues (especially Ruth Wodak) and formally entered the academic spotlight with the publication of Fairclough's *Language and Power* (1989). CDA establishes a link between language and social structure by examining how text and talk reproduce and enforce social and political domination; it explores the way in which language enables society to function, how it generates and perpetuates such things as ideology, power, and conflict. For CDA scholars, words do not only convey information or opinion but are themselves tools or "loaded pistols" that are used to achieve a certain outcome. In our case studies, we are primarily concerned with uncovering the various discursive strategies by which union and government speakers tried to legitimate their positions and convince members of their audience to adopt, or support, a particular stance or course of action.

Thus far we have argued that the study of discourse is not only the study of patterns, commonalities, and relationships between texts vis-à-vis context and occasions but, more centrally, at least in the context of labour conflict, the study of what speakers aim to achieve by manipulating language. CDA pulls back the rhetorical trappings to reveal the semantic strategies, or moves, used by speakers to elicit certain reactions. This is particularly true for political utterances, like those we examine here.

As Dedaić (2006: 700) reminds us, the purpose of political speeches is "primarily persuasion rather than information or entertainment." Persuasion is the "attempt to change human behavior or to strengthen convictions and attitudes through communication" (ibid.: 702). Chilton (2004: 46) adds that "political actors, whether individuals or groups, cannot act by physical force alone, except in the extreme case," and so it is through language that action is sought and taken. It is through language that "the inspiring orator can ... lead a people, or rather mislead them, into believing that the narrow self-interests of the governing party are actually the interest of the people as a whole" (Joseph, 2006: 13).

Political discourse is a central focus of CDA. Reisigl (2008: 98) defines political discourse as "the practical science and art of effective or efficient speaking and writing in public. It is the science and art of persuasive language use." For Reisigl, the analysis of discourse "means to analyze the employment and effects of linguistic ... and other semiotic means of persuasion in rhetorical terms" (ibid.: 97). Within this context, political discourse is analysed for the way in which it enables speakers to "assert themselves against opponents, to gain followers, and to persuade addressees to adopt a promoted political opinion" (ibid.: 98). Political speakers wield sophisticated discursive tools and draw upon a large body of cultural and national discourses. Specialized analytical instruments are required for revealing the ways in which language is being manipulated to further a particular political agenda. Political speakers do not simply transmit facts; they also try to shape and articulate a nation's deepest convictions and persuade citizens to accept and fight for these values. Frequently, such convictions and values are presented as the "right ones" and are set against the wrong principles of an adversary, such as an opposition party or another nation. Fundamentally, political discourse is about taking sides. As Chilton (2004: 6) notes, "political activity does not exist without the use of language." It is through language that sides are created in the first place.

We treat labour conflict as a web of discursive practices used by governments and unions to create realities that advance their interests. The purpose of either party is to achieve discursive dominance, which means that, when one side's representation of events is legitimated as true, it neutralizes alternative versions of the same events. This in turn should translate into more concrete, material achievements. We study how government and union speakers mobilized language to achieve such dominance through legitimation strategies. The data sources we examine – the written mass media and various institutional publications – were designed by the parties involved to inform but also, perhaps more important, to construct contexts that would make persuasion and justification more credible. The texts are therefore linguistic representations of the world according to the protagonists of the labour conflicts we explore. They provide rich information about how governments and unions use language to legitimate their own behaviour and undercut the same effort of the opposing party.

Legitimacy

In political science, legitimacy is the popular acceptance of a governing regime among those subject to its authority. According to the German political philosopher Dolf Sternberger, "legitimacy is the foundation of such governmental power as is exercised both with a consciousness on the government's part that it has the right to govern and with some recognition by the governed of that right" (1968: 244). It "involves the capacity of the [political] system to engender and maintain the belief that the existing political institutions are the most appropriate ones for the society" (Lipset, 1960: 77). A regime becomes legitimate when those people subject to its authority approve of it. Whether or not people regard a political system as legitimate depends on the extent to which the regime's legitimation efforts fit with their values, needs, and expectations. Legitimacy, in short, is evaluative. Therefore, although a government's actions during labour conflicts might be within the purview of its sovereign powers and hence legal, legitimacy is not guaranteed. This may explain why democratic governments, such as those at the centre of this study, are compelled to justify their actions during labour disputes. Put simply, widespread acceptance of their actions, legal though they may be, is not guaranteed. Governments need to secure the support of a large portion of the voting population to retain power. Legitimation efforts are an important means to achieve this goal. So why are unions engaged in legitimation activities?

Legitimacy has universal applicability, which exceeds the realm of politics. In organization studies, "legitimacy is a generalized perception or assumption that the actions of an entity are desirable, proper, or appropriate within some socially constructed system of norms, values, beliefs, and definitions" (Suchman, 1995: 574). This definition highlights the cognitive and evaluative dimensions of the concept. To be legitimate, actions should be desirable to an audience and congruent with its definitions of right and wrong, acceptable and unacceptable, proper and improper. Like governments, unions may engage in legal collective actions that may or may not be legitimate. We propose that union leaders seek legitimacy from the rank and file for three main reasons: politically, like their government counterparts, they want to retain power and remain in office; practically, they rely on internal solidarity to apply successfully their organization's collective muscle; and, as we will demonstrate later, they also work hard to convince the public at large that their agenda and behaviour are congruent with the public's values and interests, and so deserve its support. Why do they seek the public's approval for their actions? Why do they need it? Perhaps one sweeping answer is provided by Sternberger, who asserts that "the desire for legitimacy is ... deeply rooted in human communities" (1968: 244). Unions want to be accepted and valued by society. They fought hard to gain legal and popular recognition and become a legitimate institution in democratic societies, and it is in their vested interest not to alienate the public and risk losing that hard-won legitimacy. Moreover, if the public endorses a union's behaviour and positions, government might be less likely to dismiss the union's agenda as narrow, serving the interests of a greedy sectarian group. This, in turn, should help the union pressure the government to yield to its demands.

Legitimation Strategies

If indeed discourses are socially influential (Fairclough and Wodak, 1997: 258), then they are worth struggling over. And, if indeed they shape the way people perceive and judge reality, then discursive superiority provides its practitioners with a valuable advantage. It follows that labour disputes are also about achieving discursive dominance, which in turn may help achieve, or maintain, social, economic, and political supremacy. In this sense, the parties' legitimation strategies assume an importance that should not be obscured by the more tangible aspects of labour disputes, such as strikes, rallies, injunctions, demands and counter-demands, and economic wins and losses.

Van Leeuwen (2008) and van Leeuwen and Wodak (1999) have distinguished the four archetypical legitimation strategies which comprise our analytical framework. The first is "authorization," meaning legitimation by reference to authority. This legitimation strategy answers questions such as: Why should we trust your words? Why should we follow you? Why should we accept your recommendation? The answers to such questions highlight several kinds of authorization legitimation strategies (van Leeuwen, 2008: 106–9). The authorization is personal if the answer is essentially "'because I say so,' or because 'so-and-so says so,' where the 'I' or the 'so-and-so' is someone in whom institutionalized authority is vested" (van Leeuwen and Wodak, 1999: 104). In this case, authority derives from the speaker's status, which, often, is a function of their organization and their position in the organization's power structure (e.g., a premier, a minister, a union leader). No additional justification is needed, since the speaker's statements are expected to be accepted at face value because "s/he must know what s/he is talking about."

The authority may also be impersonal; that is, it may be vested in regulations, expertise, laws, budgets, or markets. An audience should accept a plan of action, or a situation, because "the market has spoken," or because "the law says so." Authorization legitimation can also be based on expertise, so that instead of providing arguments and evidence, the speaker relies on an expert's advice that is expected to carry enough weight to justify a course of action. There are three other types of authority – role model, tradition, and conformity – but they are not relevant here.

The second type of legitimation strategy, "rationalization," is legitimation by reference to the utility (e.g., goals, uses, effects) of specific actions based on knowledge claims that are accepted in a given context as relevant ("instrumental rationalization") or as true to "the facts of life" ("theoretical rationalization"). People applying the instrumental form of this strategy justify actions by reference to the purposes, or functions, the actions serve. For example, government speakers may rationalize a back-to-work order by stressing the need to end a hardship in an essential service caused by the strike. The union speakers may justify such a strike by referring to years of neglect that can be ended only by forcing the government to act.

Theoretical rationalization defends the activity to be legitimated by arguing that it is part of a natural course of events; it is appropriate "because this is the way things are" (or "this is life," or "this is part of the job and it comes with the territory," or "kids will always be kids"). In other words, this "legitimation is grounded not on whether an action is morally justified, nor on whether it is purposeful or effective, but on whether it is founded on some kind of truth, on the way 'things are'" (van Leeuwen, 2008: 115–16). For instance, a union leader may justify a strike by arguing that it is the only way a union can impress its demands upon a government with any chance of success, because "governments only understand power." A government, in turn, may argue that it has ordered striking workers back to work because that is what governments do – they protect the existing social order.

The third legitimation strategy, "moral evaluation," is legitimation by reference to specific value systems, or domains, that provide the moral basis for legitimation. Sometimes, a value is simply and clearly asserted by using words such as "bad" or "good," "right" or "wrong." On other occasions, "an activity is referred to by means of an expression that distils from it a quality which links it to a discourse of values (which 'moralizes' it)" (van Leeuwen and Wodak, 1999: 108). Then, moralization evaluation is the product of linking a practice to specific discourses of values which, in turn, legitimate that practice. Frequently, the discourses are not made explicit: "They are only hinted at, by means of adjectives such as 'healthy,' 'normal,' 'natural,' 'useful,' and so on" (van Leeuwen, 2008: 110). It is left for the audience to apply its knowledge and understanding to assign a moral quality to these concepts.

In North America, for example, a government can maintain that public-sector restructuring is needed in order to make the sector more efficient. Most likely, the government would expect the public to endorse its effort because rendering the public sector more efficient "is the right thing to do; something that you would do too were you in our shoes, because the public wants more efficient public services." The discourse of efficiency, which in this society connotes a positive value, is expected to moralize the government's restructuring campaign. The government likely assumes that few, if any, will ask, "Why do we have to become more efficient?" Or "why do we have to be efficient at all?" Sometimes the value systems that should provide the moral basis for legitimation may be masked, and then only our common-sense knowledge of the cultural context reveals their legitimating role. In general, values are expected both to motivate and to persuade people. Values, therefore, can be used to motivate workers to go on strike and persuade other stakeholders to endorse the strike and support the strikers and their cause. Defending actions in terms of social values suggests that "anyone in the same situation might reasonably have done the same" (Provis, 1996: 473–4). In brief, moralization-legitimation strategy emphasizes motives that, seemingly, are expected to be endorsed publicly.

Rationalization maintains a relationship with moralization, a relationship that can shift depending on circumstance. The utility one seeks may or may not be moralized. Occasionally, rationalization and moralization may go hand in hand, but this may not be explicit. When employing the strategy of rationalization, morality may become oblique and submerged, taking a backseat to practical functions. In their studies on the legitimation of production unit shutdowns in multinational corporations, Vaara and Tienari (2008) provide an example of instrumental-rationalization legitimation – a company shutdown is justified by references to profitability improvement and annual savings (e.g., the company can produce the same products elsewhere for less). In addition to the utility of the shutdown, "profitability" and "savings" are strong values, at least in the realm of business. In industrial relations, a union can present a strike in a hospital as a means of fighting against bed closures. The government, in turn, can justify back-to-work legislation as a step necessary to protect public well-being. These decisions can also be supported by moral justification, as being "the right thing to do."

Sometimes, however, the end value associated with a policy or a plan may not justify the tools used to achieve it. Rationalization legitimation emphasizes utilitarian purposes which might translate into narrow vested interests. Usually, interests connote concrete goals that are related to individual choices and private, often economic, advancement. Moralization legitimation emphasizes values, which are linked to needs and desires that can be presented as the correct, occasionally idealized, modes of behaviour (Provis, 1996: 479). But people who share similar values may have conflicting interests. For example, those who appreciate the value of efficient public services may not agree on the concrete steps taken to promote efficiency in this sector, since such steps might have a direct negative bearing on the interests of clients, workers, or managers. In this case, different interest groups may seek differing, perhaps even conflicting, paths to greater efficiency.

The fourth and last type of legitimation strategy is "mythopoesis," or mythmaking. It refers to legitimation that is achieved through storytelling, or the construction of narrative structures to indicate how the issue in question relates to the past or the future. Narratives and stories are concepts that are so closely related that "when we speak of narrative, we are usually speaking of story" (Scholes, 1981: 206). The difference between these two concepts is slight: "A narration is the symbolic presentation of a sequence of events connected by subject matter and related by time ... When the telling provides this sequence with a certain kind of shape and a certain level of human interest, we are in the presence not merely of narrative but of story" (ibid.: 205–6). Unlike lists, narratives and stories relate facts using a core theme and present the result in an interesting way. Seemingly, the difference between a narrative and a story is a matter of degree: "As we move from narrative to story we are forced to recognize the increasing importance of *plot*, which 'knits events together,' allowing us to understand the deeper significance of an event in the light of others" (Gabriel, 2004: 64). Stories can be conceived of as narrative delivered in a more creative, elegant manner, invoking familiar elements "to contextually ground those that are less familiar" (Martens, Jennings, and Jennings, 2007: 1125) Given the similarity between narrative and story, we use the two terms interchangeably.

Narratives and stories can be based on fictional or non-fictional material. The texts we use comprise non-fictional narratives, or sequences of real-life events that frequently are structured like stories with a beginning, a middle, and an end, and with the addition of a purpose such as legitimation (Ochs, 1997: 195). In real life, a story becomes a powerful legitimation strategy when it resonates with an audience, when people can locate themselves in it (Shaw, Brown, and Bromiley, 1998). In this way, the story enables people to make sense of a complex reality and renders them more likely to embrace and identify with the plot.

Van Leeuwen and Wodak (1999: 110) distinguish two generic types of stories, moral and cautionary: "In *moral tales* the hero or heroes follow socially legitimate practices and are rewarded for this with a happy ending. In *cautionary* tales the hero or heroes engage in socially deviant behavior that results in an unhappy ending." In moral tales, protagonists are rewarded for engaging in acceptable social practices or for protecting the legitimate order; for example, a government that abrogates collective agreements and orders wage rollbacks can tell a story about its irresponsible predecessor, who brought society to the brink of bankruptcy by recklessly spending beyond its means, while, in contrast, the current government is showing leadership by making tough decisions designed to restore financial stability. Cautionary tales are about what will happen if the protagonist deviates from the norms of social practices. In the last example, the union may counter with a story about a government that, by breaching the legal right to strike, has endangered democracy and will be punished with a strike – and, the union hopes, at the polls. Using creatively metaphors and images, the speakers can craft an elegant, coherent, and memorable plot.

A reader first coming to our study may well pause and ask why we chose to use van Leeuwen and Wodak's framework. It should be noted at the outset that our choice is not due to a lack of frameworks. In fact, a review of the literature soon reveals a landscape dominated by frameworks, classifications, and categories. As researchers we were driven by two concerns – comprehensiveness and economy. We required a framework that would allow us to express the breadth of our analysis without getting lost in the data. We also needed to express parsimoniously the most salient aspects of the data. But fundamentally we wanted to provide the topography of the landscape, so that we could demarcate the main discursive strategies employed by speakers when legitimating themselves during public-sector labour conflict.

The model put forward by van Leeuwen and Wodak satisfied our need for structure and parsimony. It provided the means for organizing our massive amount of data into four general categories, thus keeping our analysis simple but not simplistic, accessible yet sophisticated. For instance, the analytical landscape concerning only one of the strategies discussed above, storytelling, is vast and replete with possibilities. At one extreme, we may recall the renowned Russian novelist Leo Tolstoy, who remarked how "all great literature is one of two stories; a man goes on a journey or a stranger comes to town." At the other end of the spectrum, we point to Georges Polti's (1917) work, *The Thirty-Six Dramatic Situations*, in which he provides a descriptive list of thirty-six categories that contain every dramatic situation that may occur in a story or performance. Somewhere in the middle we find Christopher Booker's (2004) recent work, *The Seven Basic Plots*, which outlines seven basic plots common to all stories. The relative frugality of the van Leeuwen and Wodak model enabled us to frame storytelling as an important legitimation strategy and organize the data in a manageable, practical, and meaningful manner.

Naturally, frameworks impose artificial boundaries; in fact, this is an essential quality of their analytical strength. However, the model boundaries we selected allowed us to begin charting a new landscape, a terra incognita in industrial-relations research. Employing a framework that had demonstrated its usefulness provided us with a way to embark on this endeavour and, we hope, will enable others to follow along with us on this exciting voyage.

In summary, this study examines the legitimation efforts of union and government personnel during labour disputes. These efforts have been conceptualized as legitimation strategies, which are the ways protagonists mobilize discursive resources to impart a sense of legitimacy to their own actions and arguments while casting a long shadow on those of their opponents. Authorization, rationalization, moralization, and mythopoesis comprise the analytical framework we use to organize, present, and analyse the data. These four legitimation strategies are not mutually exclusive. Frequently, they are intertwined, as multiple legitimation is often the most effective form of legitimation.

Remember, legitimation is about creating a sense of positive, beneficial, ethical, understandable, necessary, or otherwise acceptable action in a specific setting (Vaara and Tienari, 2008: 986). Human agents create this sense. Van Leeuwen and Wodak offer a useful analytical tool for examining the role of discourse in this creative process. When combined with critical discourse analysis, this tool enables us to deal with broader social practices and the power relations of the social actors involved. Labour conflict represents one opportunity to use this tool to explore how controversial, sometimes illegal, actions are defended; how protagonists justify the use of power; and how structures of domination (e.g., union – members, government – workers) are discursively constructed and used to win discursive struggles.

The Data

As we have mentioned before, we used seven case studies of labour conflicts, with each being drawn from a different province. These conflicts involved a disagreement between unions and governments and/or the direct public employer (e.g., a school board, a health-care authority) in the media. Each of them started either with deadlocked collective bargaining or with a government policy that had attracted the unions' wrath. Regardless of the exact reason, in all the seven cases government played an active role and, perhaps because of that, the media found interest in the events. Governments, however, do not intervene in every labour dispute and the media is not attracted to every conflict in the public sector. Thus, our choice of cases was not random. We consider the cases we selected "discursive events," for they produced a discernible discourse that we could analyse in this research.

Naturally, texts are data that can be approached from various analytical perspectives and interpreted in more than one way. Four legitimation strategies that are discussed from the perspectives of two parties across seven cases produced a wide canvas, and we had to paint with a broad brush. We would have liked to offer readers an opportunity to pass their own judgment on how we used the data by including all the raw data in the body of the book. However, space limitations made that impossible. Instead, we present only selective examples to illustrate the spectrum of arguments, images, and metaphors and to substantiate our discussion.

Chapter Three

Government Intervention in Industrial Relations

Patterns of Government Intervention

How do governments, as sovereigns, intervene in industrial relations? How frequent and widespread is this phenomenon? How many employees have been affected by it? What factors can predict the likelihood of government intervention? Since data have been collected systematically only from 1978, the evidence for the 1960s and most of the 1970s is sketchy. It is known, however, that governments began to erode the rights of unions to call strikes and engage in collective bargaining soon after these rights had been secured in law following the Second World War. According to Panitch and Swartz (1988: 31), during the 1960s, governments ordered their employees back to work on thirteen occasions, whereas in the 1970s they did so forty-one times. Thompson (1986: 108) reports that, between 1975 and 1983, there were forty instances of back-to-work legislation. More recently, NUPGE (2010) has indicated that, between 1982 and 2009, the federal government alone had passed thirteen pieces of back-to-work legislation while provincial governments had resorted to this measure seventy-five times. This information does not include interventions that occurred outside the structure of back-to-work legislation, through policies, budgets, and other types of restrictive labour legislation (e.g., suspension of bargaining rights, restrictions on scope of bargaining). In total, the federal government passed 24 and the provinces 165 pieces of restrictive labour legislation between 1982 and 2009 (ibid.).

Tables 1 and 2 provide more systematic data about government intervention in collective bargaining through legislation between January 1980 and December 2009. The tables distinguish seven settlement

Table 1 Settlement Stages, Major Collective Agreements, Public Sector, 1980–2009

Settlement Stage	Period I 1980–9		Period II 1990–9		Period III 2000–9	
	Number	Per cent	Number	Per cent	Number	Per cent
Direct bargaining	1,449	49.3	1,362	60.9	1,290	62.5
During work stoppage	90	3.1	63	2.8	21	1.0
Post-work stoppage	39	1.3	16	.7	38	1.8
Legislated	396	13.5	219	9.8	51	2.5
Arbitration	278	9.4	123	5.5	150	7.4
Mediation*	321	10.9	283	12.7	318	15.4
Conciliation**	366	12.5	169	7.6	195	9.4
Total number of agreements	2,939	100	2,235	100	2,063	100

Source: Calculations based on special data request from Human Resources and Social Development Canada's Major Wage Settlements database, for major collective agreements, usually of 500 or more employees.
*Includes mediation, mediation after work stoppage, and mediation commission.
**Includes conciliation officer and conciliation board.

Table 2 Settlements Stages, Employees Covered by Major Collective Agreements, Public Sector, 1980–2009

Settlement Stage	Period I 1980–9		Period II 1990–9		Period III 2000–9	
	Employees	Per cent	Employees	Per cent	Employees	Per cent
Direct bargaining	2,610,204	37.8	3,485,295	7.2	2,966,265	52.3
During work stoppage	437,106	6.3	154,792	2.5	77,620	1.4
Post-work stoppage	90,475	1.3	44,090	.7	214,810	3.7
Legislated	1,354,500	19.6	920,831	15.2	507,860	8.9
Arbitration	669,433	9.7	324,217	5.3	447,240	7.9
Mediation*	714,764	10.4	739,800	12.2	1,008,555	17.8
Conciliation**	1,027,329	14.9	422,077	6.9	452,670	8.0
Total number of employees covered	6,903,811	100	6,091,102	100	5,675,020	100

Source: Calculations based on special data request from Human Resources and Social Development Canada's Major Wage Settlements database, for major collective agreements, usually of 500 or more employees.
*Includes mediation, mediation after work stoppage, and mediation commission.
**Includes conciliation officer and conciliation board.

stages of major collective agreements in the public sector over three time periods – the 1980s, 1990s, and 2000–2010. The first three stages comprise settlements reached by the parties themselves before, during, or after the occurrence of a strike/lockout. The fourth one includes legislated settlements. The last three stages contain settlements reached with the help of a third party. In each time period, as revealed in Table 1, more than half of the total number of collective agreements were settled by the parties themselves. Over 49.0 per cent of the cases were settled by direct bargaining without any job action. Table 2 provides information on the number of employees covered by agreements settled at each stage across the same three time periods. Overall, the number of employees covered by agreements negotiated directly by the parties exceeds 45.0 per cent of the total employees covered by collective agreements.

The data demonstrate that legislation was a significant mechanism for settling disputes during the first two periods but was used less frequently in the last period. In Period I, it was used more frequently than any other dispute-settling mechanism. In Period II, it was used more frequently than conciliation and arbitration but less often than mediation. It was used least frequently in Period III, which, after 2006, witnessed no intervention through legislation. It should be noted that in 2007, in a landmark decision, the Supreme Court of Canada declared that collective bargaining was protected by the Charter of Rights of Freedoms. Therefore, governments could not tear up at will duly negotiated collective agreements. The Court ruled:

> (§86) Recognizing that workers have the right to bargain collectively as part of their freedom to associate reaffirms the values of dignity, equality and democracy that are inherent in the *Charter* ... the constitutional right to collective bargaining concerns the protection of the ability of workers to engage in associational activities, and their capacity to act in common to reach shared goals related to workplace issues and terms of employment ...
>
> (§89) Section 2(*d*) [of the Charter, which guarantees freedom of association] imposes corresponding duties on government employers to agree to meet and discuss with [their employees]. It also puts constraints on the exercise of legislative powers in respect of the right to collective bargaining ... (Supreme Court of Canada, 2007)

Whereas the effects of 2007 Supreme Court decision are yet to be systematically studied, the material decline in legislated collective agreements in the third period (see Table 1) might be related to it. The Court, however, did not preclude government intervention in labour conflicts through legislation. Governments are still free to terminate legal strikes using back-to-work legislation. In January 2009, for example, the Ontario government passed Bill 145 (An Act to Resolve Labour Disputes between York University and Canadian Union of Public Employees, Local 3903), which ended an eighty-five-day strike at York University by ordering back to work 3,350 contract faculty and teaching assistants. The preamble to the bill stipulated that "the public interest requires an exceptional and temporary solution to address the matters in dispute so that new collective agreements may be concluded through a fair process of mediation-arbitration, staff and students can return to class and the University can resume providing post-secondary education." And so the workers returned to work, but the government did not impose an agreement on them; instead, it referred the case to a mediator-arbitrator. Yet the mediator-arbitrator's proverbial hands were tied by the following legal restrictions:

§15 (2) In making an award, the mediator-arbitrator shall take into consideration all factors that he or she considers relevant, including the following criteria:
1. The employer's ability to pay in light of its fiscal situation.
2. The extent to which services may have to be reduced, in light of the award, if current funding and taxation are not increased.
3. The economic situation in Ontario and in the Greater Toronto Area.
4. A comparison, as between the employees and comparable employees in the public and private sectors, of the nature of the work performed and of the terms and conditions of employment.
5. The employer's ability to attract and retain qualified employees.

We return to this case in chapter 9.

Research suggests that government intervention may be associated with the prevailing economic situation and the government's orientation towards organized labour and collective bargaining in the public sector. According to Lewin and Goldenberg (1980: 251), "the combination of a more strained economic climate and a political climate which is less supportive of unionism and collective bargaining for public employees may spur further restrictions, including legal restrictions, on the scope of public sector bargaining." Indeed, during the 1980s, most of the restrictive legislation was a result of the Liberal federal government's Public

Sector Compensation Restraint Act (known as the "6 and 5" program). The initiative, which was embraced by most of the provinces, occurred between 1982 and 1984. It was designed to curb annual double-digit increases in inflation by restraining collective bargaining-based wage increases, and it specifically targeted the public sector. In Period I, 291 of 396 legislated settlements occurred in 1983.

In Period II, the first four years were ones of "retrenchment" (Rose, 2004). Governments tried to restructure their public sectors in an attempt to control expenditures, reduce budget deficits, and address public debt. Legislated wage rollbacks were one policy tool governments used to facilitate their efforts. Between 1991 and 1994, governments legislated 208 wage settlements. The total number of legislated settlements for the 1990s was 219. As previously noted, Period III experienced a sharp decline in legislated agreements. Between 2000 and 2009, governments legislated fifty-one settlements, thirty-five of which occurred in Quebec in 2005. In December of that year, the Quebec Liberal government passed Bill 142, which applied to more than 500,000 hospital workers, teachers, civil servants, school-support staff, and other provincial employees. It imposed a thirty-three-month wage freeze (retroactive to 30 June 2003) and an annual wage increase of 2.0 per cent in the last four years of an almost seven-year contract. Taken together, the bill gave public-sector employees an average 1.2 per cent wage increase per year. The average inflation rate for the period was about 2.0 per cent per year.

More than a decade ago, Gunderson and Hyatt (1996: 264) pointed out that "legislated intervention, such as wage controls, back-to-work legislation, or 'social contracts,' are now more common means of dispute resolution in the public sector than are arbitration and the strike combined." Some researchers believe that the phenomenon is here to stay. Rose (2004: 289–90) speculates that, even when they experience economic expansion, "governments are not prepared to restore a genuine collective bargaining system and unions are not in a position to compel them to do so," and so "constrained collective bargaining will likely remain a fixture of the public sector labor relations for years to come." In a similar vein, writing in the 1980s and early 2000s respectively, Weiler (1986: 39) and Gunderson (2005: 406) expected that public-sector unions would continue to be subjected to legislated wage restraints, whether in the form of a wage freeze or wage guidelines, with their ability to strike either eliminated or circumscribed through such means as back-to-work legislation, a prohibition on strikes through the designation of workers as essential, or a freeze on existing agreements. Time will tell if the recent decline in legislated settlements is a long-term trend or just a temporary lull.

Notwithstanding their frequent intervention, Canadian governments did not engage in an all-out attack on industrial-relations institutions (Thompson, 1986; Adams, 2001: 223). This is why government intervention was not translated into a historical defeat of the Canadian labour movement that could mark the beginning of a new era in industrial relations. Consequently, "collective bargaining might be restricted at will, but it still exists within a solid legal framework; unions might be marginalized, but they are not eliminated" (Reshef, 2007: 679). Put differently, continuity rather than a radical break with the past has characterized the federal and provincial industrial-relations systems (Thompson and Rose, 2003: 321). Possibly, therefore, labour's right to strike and collective bargaining have been gradually eroded, their vitality slowly sapped. As a result, "in the public sector of the future, we may see a highly organized work force employed under conditions established unilaterally by the employer" (Thompson and Swimmer, 1995: 434).

The notion that, generally, Canadian governments accept the structure and role of the existing industrial-relations institutions has received additional support from Haddow and Klassen (2006). They compare the impact of partisan differences among governing parties on labour-market policy making from 1990 to 2003 in four Canadian provinces: Ontario, Quebec, British Columbia, and Alberta. The period they researched perhaps witnessed the most significant change in Canadian labour-market policy, with Canadian governments, provincial and federal, rethinking their role as service providers, introducing deep budget cuts to eliminate deficits and debts, and streamlining public sectors to facilitate those cuts. This era provided governments with propitious opportunities to cripple organized labour for the long haul. Yet none of the four governments took advantage of those circumstances to transform industrial relations. Even when Ontario's Progressive Conservative government did introduce anti-labour legislation in the second half of the 1990s, it was aimed to offset its predecessor's pro-labour actions, which had swung the pendulum in favour of organized labour.

The above discussion highlights several attributes of government intervention in industrial relations. It describes the form and scope of the intervention; suggests that, although the phenomenon declined in the first decade of the 2000s, it is not likely to disappear completely any time soon; and maintains that, despite frequent government interventions, unions and collective bargaining have not become "a thing of the past."

Unfortunately, little is known about the mechanics of government-union interactions during conflicts. How do the parties act out their feuds? How do they try to influence each other and others? How do they manipulate language to this end? What arguments do they craft to justify their behaviour and condemn that of their opponents? In the case studies examined here, we address these questions by focusing on how unions, employers, and governments mobilized language to legitimate their actions and arguments during public-sector labour disputes.

General Context

"Discourse is not produced without context and cannot be understood without taking context into consideration" (Fairclough and Wodak, 1997: 276; also Hardy, Palmer, and Phillips, 2000: 1233; Grant and Hardy, 2003). What were the main features of the social, economic, and political contexts of our case studies? Each dispute occurred in and was shaped by its own local context, which comprised such elements as the industry, relevant laws, various customs and practices, the identity of the government party, the government and union agendas, past experiences, and the economic situation. But, at the same time, they were all subjected to similar features of the national political, social, and economic systems. One such feature has already been discussed, that is, the tendency of Canadian governments to intervene in industrial relations and labour disputes. Below, we discuss two additional ones.

The events analysed herein took place between 1994 and 2005. Since the early 1980s, government decisions and actions had occurred in broad economic, political, and ideological contexts emphasizing the discourses of neo-liberalism and New Public Management (NPM). During this period, the language and ideas of neo-liberalism permeated Canada and acquired a powerful ideological as well as analytical dimension (Swimmer, 2001b; Reshef and Rastin, 2003; Haddow and Klassen, 2006. [Useful sources about neo-liberalism are Bourdieu, 1998; George, 1999; Martinez and Garcia, 1996.]) It became a tool in the hands of policy makers and other change agents, promoting the restructuring of the government, reduced investment in social services, moderation in wages, and greater flexibility in work organization. Over time, these actions assumed positive value connotations. In many provinces, a majority of voters were convinced that policies such as public-sector restructuring, budget cuts, and privatization were necessary and appropriate, and therefore gave their support to parties advocating a neo-liberal agenda.

These programs sanctified the power of markets in the name of economic efficiency, growth, and prosperity and sought the abolition of administrative and political barriers to competition. Neo-liberal discourse was further augmented by the discourse of New Public Management, which injected the logic of the free market into the public sector.

During the 1980s and 1990s, the field of public administration was dominated by NPM, which, as Andresani and Ferlie (2006: 416) point out, was often referred to as the grand narrative of public-management reform. Fattore, Dubois, and Lapenta (2012: 218) argue that NPM should be regarded as "sets of ideas rather than as paradigms." Its origins lie in the consolidating of new institutional economics (public choice, transaction cost, and principal-agent theory) and scientific management-based business philosophies. NPM's focus is on intra-organizational processes and management. It emphasizes the efficiency of those processes and the appropriateness of management principles and structure in producing public services (Osborne, 2006). NPM elevates the powerful combination of an empowered and entrepreneurial management over the more traditional view of autonomous public-sector professionals and administrators. Rather than the customary attention paid to the central activity of planning, NPM favours the use of quasi-market forces. In addition, it places a greater emphasis on the use of performance measurement, monitoring, and audit systems (Andresani and Ferlie, 2006). In place of more collaborative reforms, NPM developments are typically top-down in nature, driven by a "reformist" central government seeking to maximize the utility of large operational agencies and functions. Fattore, Dubois, and Lapenta (2012: 219) argue that the central aim of NPM is to "enhance government performance by promoting the 'three Es' (economy, efficiency, and effectiveness) and by introducing management principles that often have been transferred from business."

A common NPM prescription is that governments, like their business counterparts, should downsize and outsource at least some of their operations. Osborne and Gaebler (1992) provide a popular image of how government can increase its entrepreneurial nature by arguing that it should distinguish between "steering" and "rowing." "Steering" is shorthand for setting policies, delivering funds to operational bodies (public and private), and evaluating performance, together with reducing the government role in operations. "Rowing" refers to operational management. Governments should focus on steering while minimizing their involvement in rowing. Thus, NPM re-establishes the traditional dichotomy between government policy and administration function with a clear line drawn between the two (Metcalfe and Richards, 1990). Not surprisingly, NPM figures prominently in the thinking of those who believe that smaller governments are preferable to larger ones. As well, for those trumpeting the virtues of NPM, discussions are often concerned with how budgets can be streamlined rather than with how outcomes can be enhanced.

An early proponent of these developments was British Prime Minister Margaret Thatcher (1979–90), who, upon election, reformed British government by reducing the autonomy of the civil-service arm of the government, making government operations more economical and efficient, and enhancing the freedom of individual citizens (Aucoin, 1995: 1). To facilitate these reforms, the Thatcher government introduced major changes in organizational design and managerial practices in the public sector. These changes were crystallized by a new managerial discourse, that of NPM. It emphasized a leaner, more efficient public sector, reflecting the government's new focus on policy formation and regulation and its reduced involvement in service delivery. Thatcher identified unions as a major roadblock to the efficient operation of the market and the public sector. Consequently, a cornerstone of Thatcherism was a profound anti-union sentiment, which found expression in a string of labour laws geared to undercutting the unions and a bitter one-year dispute with the National Union of Mineworkers (1984–5).

Neo-liberalism and New Public Management found strong support in Canada (Swimmer, 2001a: 8–9; Schwartz, 1997; OECD, 1993: 44–5). We note, however, that in recent years it has become more difficult to assess the extent to which governments draw consciously on the NPM model. In fact, there is evidence that as a coherent approach "NPM is dead," even though elements of the model can still be found (Dunleavy et al., 2006). As a result of the 1990–1 recession, which led to falling tax revenues and increased social-welfare expenditures, every provincial government experienced a growing debt and budget deficit. To make matters worse, federal grants to the provinces for social programs were reduced by $6 billion (or 37 per cent) between the 1995–6 and 1997–8 fiscal years (Swimmer, 2001a: 3). The 1990s also witnessed mounting accumulated debt levels across all provinces, a consequence of a decade of government deficits and high interest rates. As Swimmer (ibid.) observes, "provincial debts climbed steadily between 1988 and 1996, with big jumps between 1992 and 1994, reflecting the large deficits in that period." Fiscal calamity loomed large, rendering drastic budgetary restraint imminent.

Several provincial governments launched a blitzkrieg on budget deficits and provincial debts, with the heavy artillery being reduced investment in social services and public-sector restructuring. The campaigns were guided by a philosophy that stressed leaner and more efficient governments with significantly reduced service-provider roles. In the name of market supremacy and service efficiency, governments pursuing neo-liberalism and NPM did not hesitate to subordinate industrial-relations institutions to political agendas and business interests. They tried to emancipate the public sector from the yoke of unions and collective agreements, which restricted governments' freedom to modernize their public sectors (i.e., downsize and privatize public services). In this context, when a government intervened in industrial relations, it was likely to undermine a union's capacity to protect its members by, for example, rendering job action less probable or short-lived, forcing acceptance of the employers' last offer, and limiting the scope of future collective bargaining.

In this context one should recall that an important component of Thatcherism was a profound anti-union sentiment. One of her 1979 campaign slogans, "Who rules England?" implied that if she were elected, she would not let the unions dictate any agenda to her government. In contrast, unions in Canada were not made the primary target of public-sector restructuring. On a few occasions, for ideological reasons, governments acted with the premeditated intention of undermining organized labour (Reshef, 2007; Rastin and Reshef, 2003: 19–20, 95). But in most cases, provincial governments set their sights on curbing inflation, trimming budgets, or restructuring the public sector, and the unions were caught "in the line of fire."

In Haddow and Klassen's study (2006), not even one of the four governments examined – British Columbia, Alberta, Ontario, and Quebec – took advantage of being in power during difficult economic times to launch an assault on unions. In the cases of British Columbia and Ontario, newly elected centre-right governments replaced pro-labour, centre-left governments in 2001 and 1995 respectively. In each province, the government introduced policies that reversed the situation in industrial relations to what it was before the pro-labour parties took office. Generally, notwithstanding their frequent and mostly anti-union intervention in industrial relations, Canadian governments did not have an anti-union agenda. For them, industrial relations were non-problematic until ad hoc events proved otherwise. Only then did they step in with measures that frequently undermined unions by, for example, abrogating existing collective agreements and/or banning legal strikes.

The following three cases illustrate many of the points made above, and provide additional details on the growing tensions between governments struggling to achieve fiscal stability and unions refusing to let that happen on the backs of their members. During the 1990s and early 2000s, the Alberta, Ontario, and British Columbia governments were prominent proponents of neo-liberalism. Their efforts served as templates for other provinces facing fiscal challenges. In terms of public-sector industrial relations, the legacy of their ideologies, policies, and public-sector restructuring techniques lingered for years following the "official" conclusion of their campaigns to balance budgets and eliminate debts. In fact, it seems that in some ways those campaigns are not over, as evidenced by how some provincial governments still try to deal with budget deficits and provincial debts. The following overview, relying partially on Reshef and Rastin (2003), aims to illuminate the origins and nature of the labour conflicts we discuss.

Alberta: Welcome to Ralph's World

Upon election in June 1993, Premier Ralph Klein and his Progressive Conservative government embarked on an ambitious plan, popularly known as the Klein Revolution, to balance the budget within four years without raising taxes and to eliminate the provincial debt by 2010. Budget cuts and public-sector restructuring were the two main policy tools. Between 1993 and 1996, the budget for basic education was cut by 5.6 per cent, higher education by 15.3 per cent, health care by 17.7 per cent, and general welfare by 19.1 per cent. Other departments would take average budget cuts of 20.0 per cent. Consequently, between 1993 and 1996, Alberta brought its level of provincial spending to an exceptionally low level, "by a considerable measure, the lowest per capita in Canada" (McMillan, 1996: 15).

In its battle to put the province back on solid financial ground, in 1993 the government enacted the Deficit Elimination Act, which saw Alberta's deficit wiped out in less than three years. In 1995 the government tightened its grip on its fiscal goal by enacting the Balanced Budget and Debt Retirement Act, which forbade deficit spending. Section 2 of the act provided that "expenditures during a fiscal year must not be more than revenue." The act outlined procedures the budget-planning process must follow to prevent unplanned deficits. In addition, it required that any surplus the government realized must be directed to paying down the provincial debt. To guarantee the elimination of

Alberta's accumulated debt, in early 1999 the government enacted the Fiscal Responsibility Act, which called for Alberta's accumulated debt to be wiped out in twenty-five years and set five-year milestones to ensure progress.

To facilitate the deficit-elimination process, in October 1993 the government asked all health-care employees to voluntarily take a 5.0 per cent pay cut followed by two years of wage freeze. In November 1993 it announced that the salary budgets for health, education, advanced education, and public administration were being cut by 5.0 per cent. Consequently, all public-sector employees were expected to take a 5.0 per cent wage rollback followed by zero wage increases in each of the next two years. Unions were expected to voluntarily negotiate the –5,0,0 scheme with their respective employers, and most complied. Arbitrators imposed the scheme in the few cases where unions had resisted.

A comprehensive restructuring of the civil service was a major component of the Klein Revolution. This thrust had been driven by a business-planning approach, privatization of government services, and human resources management (HRM) innovation. Following the 1993 budget, each government agency developed a three-year business plan that indicated its needs, goals, achievement tactics, and performance measures. The business plans were meant to reflect the government's commitment to "transparency" and "accountability." By defining concrete goals and clearly describing strategies for their achievement, the plans were intended to make it possible for the public to evaluate the government's performance. In addition, the business plans were designed to facilitate the government's scheme to minimize its role in the marketplace, or, in Klein's parlance, to "get out of the business of business." The Klein government privatized several services, such as highway maintenance, payrolls, automobile licensing and registries, corporate records, boiler inspection, and treasury branches. As a result of the restructuring campaign, between 1993 and 1997, the number of government employees dropped by 23.5 per cent, from 27,705 to 21,193, a milestone on the government's road to becoming leaner and more efficient (Alberta Personnel Administration Office, 1995, 1996, and 1997).

In education, 60 new school boards replaced 146 boards. But, more important, in 1994 the government enacted the School Amendment Act, which strengthened the role of the education minister at the expense of local, especially public, school boards by transferring their taxation powers to cabinet. The effort to restructure the education system included a reduction of the teaching workforce. By early 1997, there were about fifteen hundred (about 5.0 per cent of the 1993 teaching workforce) fewer teachers than three years earlier (Johnsrude, 1997).

In health care, a regionalization process was carried out to promote the integration of institutions and services within a regional structure and decentralize decision making (Alberta, Health Planning Secretariat, 1993). Consequently, 17 regional health authorities replaced some 200 hospital boards. Every hospital has been incorporated with all, or most, other health-care facilities in its region, and the site-based decision-making process has assumed a regional focus. Following regionalization, sometimes, different groups of employees under different collective agreements performed similar work for the same employer. Occasionally, members of similar bargaining units would work side by side, a situation known as "intermingling." To resolve the problem, the Alberta Labour Relations Board provided the following rule: if one or the only union represented between approximately 20 per cent and 80 per cent of employees in the consolidated unit, the board would conduct a representation vote to determine employees' wishes on representation. A union representing less than 20 per cent of the union-eligible workforce would not be included on the ballot for the vote. Thus, where health-care services were merged across existing bargaining unit boundaries, some unions would lose their bargaining rights without a representation vote if they represented less than 20 per cent of a bargaining unit. If one union represented more than 80 per cent of the workers in the consolidated unit, it would become the bargaining agent for the consolidated unit without a vote. In addition, to cope with budget cuts, between 1993 and 1995, the Alberta health-care workforce declined by 21.2 per cent, from 65,512 to 51,639 employees (Alberta Health, 1994 and 1995).

The above developments were important landmarks in the Alberta government campaign to promote the "Alberta Advantage," which implied that flexible labour policies, privatization, and low overall labour costs were an effective business-promoting strategy. The first few years following the end of the Klein Revolution in 1997 witnessed an economic upswing that raised worker expectations for higher wages and improved working conditions. The Alberta case presented in this book is a result of such rising expectations among teachers and the government's reluctance to meet them.

More recently, like the rest of the modern global economy, Alberta has been suffering the repercussions of the 2008 economic crisis. That year, natural-gas revenues were $5.8 billion. In 2012–13 it was estimated that natural-gas revenues would be $1.2 billion, or about one-fifth of what they were just four years ago. The strong value of the Canadian dollar also affected the bottom line. In 2012–13, for every one-cent increase in the exchange rate over a course of twelve months, Alberta would receive $247 million less in revenue (Liepert, 2012). Not surprisingly perhaps, following the recession of 2008–9, Alberta lost 28,000 jobs. However, Alberta's recovery was impressive. By June 2011, all of those jobs had been recovered, and then some. In early 2012 Alberta's economy was forecast to grow by a healthy 3.8 per cent, up from 3.5 per cent in 2011. That year, the government posted a budget deficit of $886 million. It forecast a balanced budget the following year, and a $5.2-billion surplus by 2014–15. Increasing revenues were mainly due to higher income-tax returns, a result of the strength of the economy, and rising oil prices.

Unfortunately, by late 2012 this rosy picture was severely tainted. Falling oil revenues and a volatile global marketplace led Finance Minister Doug Horner to announce that the projected deficit for 2012–13 could rise to between $2.3 billion and $3.0 billion. In the first three months of the fiscal year, overall revenue decreased by $400 million. To reach a balanced budget by 2014, all government departments were directed to spend less than their budgets and find other efficiencies to save at least $500 million in total. According to Horner, "there will be no new money for public-service sector negotiations until we see improvement" (Bennett, 2012). Premier Alison Redford stated that the province might have to borrow to build roads, schools, and hospitals. The rhetoric was tailored to justify what had been a faux pas in the preceding twenty years: "There's lots of different ways to talk about deficits, but one thing we can't have is an infrastructure deficit," Redford said. "We have to make sure we're keeping up with what you need and with what your communities need" (O'Donnell, 2012). What this means in practice is yet to be seen.

Ontario: Harris's Common Sense Revolution

In June 1995, led by Mike Harris, the Progressive Conservative Party of Ontario returned to power after a ten-year hiatus. A year earlier, in May, Harris made a bold move when he unveiled his Common Sense Revolution in a document so entitled. Patterned after the Klein Revolution, it advocated the elimination of the deficit over five years along with 13,000 government jobs; a cut of 20 per cent in all government expenditures except health, law enforcement, and classroom funding; a reduction in the personal income-tax rate of 30 per cent; a reduction in welfare benefits to 10 per cent above the national average, with mandatory "workfare" and "learnfare" for all except single parents with young children; and a repeal of the Rae government's Bill 40 (Ontario Progressive Party, 1994; Dyck, 1996: 361). In 1992, less than two years after leading his New Democratic Party to its historic victory, Premier Bob Rae had tabled Bill 40, which introduced several pro-labour amendments to the Labour Relations Act. In Rae's words, Bill 40 "made it easier for employees to unionize, and harder for an employer to break a union. It brought cases to the labour board faster, allowed for the reinstatement of workers found to be unfairly harassed by an employer, and prevented the use of replacement workers during the course of a legal strike" (Rae, 1997: 266). Bill 40 came into force in January 1993.

In 1999–2000 the Harris government achieved its balanced-budget target. As promised, the road to this destination was paved with budget cuts to the tune of $4 billion, reduced welfare benefits, the elimination of employment equity and its quotas, and a significant reduction of the public-sector workforce. For example, the government cut over 14,000 of 81,251 full-time-equivalent public-service positions (*Canadian Business*, 1995: 15; Courchene and Telmer, 1998: 175–6). Contrary to prior promises, cuts were made to the education and health-care budgets. Workforce adjustments were to follow promptly. In education, in 1992–3 there were 125,334 teachers in Ontario's elementary and secondary schools. The comparable figure for 1996–7 was 115,740 (Statistics Canada, 2000; Dare, 1997: 20–6). At the same time, the number of students grew by close to 40,000 (Ontario Ministry of Education, 1996–7) In health care, in 1993, the Ontario hospitals employed 176,000 employees, whereas in 1997 the figure dropped to 158,400 (Statistics Canada, 1998).

Given the heavy unionization rate of the Ontario public sector, union opposition to the budget cuts and associated public-sector restructuring was inevitable. How did the government heed the union concerns? Rose's conclusion about the implications of the Common Sense Revolution for unions and labour relations is worth repeating at length:

> The Harris Government represents a departure from the past in three important respects. First, consultation with organized labour and the search for consensus have been abandoned. Second, accommodating organized labour is no longer deemed essential to attracting business investment. There has been a major shift in emphasis – labour relations [sic] is no longer considered a *qui pro quo* for attracting investment. Third, pragmatism has given way to a doctrinaire approach to labour reform and economic adjustment. It should be noted that the Harris Government has not limited

itself to reducing public expenditures and restructuring the broader public sector. A number of initiatives have rescinded union rights that have been in place for decades (e.g., card-based certification and successor rights). In the process, the province's rich tradition of promoting harmony and cooperation has been replaced by confrontation with organized labour. (1998: 48; emphasis in original)

Harris, perceiving unions as a potential barrier to smooth implementation of his agenda and perhaps being ideologically opposed to them, had decided to confront and undercut organized labour. His government used extensive legislation to alter the industrial-relations rules of the game, thereby undermining the unions' capacity to derail the restructuring campaign by working within the system through established industrial-relations institutions (Dare, 1997). For example, in October 1995, the government passed Bill 7, the Labour Relations Employment Statutes Law Amendment Act, which restored the status quo ante by repealing the New Democratic Party (NDP) labour-law amendments (Bill 40). Among the other elements of Bill 40 that Bill 7 overturned were: the prohibition on the use of strike-replacement workers; protection for striking employees, including continuation of benefits during a strike or a lockout and return-to-work provisions based on employee seniority; automatic access to first-contract arbitration; and the right of unions to picket or organize on private property to which the public normally has access (e.g., shopping malls).

While Bill 7 targeted all unions in Ontario, it had special implications for civil servants and their union, the Ontario Public Service Employees Union. The bill removed civil servants' successor rights from the Crown Employees Collective Bargaining Act. Successor rights – labour-code provisions that allow the continuation of a collective agreement, and that recognize a union's right to continue to represent employees in a bargaining unit, when a cohesive business or function is sold, transferred, or otherwise divested – had been granted to the Ontario civil servants in 1975 (Rapaport, 1999: 46). Their elimination was to pave the road for efficient privatization of government services. In addition, to ensure the smooth reorganization of government offices and agencies, Bill 7 removed civil servants' arbitration rights in job-classification disputes.

Like its Alberta counterpart, the Ontario government used NPM to streamline its public-sector performance. It is worth recalling that NPM was "never all that new, it was mainly borrowed. It was never public, it was mainly derived from private sector experience. It was never strictly management, there was always a strong ideological component in the approach" (Thomas, 2003: 3). The driving force behind the policy decisions of the Harris government was a focus on cost cutting and determining how ministries could do more with less, rather than what should be done regardless of costs. According to McLellan (1997), Harris's administration developed a centralized policy for all government ministries, as opposed to previous efforts that were piecemeal and decentralized. The centerpiece of its plan for streamlining and reinvigorating government was the promise to reduce the size of the public service by 13,000 positions over five years, encourage more business and private involvement, and increase the quality of services by creating a new kind of government (White 2000).

The potential consequences of focusing on trimming budgets and the subsequent emphasis on contracting out, however, were cast in stark relief by the events of the 2000 water tragedy in which an E. coli outbreak killed seven people, and infected twenty-five hundred more, in Walkerton, Ontario. The Walkerton Inquiry Report found that a weakened Ministry of Environment was unable to detect problems with Walkerton's newly privatized water supply. Harris's government had changed many of the core functions of the department but ensured that only 28.0 per cent of its former responsibilities were being performed by outside organizations or municipalities. In this case, the privatization of drinking water was not accompanied by a proper regulatory regime that could effectively respond to an E. coli outbreak. Under Harris, numerous public-service positions had been cut in the name of NPM, but the loss of key services had not been addressed.

The years following the Common Sense Revolution were tumultuous. In October 2003 the Liberal Party returned to office after spending fourteen years in opposition. Upon election, Dalton McGuinty, the premier-designate, asked former provincial auditor Erik Peters to conduct an independent review of the province's finances. Peters concluded that Ontario faced a projected deficit of $5.6 billion for 2003–4. The 2003 Economic Outlook and Fiscal Review, released by the minister of finance in December, showed that the deficit identified by Peters was not a one-year anomaly in an otherwise healthy fiscal situation. It was a chronic, structural deficit caused by several years of much faster growth in program spending than in government tax revenues. Unless addressed, this imbalance would lead to continued budgetary deficits over the medium term. The 2004 budget followed. As part of the government's multi-year fiscal plan, the interim deficit of $6.2 billion in 2003–4 would be reduced to $2.2 billion in 2004–5, $2.1 billion in 2005–6, and $1.5 billion in 2006–7. Ontario's books would be balanced by 2007–8. The recovery program progressed according to that plan. In 2007 a jubilant Greg Sorbara, the minister of finance, announced that the 2007–8 budget "is a budget that we can all celebrate. It ushers in an era of new economic strength for Ontario. An era as welcome as spring" (Sorbara, 2007: 1). Alas, that spring was short-lived. In 2009 Ontario was "in the grip of a global economic crisis" (Duncan, 2009). Owing to plunging tax revenues, the budget for that year posted a record $14.1-billion deficit.

In 2011 the premier established the Commission on the Reform of Ontario's Public Services to advise the government on how to return to a balanced budget no later than 2017–18 and how to get more value for taxpayers' money. Former Toronto Dominion Bank chief economist Don Drummond headed the commission. Early in its work, it concluded that the deficit, $14 billion in 2010–11, was on track to rise to just over $30 billion by 2017–18. In early 2012 Drummond released the commission's 362 recommendations. These included a cap on growth of health-care spending at 2.5 per cent each year to 2017–18; moving more patients away from hospital care to cheaper forms of health care; increases in school class sizes; tighter controls over public-sector wages; a cap on growth in primary and secondary education spending at 1.0 per cent each year to 2017–18; and a cap on growth in post-secondary education spending (excluding training) at 1.5 per cent each year to 2017–18. Was this a sequel to the Common Sense Revolution? If so, should we brace for a new round of confrontations with organized labour?

British Columbia: Campbell's Neo-Liberal Version

On 16 May 2001 Gordon Campbell led his Liberal Party to a landslide victory in the British Columbia provincial elections. With seventy-seven seats in a seventy-nine-seat legislature, the Liberals triumphantly ended the NDP's ten-year rule as well as their own forty-nine-year political drought (the last Liberal premier was Byron Johnson, who was in power from 1947 to 1952). Campbell was well positioned to serve British Columbians his own version of neo-liberalism. (The B.C. Liberal Party is not connected to any earlier Liberal government in the province – the last one was in office between 1947–52 – or to its federal counterpart of the same name. The B.C. Liberals are described as "a broad, heterogeneous coalition of conservatives, many of whom used to support the Social Credit and BC Reform parties" [*Globe and Mail*, 2001]).

Campbell inherited a $3.4-billion deficit, which was projected to grow to $4.4 billion by 2003. Before his election, he had promised to balance the budget by 2004–5 using the now proven cocktail of budget cuts, layoffs, legislation, and restructuring. Tax cuts also figured prominently in his election platform. Campbell began to deliver on his campaign promises as soon as he started his new job. On his first official day in office, he announced a 25.0 per cent across the board income-tax cut. But the gist of the Liberal government plan was announced in January 2002. Then, British Columbians learned that, in the next three years, some 11,700 public servants would be laid off, thus shrinking the 34,000-strong public-sector labour force by almost a third. In addition, eight jails and twenty-four out of sixty-eight courthouses would be closed. Total government spending would be reduced by $1.9 billion, an 8.0 per cent cut over three years. Later that month, the seventy-seven Liberal MLAs voted in favour of a 5.0 per cent pay cut and a three-year wage freeze. They also legislated to cut ministers' salaries by 20.0 per cent if they did not meet their budgets. There was no plan to roll back salaries in the B.C. public sector.

But, taking a leaf from Harris's book, the Campbell government soon capitalized on its political momentum and passed legislation to undermine the unions and weaken their resistance. On 16 August 2001 the government passed Bill 18, the Skills Development and Labour Statutes Amendment Act, which restored secret-ballot voting for union certification. Under the new rules, if fewer than 45 per cent of the employees in the bargaining unit are members of the union when the union applies for certification, the B.C. Labour Relations Board will dismiss the application; if the evidence shows that at least 45 per cent of the employees are members in good standing, the board will order a representation vote.

Education was a prime target for restructuring. To keep in check the militant B.C. teachers, Bill 18 designated education, not just teaching, an essential service, reversing a 1993 decision made by the NDP government. Consequently, the labour minister could direct the Labour Relations Board to designate school-support staff, facilities, or services as essential if a labour dispute threatened school programs.

Like their Ontario and Alberta counterparts, the B.C. government also planned major changes to health care. To smooth the process, on 27 January 2002 the government passed Bill 29, the Health and Social Services Delivery Improvement Act. The bill annulled "sweetheart deals" made by the NDP with health-care unions, making it possible to contract out thousands of "non-clinical" jobs, such as laundry, maintenance, and food and technology services, to the private sector. Responding to the protests of public-sector unions, the minister of health services, Colin Hansen, snorted: "We are not a job-creation program" (Sullivan, 2002).

In the face of these moves, the public-sector unions did not sit idly by. During the last weekend of February 2002, fourteen anti-government rallies were held across British Columbia, the largest attended by some twenty thousand people in the province's capital, Victoria. The government, however, did not stray from its original course, reaffirming the resolve and commitment to the new discourse it had displayed a few weeks before when confronting the province's teachers.

The B.C. teachers were one of the first groups of public-sector employees to feel the fallout of the 2001 political upheaval. In 1994 the Public Education Labour Relations Act had provided for collective bargaining in British Columbia's education system and established one bargaining unit for all public-sector teachers, with the BC Teachers' Federation (BCTF) as the bargaining agent and the BC Public School Employers' Association (BCPSEA) as the employers' association. Cost provisions, including salaries, benefits, workload, and class-size restrictions, were deemed to be provincial matters, to be negotiated by the BCTF and BCPSEA. Since then, the parties had only one successful round of collective bargaining. In 2006 they negotiated, on their own, a five-year agreement that provided 16 per cent wage increase over five years and a signing bonus.

Among other challenges that Campbell inherited from the NDP government was a deadlocked wage-bargaining process between the province's forty-five thousand teachers, represented by the BCTF, and the BCPSEA. Just prior to the government's taking office, a new bargaining round between the BCTF and BCPSEA had begun. In March 2001 the BCTF demanded a 34.0 per cent wage increase over three years. The BCPSEA offered about one-fifth of that figure, 7.5 per cent over three years. A stalemate was unavoidable. Over the next few months, the teachers revised their wage demand to a 16.0 per cent raise over three years plus a 6.0 per cent market adjustment. The BCPSEA stuck to its initial proposal. As the teachers were contemplating their next move, they were hit by Bill 18, which designated education an essential service. The teachers began the 2001–2 school year by withdrawing their extracurricular services. Later, a Labour Relations Board ruling clarified that the teachers could indeed withdraw from most extracurricular activities such as sports and music programs. The teachers also could, and did, refuse to supervise students or meet with parents outside class hours; meetings with administrators could be declined as well.

In January 2002 the government lost its patience and decided to intervene in the dispute. On 27 January, the same Sunday it passed Bill 29, the

B.C. government passed two additional bills. Bill 27, the Education Services Collective Agreement Act, imposed the employers' first and only offer. Bill 28, the Public Education Flexibility and Choice Act, dealt a major blow to the union's bargaining capacity. The act narrowed the scope of collective bargaining by eliminating key provisions that teachers had negotiated over many years. Staffing levels, caseloads, and teaching loads were removed as permissible subjects of bargaining. Class-size limits for primary students were increased province-wide. Kindergarten class sizes went up from twenty to twenty-two students (the average per district was set at nineteen), and grades 1–3 went up from twenty to twenty-four students (the average was then twenty-one). The average for the rest of the classes was set at thirty students. The teachers' reaction was swift. On the following Monday, 28 January, thousands of teachers staged a one-day walkout and about forty rallies across the province affecting some six hundred thousand students. The government, however, did not budge.

The BCTF challenged the legislation, calling it unconstitutional. In April 2011, in line with the 2007 Supreme Court decision, the British Columbia Supreme Court found in the teachers' favour and gave the province a year to fix the faulty legislation According to Justice Griffin:

> § (293) Taking away the right to bargain these matters [i.e., staffing levels, caseloads, and teaching loads] seriously eroded the bargaining strength of teachers and increased the bargaining strength of the employer. Without the ability to collectively bargain these issues, teachers can have little individual influence over these matters.
>
> § (295) It is clear from the history of teachers' labour relations that they have long considered their working conditions a significant priority to be negotiated collectively, and this includes the conditions of class size and composition, non-enrolling issues, and hours of work. I conclude that the legislation purging the collective agreement of these matters, and prohibiting future collective bargaining over these matters, interfered with the teachers' ability to come together to collectively pursue goals, and significantly undermined the teachers' s. 2 (d) *Charter* guarantee of freedom of association. (*British Columbia Teachers' Federation v. British Columbia*, 2011 BCSC 469; emphasis in original)

The years 2002–11, the period between that controversial legislation and the court decision, did not bring British Columbia to the promised land of fiscal stability. In 2004, for example, in her Speech from the Throne, Lieutenant Governor Iona Campagnolo announced:

As we strive to create the sound financial footing that is critical to the next generation of British Columbians' future, everyone must share in the burden of the transformation that is taking place.

Already many public-sector servants have accepted that responsibility, as 27 separate agreements have been concluded within the government's cost neutral negotiating mandate. (Campagnolo, 2004: 25)

In 2011 Lieutenant Governor Steven L. Point told British Columbians that "the fiscal situation is significantly more challenged than was envisioned during the last round of collective bargaining" (Point, 2011: 10). In early 2011 Minister of Finance Colin Hansen (2011: 3) forecast a deficit of $1.265 billion for the fiscal year just ending. The deficit was expected to fall to $925 million in 2011, and fall again to $440 million in 2012. Among other deficit-elimination measures, in 2010 the B.C. government imposed "net-zero" mandate for negotiations. It meant that public-sector unions and employers must settle for two-year deals at no additional cost. The teachers refused to comply with that diktat. They asked for a 15.0 per cent wage increase over three years and a renewed negotiation over class size and composition. The government rejected the demands. Next, it had to decide how to deal with the teachers' refusal to sign a "net-zero" agreement, something that more than 130 bargaining units covering about 75 per cent of the B.C. public-sector workforce had done.

The grace period provided by Justice Griffin, which suspended the declaration of invalidity of specific sections of Bills 27 and 28 for a period of one year to allow the government time to address the repercussions of her decision, ended in April 2012. Still, the B.C. government did not hesitate to introduce Bill 22, the Education Improvement Act, in March 2012 in order to end the dispute. It imposed a six-month cooling-off period and brought in a government-appointed mediator bound by the province's net-zero mandate. In addition, the mediator was not allowed to consider class size and composition, items that should have been restored to the bargaining table following the 2011 Griffin decision. According to Bill 22, these items would become negotiable in the next round of bargaining in the summer of 2013. Following the mediation process, if there was no significant position shift by either side, a contract would be legislated. The government allowed members of the Legislative Assembly to debate the bill for two weeks.

In late June, the teachers voted to accept a new contract. According to the BCTF president, Susan Lambert, the union "was bullied into" a deal (Hutchinson, 2012). Lambert added that "this settlement does nothing to alleviate the working conditions and learning conditions in schools, it does nothing to decrease classroom sizes, it does nothing to increase programs that support children with special needs" (Nursall, 2012). The union recommended accepting the agreement to avoid having a legislated agreement.

Reviewing the Record

How did developments in Alberta, Ontario, and British Columbia influence industrial relations? How did they affect the ability of unions to negotiate collective agreements and call strikes in the public sector? What impact did they have on governments' ability to end industrial disputes on their terms? Some answers to these questions are provided by the cases discussed in this book. Yet the effects of the more recent developments are still not fully understood. For example, union leaders may have learned that, if they push government too hard, they will likely face legislation to end the dispute, jail terms, and heavy fines. This, in turn, may moderate their negotiation tactics. In the B.C. case reported above, the union president preferred to be "bullied into" a deal than to keep fighting the intractable government and face a legislated agreement. In the political climate of the day, governments might have concluded that, if they made what looked like a sincere effort to settle a dispute before legislating an end to it, they likely would not suffer. At most, they might be forced to allow time for parliamentary debates (e.g., two weeks in the B.C. case mentioned above), meetings between the parties, and public input before terminating a labour conflict without breaching any legal imperatives or incurring a political cost. Thus, despite the 2007 Supreme Court of Canada and the 2011 British Columbia Supreme Court decisions, the B.C. government was ready to restrict collective bargaining and impose a collective agreement on teachers.

Are organized labour's rights to engage in free collective bargaining and call strikes still exposed to government assault? More generally, can unions challenge effectively recent government efforts to restore economic stability using the infamous tools of public-sector restructuring, downsizing, and wage rollbacks? After a period of relative lull, are we bound to witness a surge in public-sector labour conflicts and restrictive legislation? It remains to be seen how governments and unions have adapted to changing circumstances and rules of the game.

Chapter Four

The Case Studies

As we have stated before, this book focuses on language and how government and union personnel mobilized it to legitimate their behaviour during labour conflicts. The context provided in chapter 3 frames the conflicts vis-à-vis various economic, legislative, and legal developments. Generally, the conflicts were a result of a clash between governments trying to balance the books and unions that refused to let that happen at the expense of their members. Our research uses material from seven cases of government intervention in public-sector industrial relations through restrictive legislation or policy.

Table 3 presents skeletal background information and the main features of these cases. The events span six years, from 1999 to 2005. In four cases, a Progressive Conservative government was in office; in two, the government was Liberal; a New Democratic government was involved in one case. The last column in Table 3 shows the party that won the first election following the conflict, and the change in the number of seats it won compared with the previous election. According to our data, governments were likely to survive those elections that followed a labour conflict in which they had intervened. In fact, in none of the cases did the government party lose the next election. Therefore, like others, we argue that the political cost of government intervention in industrial relations seems to be endurable (Swimmer and Bartkiw, 2003: 583). However, interestingly, only in one case did the re-elected party increase the number of its members in the elections following the conflict. In six cases, the government party was re-elected with fewer seats in the legislature.

Why did intervention in labour conflicts not exact a higher cost from the governments responsible? Perhaps voting patterns in the wake of

Table 3 The Events

Province	Government Party	Year	Event Background	Details of Intervention	Party Winning Post-event Elections (Change of Seats in Legislature)
Saskatchewan	New Democratic Party	1999	In late 1998 the Saskatchewan Union of Nurses (SUN) started negotiations with the Saskatchewan Association of Health Organizations (SAHO). SUN asked for wage increases of up to 22 per cent, to a top rate of $52,133 a year. SAHO offered 6 per cent over 3 years plus 1 per cent for adjustments. That was in line with the government's wage cap for public-sector employees. Negotiations resulted in an impasse. On 8 April 1999 SUN called a province-wide legal strike. Saskatchewan did not have a designation system, but SUN promised to maintain essential services. The strike ended on 18 April.	Six hours after the start of the strike, the labour-oriented government passed Bill 23, an Act Respecting the Resumption of Services by Nurses. The act ended the strike, extended the expired collective agreement, and imposed a 2 per cent wage increase per year for the following three years. The act also allowed for a 1 per cent increase for benefits and a 1.2 per cent increase for wage parity. The nurses did not budge, staying on the picket lines for another week despite a court injunction and threats of high fines. On 19 April the parties signed a memorandum of understanding that gave the nurses a few more benefits in addition to the above raises. The government repealed Bill 23 in August. In June, SUN faced a contempt-of-court-hearing. In response to a ruling that would have levied a fine of $120,000, SUN agreed to "purge its contempt" by donating the money to hospital foundations.	NDP (−13)

New Brunswick	PC	2001	Following deadlocked bargaining and the government's rejection of a conciliation board's recommendation, on 21 February 94 per cent of New Brunswick's 6,000 hospital workers (maintenance and janitorial staff, food and laboratory workers, clerical staff, and registered nursing assistants) voted to strike. Money was the main issue at dispute. There was a wide gap between the 12.5 per cent for a four-year contract the province was offering, and the 18 per cent the union was seeking in a new three-year contract.

PC (−16)

The strike commenced on 2 March. Over half of the hospital workers were designated essential. About 2,500 workers were allowed to hit the picket lines. Just hours after the workers had gone on strike, the government said it would force them to return to work.

On 5 March the government passed Bill 30, an Act to Ensure the Continuation of Certain Public Services in the Public Service. The act was never proclaimed. If it had been, Bill 30 would have given the government the right to impose a contract on the workers and to fine them according to the above schedule.

On 6 March the workers ratified a new four-year collective agreement. The deal gave the workers an average wage increase of 12.5 per cent over four years. That worked out to an annual pay increase of 2 per cent, with an additional 4.5 per cent to be distributed among a majority of the members through adjustments such as pay equity and reclassification.

(Continued)

Table 3 (Continued)

Province	Government Party	Year	Event Background	Details of Intervention	Party Winning Post-event Elections Change of Seats in Legislature)
Newfoundland and Labrador	PC	2004	In 2004 the province was expected to have a budget deficit of $840 million. If left unchecked, the accumulated debt was forecast to balloon to $15.8 billion in 2007–8, from the current $11.5 billion. As a way to deal with the financial exigency, Premier Danny Williams broke a campaign promise to public-sector employees and announced massive job cuts. On 30 March, Williams put forward a series of reforms in his government's first budget, which included cutting 4,000 jobs over four years from the province's 32,000-member civil service. Most of the job elimination was expected to occur through retirement and normal attrition. In addition, the premier told public-sector employees that they would have to accept a four-year contract that included a wage freeze in its first two years.	On 1 April, Newfoundland's public-sector unions began a massive strike that had more than two-thirds of the 30,000 provincial employees on the picket lines. Lab technicians, government office personnel, school custodians, teacher's aides, school secretarial staff, and liquor store employees were off work, protesting the financial deal the government offered – 0–0–2–3. The unions agreed to the wage freeze but wanted more money in the final two years of the contract. On 26 April, the government tabled Bill 18, the Public Services Resumption and Continuation Act, to end the massive strike. The workers went back to work on the following day, pre-empting the actual enactment of the bill. The bill was eventually passed on 4 May. It ended the twenty-seven-day strike and imposed a four-year collective agreement with a two-year wage freeze and wage increases of 2 and 3 per cent in the third and fourth year of the legislated contract. The legislation reduced sick leave for new employees by half and allowed the dismissal of anyone who failed to comply.	PC (+10)

| Nova Scotia | PC | 2001 | In 2000 all collective agreements for registered nurses (RNs), licensed practical nurses (LPNs), clerical and support staff, and other Health Care unit employees (e.g., laboratory technologists, physiotherapists, ward aides) expired. By mid-2001, the Nova Scotia Nurses' Union (NSNU), representing 3,600 RNs and 345 LPNs, and the Nova Scotia Government and General Employees' Union (NSGEU), representing 2,300 RNs, 455 LPNs, and 2,900 Health Care unit workers, had settled all terms and conditions for the new collective agreements, other than wages, by negotiation.

Following strike votes, the RNs and LPNs were in a position to withdraw their services beginning mid-July and 27 June 2001 respectively. In May a tentative agreement was reached for the Health Care unit. However, only the clerical and support-services units accepted it and entered into a collective agreement. The rest of the health-care workers took a strike vote on 30 May–1 June and decided in favour of a strike.

On 12 June a mediator was appointed to attempt to bring about a settlement with the Health Care unit workers. The workers voted to reject the proposed agreement. | On 14 June 2001 the government introduced Bill 68, the Health Care Continuation (2001) Act. The legislation was designed to prevent a strike of health-care workers by suspending the right of these employees to strike until 31 March 2004. The bill gave cabinet the power to impose new collective-agreement terms if they could not be bargained. In addition, section 13 did not allow the dispute to go to arbitration.

The NSGEU began a legal strike on 27 June. Within hours, the government applied Bill 68 to the strikers, rendering their job action illegal.

The strikers ended the illegal action on the 28th. However, in retaliation against Bill 68, the NSGEU began gathering resignation letters from members to be submitted to the employer if the dispute was not resolved in a different way.

On 5 July the government withdrew Bill 68, and the parties agreed to invoke a Final Offer Selection arbitration process. The arbitrator selected the union offer in the case of the RNs and the employer offers in the cases of the LPNs and Health Care unit workers. | PC (–5) |

(Continued)

Table 3 (Continued)

Province	Government Party	Year	Event Background	Details of Intervention	Party Winning Post-event Elections (Change of Seats in Legislature)
British Columbia	Liberal	2004	Since coming to power in 2001, the Liberal government had eliminated more than 4,000 hospital jobs (close to 6,000 according to the union). In 2004 the Health Employers Association of British Columbia (HEABC) planned to cut $250 million in wages and benefits per year over the next three years by, according to the union, laying off an additional 2,500 workers. On 25 April 2004 health-care employees across British Columbia went on strike after contract talks broke down and a seventy-two-hour strike notice had been issued. Eleven unions represented some 43,000 workers. Forty thousand of them belonged to the Hospital Employees' Union's (HEU). Central to the HEU's concerns was the government's refusal to put layoffs and privatization plans on hold during contract talks.	On 28 April the government passed Bill 37, the Health Sector (Facilities Subsector) Collective Bargaining Act, which required the striking workers to return immediately to work. In addition, the act imposed a new collective agreement on the parties which provided for a total savings of 15 per cent on wages. Four per cent of these savings would be achieved by going from a 36- to a 37.5-hour workweek. Alternatively, if within the next fourteen days the union asked for an arbitrator to assist the parties to negotiate reductions in wages and/or benefits, the reduction would be 14 per cent in total compensation – again including 4 per cent savings from the extended workweek. The collective agreement constituted under the act was retroactive to 1 April and expired on 31 March 2006. The following day, the union turned the strike into a protest, and the picket lines became "protest lines."	Liberal (−31) (Gordon Campbell was the first premier to win back-to-back majorities since former Social Credit premier Bill Bennett in 1983

Among the strikers were licensed practical nurses, care aides, laboratory assistants, X-ray and EKG technicians, and many support-services employees including housekeeping, laundry, dietary, and maintenance.

On 30 April, when the back-to-work legislation became effective, the HEABC went to the Labour Relations Board in an effort to get the strike declared illegal. On that day, the board ordered the union leaders to get their workers back on the job immediately. The union was defiant and the workers stayed on the "protest lines."

On 2 May the parties signed a tentative deal which included a cap on further contracting-out at 600 full-time jobs over the next two years, and a $25-million severance package for affected employees. The union's workweek would increase to 37.5 hours from 36, which would contribute a 4 per cent saving for the province. The balance of the savings, as specified in Bill 37, would be determined through negotiations on monetary and non-monetary benefits and, if necessary, arbitration. In addition, there would be no retroactive payback on wage rollbacks, and no recriminations for any union members or unions, following workers' return to work on Monday, 3 May. On 2 May, acting on an earlier motion by the HEABC (which was unrelated to the tentative deal), the court charged the union with civil contempt for defying the government's back-to-work legislation. On 11 June 2004 Justice Robert Bauman fined the union $150,000. This was the highest contempt fine ever imposed on a union in British Columbia.

(Continued)

Table 3 (Continued)

Province	Government Party	Year	Event Background	Details of Intervention	Party Winning Post-event Elections (Change of Seats in Legislature)
Alberta	PC	2002	In April 2001, in its new budget, the government created Teacher Salary Enhancement Funding, through which it set aside money for school boards to give teachers a 4 per cent raise in September 2001, and an additional 2 per cent increase in the following year. It is noteworthy that, in its original form, the budget had a surplus of $817 million. However, the economic downturn following the terrorist attacks of 11 September forced the government to trim its richest budget in history.	After a failed mediation process, on 4 February 2002, the Alberta Teachers' Association (ATA) managed an unprecedented feat. For the first time in its history, the union coordinated a series of strikes across nineteen of Alberta's sixty-two school districts. The walkout of 14,538 teachers kept 250,196 students at home. Two weeks later, as the strike activity spread to three more school districts, the number of striking teachers rose to 20,947. At that point, 356,845 students were affected. The strikes, which lasted thirteen working days, ended on 21 February, when the government, just two days after saying it didn't have enough evidence to declare a public emergency and order the striking teachers back to work, did just that.	PC (−12)

In March the government passed Bill 12, the Education Services Settlement Act, which outlined a process to enable the parties to reach settlements through arbitration. Any school district that had not reached a negotiated settlement would be referred to a three-member panel for binding arbitration.

In July the arbitration tribunal submitted its awards, which gave teachers a raise of 6.25 per cent retroactive to 1 September 2001, and an additional 3.75 per cent (compounded) increase effective 31 August 2002, for an end-rate for 2001–2 of 10.23 per cent. For 2002–3, teachers would receive an additional 3.5 per cent effective 1 March 2003, for an overall end-rate of 14.09 per cent over two years.

(Continued)

Table 3 (Continued)

Province	Government Party	Year	Event Background	Details of Intervention	Party Winning Post-event Elections (Change of seats in legislature)
Quebec	Liberal	2005	In 2004 it became apparent that the Liberal government and its 550,000 employees were heading towards a confrontation over salary demands. The government offered 12.6 per cent over six years and nine months, including pay equity; the unions asked the government for a 12.6 per cent increase over three years, with pay equity being settled though additional talks (as called for under Quebec's pay-equity law). In October 2005 a common front formed by the Confédération des syndicats nationaux (CSN) and the Quebec Federation of Labour (QFL) – together representing 200,000 public-sector workers – was given a strong strike mandate. Almost immediately, the unions started with rotating short strikes in schools, hospitals, and other services.	On 15 December 2005 the government decided to step in. Using a unique manoeuvre – adjourning the National Assembly and calling it back into emergency session the next day – the government passed Bill 142, an Act Respecting the Conditions of Employment in the Public Sector. The act imposed wages and working conditions on 500,000 public-sector workers until March 2010. It imposed a thirty-three-month wage freeze retroactive to 30 June 30 2003, and annual wage increases of 2.0 per cent in the last four years of the legislated contract. With the annual inflation rate in Quebec averaging 2 per cent for the past five years, and expected to remain around that level for the next few years, the workers would see a real decline in their wages of close to 6 per cent between 2003 and 2010.	Liberal (−28)

The pay-equity issue was settled through additional talks.

Importantly, Bill 142 had nothing to do with stopping an illegal strike or forcing workers on a legal strike back to work. At the time the legislation was introduced, negotiations were going on and the only job action that had been taken consisted of one- and two-day regional walkouts that had no significant impact on the provision of essential services.

labour conflicts largely reflected the public's reaction to the way in which the protagonists behaved during the conflicts, and these reactions may in turn be at least partly attributed to the legitimation strategies of the governments and unions. The data did not allow for a causal analysis of the relationship between the parties' legitimation efforts and post-conflict voting patterns. Still, we should not disregard the fact that an important aspect of the union-government confrontations was played out in the media, which, in politics, are a key forum in which contests occur. It is reasonable to assume that, as a matter of course, people have to be encouraged and organized to strike, demonstrate, vote for a certain party, and accept and reject agendas and game plans. To be successful, the mobilization processes should create a strong bond between the interpretive orientations of the individual and the protagonist, "such that some set of individual interests, values and beliefs and [the protagonist] activities, goals, and ideology are congruent and complementary" (Snow, Rochford, Worden, and Benford, 1986: 464). Framing this alignment is an important part of the parties' legitimation strategies, for through these strategies the parties convince stakeholders to embrace their own and reject their rivalries' positions, agendas, and action plans. How they perform these strategies in the context of labour conflict is the subject matter of this study.

Labour Conflict in the Provinces

Saskatchewan

In October 1991 the labour-oriented New Democratic Party won Saskatchewan's general elections for the first time since 1982, when it had lost to the Progressive Conservative Party. At the time, the province's fiscal situation was dire. The new government quickly discovered that the previous year's deficit was $846 million, rather than the $265 million predicted by the Tories. The accumulated debt was pegged at $13.9 billion. It would climb to $15 billion by 1994. Even if Saskatchewan were to sell off all its assets, it still would be $6.5 billion in debt. With fifty-five of the Legislative Assembly's sixty-six seats, the newly elected premier, Roy Romanow, did not waste time – his assault on the budget deficit and provincial debt commenced at once. When then-Finance Minister Ed Tchorzewski tabled his first budget, in 1992, he said: "Saskatchewan faces a financial crisis of immense proportion ... Let us look forward to the day when we can tell our children that, though we entered the 1990s plagued by financial crisis, we made the difficult decisions. We turned a new page in our history and put this Province firmly on the path to prosperity" (Tchorzewski, 1992: 11; Oake, 1992; Cline, 1999: 2). When the minister tabled the sixth consecutive balanced budget seven years later, in 1999, the province's debt was $11.5 billion, down from $15 billion in 1994.

In June 1998 the government reached a new three-year deal with its civil-service employees. The new agreement increased salaries by 6.0 per cent over the next three years and guaranteed the jobs of all permanent employees. The government expected other public-sector groups to sign similar deals. Later that year, the Saskatchewan Union of Nurses started negotiations with the Saskatchewan Association of Health Organizations on behalf of its 8,400 members. SUN was seeking wage increases of up to 22.0 per cent, to a top rate of $52,133 a year. SAHO offered 6.0 per cent over three years plus 1.0 per cent for adjustments, a significant gap that soon led to an impasse. On 8 April 1999 SUN called a province-wide legal strike. Saskatchewan did not have a designation system that would ensure an acceptable level of services during strikes in health care, but SUN promised to maintain essential services. On the very same day – six hours after the beginning of the strike – the government passed Bill 23 (an Act Respecting the Resumption of Services by Nurses and the Concluding of a New Collective Bargaining Agreement between the Representative Employers' Organization and the Union), which ended the strike, extended the expired collective agreement, and imposed a wage settlement for the next three years. The nurses defied Bill 23 and stayed on the picket lines for another week despite a court injunction and the threat of high fines. Ten days later, on 28 April, the government agreed to remove the "impediments of Bill 23," thus paving the way for the signing of a new collective agreement between SUN and SAHO. In August the government repealed Bill 23.

The total value of the monetary package in the new collective agreement amounted to a 13.7 per cent wage increase, well above the employers' initial offer. Being steadfast supporters of the NDP (Haiven, 2003: 183), SUN, and other unions as well, found the government's behaviour tough to swallow. Bill 23 was regarded as both an assault on their basic rights and treachery by a supposedly close ally.

New Brunswick

On 7 June 1999 the Progressive Conservative Party returned to office after having lost the previous three elections in 1987, 1991, and 1995. With forty-four of the fifty-five seats in the Legislative Assembly, Premier

Bernard Lord was ready to confront the challenges ahead. In March of the following year, Finance Minister Norman Betts delivered the first budget of the new government. He identified major economic pitfalls, and proposed policy tools to negotiate them. The budget address set an ominous tone for the public-sector employees who were preparing for the upcoming collective bargaining:

> The estimated surplus for 1998–1999 of $18.5 million turned out to be a deficit of $164.3 million. This resulted in a corresponding increase in net debt.
>
> ... looking ahead, the situation would get worse, not better. If this trend were to continue, New Brunswick would find itself in a precarious fiscal position characterized by a widening gap between expenditures and revenues.
>
> How have we arrived at this point? In the past 20 years, deficits have totaled more than $3.5 billion while surpluses totaled only $141 million. The result has been a significant addition to the Province's net debt. The estimate for the fiscal year ending March 31, 2000, is for a cumulative net debt of $6.86 billion.
>
> The real picture is beginning to take shape. Expenses are growing faster than income. Borrowing has increased to make up the difference. Contributions from federal transfers have been reduced. Gross debt and debt service costs are climbing. When you combine these factors, the result is a serious financial problem for the Province. If left unchecked, New Brunswick taxpayers would face annual deficits of close to half a billion dollars within four years.
>
> Mr. Speaker, we will not let it happen ... The price of admission to a new century is a balanced budget. It is the foundation for a more competitive, more compassionate New Brunswick.
>
> ... we know that for New Brunswickers, there are some things that matter above all: ensuring quality health care; educating our children; helping those who cannot help themselves; protecting the health and safety of New Brunswickers; supporting job creation, and safeguarding Crown assets.
>
> The government will treat its employees fairly and compassionately and will offer those affected by Program/Service Review a range of options such as reassignments, transfer, redeployment, and temporary placement.
>
> The budget continues to provide for modest and reasonable increases in public sector wages. This year, we will be at the bargaining table with a number of public sector unions representing more than 25,000 public service employees. I look forward to signing agreements with them at the conclusion of the collective bargaining process.

> ... I am pleased to announce today that for the fiscal year 2000–2001, the first of this government, there will be a modest surplus of $21.3 million [following 9/11, this figure was revised to $8.7 million]. (Betts, 2000: 7, 9, 12)

On 2 March 2001 some 2,500 hospital workers (maintenance, janitorial, food, laboratory, and clerical workers, and registered nursing assistants) commenced a legal strike. About 3,500 workers, the rest of the bargaining unit, were designated essential and therefore had to stay on the job. The main issue in contention was money. The government, which was also the direct employer, offered an average increase of 12.5 per cent in a four-year contract, for a total cost of $18 million. The union demanded an 18.0 per cent wage raise plus a wage adjustment of more than 6.0 per cent. Three days later, the government passed, but did not proclaim, Bill 30, An Act to Ensure the Continuation of Certain Public Services in the Public Service. The bill terminated the strike and extended the existing collective agreement. To avoid proclamation of the bill, on 6 March, the workers ratified a new collective agreement that was based on the employers' last offer of an average pay raise of 12.5 per cent over four years.

Newfoundland and Labrador

In October 2003 the Progressive Conservative Party won the provincial elections, ending the fourteen-year-old Liberal administration. In early 2004 the province was due to begin negotiations with 32,000 public-sector workers. In their last collective agreement, these workers had received a total raise of 15.0 per cent over three years, after a decade of wage freezes. They had good reason to be sanguine about the upcoming round of bargaining. In March 2003 the Liberal minister of finance, Joan Marie Alyward, had delivered the last budget address of her Liberal government. Despite a predicted deficit of $286.6 million, the overall message was upbeat:

> Rushing to cut social programs now by in [sic] excess of $200 million to achieve a balanced budget is just not good public policy. As a government, we believe there is no need to take this course of action given the positive outlook for our economy and our revenues. Accordingly, this budget contains no cuts to social programs or other public services. In fact, it enhances social programs selectively where we determined it would be prudent and responsible to do so ... We have set achievable targets to bring the deficit

down responsibly to a balanced budget position over the term of our next mandate. Rather than unnecessary program cuts, we are confident this can be done by our strongly performing economy, one that leads the nation. (Alyward, 2003: 11, 39)

Less than a year later, that buoyancy had morphed into doom and gloom. On 5 January 2004 the recently elected premier, Danny Williams, issued a warning about the province's dire financial situation in a dramatic live television address. The trigger for the speech was the release, in late December, of an independent audit of the province's fiscal situation. The audit found that the projected deficit for the 2003–4 fiscal year had ballooned to $827 million (PricewaterhouseCoopers, 2003: 2). The province's debt was pegged at $11 billion.

Williams used his television broadcast to set the stage for the austerity measures that a few months later would trigger a province-wide strike by some 20,000 public-sector employees. He began the speech by stating that "on October 21, the people of Newfoundland and Labrador elected a new government because you wanted a new approach, that will see the true potential of our province fully realized in a meaningful way." Then he delivered the bad news:

> The numbers are staggering to the point where it is difficult for many of us to understand just how serious the situation is ... If this situation continues, we are in very real danger of drowning in our own debt. Out of our annual 4.2 billion dollar budget, we now spend more than a billion dollars a year – that's 25 cents of every dollar – to pay for the interest on our debt ... We must address this situation now. We are digging ourselves deeper into a hole and that's been our problem for far too long ... This will require hard work and sacrifice by everyone. We cannot expect to improve our lives without first enduring some short-term pain in return for long-term and meaningful benefits. We have a plan that focuses on achieving a balance. It's about making decisions for the right reasons – not for political reasons. That irresponsible practice has gotten us where we are today ... Our government may have inherited this serious fiscal situation but we have absolutely no intention of letting our children and grandchildren inherit it from us.
>
> There is no money available for salary increases at this time ... We can only conduct collective bargaining based upon the fiscal realities we all face, and we should only reach agreements that we can afford. Otherwise we only postpone the inevitable. (Williams, 2004)

Organized labour responded quickly and ominously: "If he carries on the way he is, we will have absolute chaos in this province as the contracts come due" (Reg Anstey, president of the Newfoundland and Labrador Federation of Labour, *Sudbury Star*, 2004). "They may decide to strike," responded the premier, who added, "That's their prerogative. I would like to think that they won't" (ibid.). In their last collective agreement, public-sector employees had received a total raise of 15.0 per cent over three years, after a decade-long wage freeze. According to the audit, that raise had added approximately $350 million to the annual salary bill of the government, which represented approximately 52.0 per cent of the entire provincial budget (PricewaterhouseCoopers, 2003: 21).

On 30 March 2004 Finance Minister Loyola Sullivan delivered his first budget speech, "Protecting Our Future." As expected, he painted a threatening picture of the province's financial situation, described how his government's predecessors had driven the province to the brink of bankruptcy, and alluded to the measures government would implement to meet the crisis:

> When we came into this office less than five months ago, our government fully expected to find a serious fiscal situation for 2004–05. But the more fundamental, and unexpected, problem was the magnitude of the deficits projected for the coming years, which would cause the debt to grow to a level that would compromise the fiscal integrity of the province ... a period of restraint would have to be endured to turn the deficit momentum around. No responsible government can ignore the stark arithmetic ... in recent years, [the previous Liberal] government has created a serious problem with money management. It has not been a good steward of the taxes Newfoundlanders and Labradorians pay every year for the services they need and value.
>
> We must bring the deficit progressively and strategically lower each year in order to protect the province's credit rating ... The consequences of a rating decline would be higher interest rates, reduced access to capital markets and increased exposure to foreign exchange fluctuations.
>
> We face a historic challenge ... We have to make some very difficult decisions. And we have more difficult decisions to make ... an inevitable result of any significant fiscal restraint exercise is some impact on jobs. Almost two thirds of government's discretionary expenditures are salaries. There will be fewer positions in the public sector as a consequence of the measures in this budget. (Sullivan, 2004: 1, 2, 8, 10, 13)

Against the backdrop of "a historic challenge," the Treasury Board began negotiations with the Newfoundland and Labrador Association of Public and Private Employees (NAPE), which represented about 16,000 workers, and the Canadian Union of Public Employees (CUPE), which represented about 4,000 employees. During several rounds of bargaining, the parties exchanged various proposals. In its last one, the government offered a four-year contract with a 0-0-2-3 wage freeze/increase scheme. The unions agreed to a wage freeze during the first two years of the contract but demanded higher increases in the subsequent two years. The government refused and so a stalemate soon ensued. On 1 April some 20,000 government workers took to the streets in what was the largest public-sector strike in Newfoundland and Labrador's history. After more than three weeks, on 26 April the government passed Bill 18, the Public Services Resumption and Consolidation Act, which ended the strike and imposed the government's final offer on the workers.

Nova Scotia

In July 1999, following six years of Liberal rule, Dr John Hamm led the Progressive Conservative Party to office. With thirty members in the fifty-two-seat House of Assembly, the new government was ready to attack the budget deficit and provincial debt. In March 2001 the minister of finance, Neil Leblanc, delivered his second budget address. The government's four-year fiscal plan was "on course, on time, and on budget" (Leblanc, 2001: 1). The budget forecasted a deficit of $91 million. This should have been the last deficit budget for this government. The debt was pegged at $11 billion. To facilitate its fiscal plan, the government had reduced the size of its civil service by about 4.0 per cent, from 9,926 to 9,503 employees. Much of that reduction was achieved through natural attrition and the elimination of vacant positions (ibid.: 8). In his budget, Leblanc cautioned public-sector employees and unions who were in the midst of collective bargaining: "Across Nova Scotia, public-sector employees and the unions that represent public servants are in various stages of the collective bargaining process. Any increase in wages puts pressure on the public treasury. To date, reasonable, responsible agreements have been reached. The government hopes, and has a responsibility to ensure, that the trend continues" (ibid.).

On 16 June 2001 negotiations between the province's nine District Health Authorities and the unions representing health-care workers – the

Nova Scotia Government and General Employees' Union and the Nova Scotia Nurses' Union – reached an impasse. The NSGEU was the largest union in the province, representing 2,300 registered nurses and 2,900 other health-care workers including licensed practical nurses, medical laboratories technologists, physiotherapists, ward aides, social workers, and X-ray technologists. The 2,900 employees belonged to a single Health Care bargaining unit. The NSNU represented 3,600 registered nurses and 350 licensed practical nurses. For nurses, the unions were seeking wage increases of between 21.0 and 25.0 per cent over three years, plus a lump-sum payment of $1,500. Following mediation, workers in the Health Care bargaining unit were offered an 8.0 per cent wage increase over three years, plus a 1.5 per cent increase to wage rates as a classification-review advance, and $750 to be paid to each employee in the bargaining unit upon ratification of the agreement. On 16 June the workers rejected the offer. As a pre-emptive measure, on 14 June, the government introduced, but did not proclaim, Bill 68, the Health Care Continuation (2001) Act. The bill was designed to prevent a strike in health care by suspending the employees' right to strike for three years. In addition, it gave the government the right to determine the provisions of any collective agreement.

Nova Scotia made no use of the designation model for any part of the workforce. Therefore, the employees were allowed to strike without any restrictions beyond the standard requisites in the Trade Union Act (Adell, Grant, and Ponak, 2001: 28). On 27 June the NSGEU commenced a legal strike. Within hours, the government proclaimed Bill 68 in respect to the Health Care bargaining unit, rendering a continuation of the strike illegal. According to arbitrator (final offer selector) Susan Ashley, "Bill 68 provoked a significant and negative response within the labor community and beyond, and exacerbated an already difficult situation" (NSGEU and NSNU and Province of Nova Scotia, 2001: 7).

The workers ended the illegal action on 28 June. However, in retaliation, the NSGEU began gathering resignation letters from members to be submitted to the employer if the dispute was not resolved differently. On 5 July the government withdrew Bill 68 and the parties agreed to a Final Offer Selection arbitration process. The arbitrator selected the union offer in the case of the registered nurses, and the employer offers in the cases of the licensed practical nurses and Health Care unit workers.

British Columbia

Some of the more general context for this case has already been presented in chapter 3. Therefore, we repeat it only briefly here and add new material that is more specific to the case.

On 16 May 2001 Gordon Campbell led his Liberal Party to a landslide victory in the B.C. provincial elections. With this win the Liberal Party, which had not been in office since 1952, ended a ten-year NDP administration. Campbell inherited a $3.4-billion deficit, which was projected to grow to $4.4 billion by 2003. Before his election, Campbell had promised to balance the budget by 2004–5 by delivering the now-proven blend of budget cuts, legislation, and public-sector restructuring. There was no plan to roll back salaries in the B.C. public sector.

As a part of an overall effort to restructure the public service, the new government tackled health care. Importantly, during his election campaign, Campbell had promised to uphold contract provisions barring any service privatization. On several occasions, he expressed his unequivocal opposition to private health care:

> I don't think there is any appetite in British Columbia to do any kind of privatizing of health care. And, indeed I don't believe we need to do that ... We have a long way to go in British Columbia before we maximize or optimize the benefits to the public health care system and we are committed to helping the public health care system. (Premier Gordon Campbell on the Bill Good Show, CKNW-Radio, 3 March 2000)

> I don't think [the Hospital Employees' Union members] have to worry about [service privatization]. Their sense should be that Gordon Campbell and the B.C. Liberals recognize the importance of HEU workers to the public health care system in this province. They are front line workers who are necessary. You can't talk to anyone in the health care system who doesn't recognize that. I want HEU workers, like other workers in the public health care system or in the public service, to recognize their value. And we will value them. (*Guardian* [an HEU magazine], interview with Gordon Campbell, November/December 2000)

> ... I don't believe in ripping up agreements ... I think the question today is how you maintain the quality and the talent of the people who are in this system.... I think the fundamental is I'm not tearing up agreements. I have never said I would tear up agreements ... I am not tearing up any agreements. (ibid.)

Thus, the future premier of British Columbia had passionately and solemnly pledged that he would not abrogate collective agreements that protected health-care workers from layoffs following restructuring. Such agreements had originated with the Employment Security Agreement/ Health Labour Accord, which had been signed by the NDP government and the British Columbia Nurses' Union, the Hospital Employees' Union, and the Health Sciences Association in July 1993. The accord guaranteed health-care workers that there would be no layoffs during and following reform to their sector. In addition, it provided for job retraining, job sharing, and fully paid re-education, with the operations handled by local committees that included union representatives.

Shortly after winning office, however, Campbell began to renege on his campaign promises. To facilitate the restructuring of health care, on 27 January 2002, the government passed Bill 29, the Health and Social Services Delivery Improvement Act. The bill made it possible to contract out thousands of "non-clinical" health-care jobs, such as laundry, maintenance, food, and technology services, to the private sector. In response to the protests of public-sector unions, the minister of health services, Colin Hansen, stated, as noted in chapter 3: "We are not a job-creation program" (Sullivan, 2002). Eventually, more than 4,200 hospital jobs were contracted out, according to the Health Employers Association of British Columbia (6,000 according to the unions) (Armstrong, 2004).

In July 2002 doctors received increases averaging $50,000. This generosity vanished in 2003, when eleven unions representing 43,000 support staff and paramedical workers prepared to begin collective bargaining with the HEABC. In 2003 the employers sought $900 million in cost saving to go to "direct patient care." Consequently, they wanted concessions in wages and benefits, along with privatization that would eliminate thousands of jobs. In April 2003 the unions and government achieved a tentative framework agreement (TFA) that mitigated the impact of contracting out on union members and extended the current agreement by two years, to 31 March 2006. In exchange for longer hours of work and wage reductions, government agreed to cap the number of positions that could be contracted out. According to the HEU, representing some 40,000 hospital workers, the cap on contracting out – set at 3,500 full-time equivalents, or 5,000 jobs – was significantly less than the government's original target of 20,000 jobs. The unions agreed to recommend that their members vote in favour of the terms of settlement (Hospital Employees' Union, 2003). Eventually, however, the membership rejected the TFA.

The parties resumed negotiation in early 2004 but failed to overcome their differences. A province-wide strike loomed large, and health-care workers hit the picket lines on 25 April. (In British Columbia, only registered nurses and transit operators are designated essential employees.) Three days later, the government passed Bill 37, the Health Sector (Facilities Subsector) Collective Agreement Act, which ordered the workers back to work and imposed wage and benefit cuts and a longer workweek. The unions, however, defied the legislation and refused to end to the strike. On 30 April the British Columbia Labour Relations Board ordered the strikers to "immediately resume their duties and work schedules of employment with the HEABC" (British Columbia Labour Relations Board, 2004: 3). Still, the HEU advised its members to disregard a law that it said disrespected them (*Globe and Mail,* 2004). The workers returned to work on 3 May.

Alberta

As in the B.C. case, the reader should refer to chapter 3 for more detail on this case's general context.

At the end of August 2001, existing teacher contracts expired in fifty-two of the sixty-two Alberta school districts. An unusual government policy prompted the Alberta Teachers' Association to launch unprecedented coordinated bargaining, which culminated in twenty-two synchronized strikes, in February 2002. The seeds of these strikes had been sown nearly ten years previous. As explained in chapter 3, upon his election in 1993, Premier Ralph Klein had spearheaded a series of socio-economic policies popularly known as the Klein Revolution. In 1994, among other austerity measures, the Progressive Conservative government reduced its total education budget by 13.0 per cent over three years. To facilitate the new spending target, the government undertook two initiatives with far-reaching industrial-relations implications. First, in 1994, it asked all public-sector employees to accept voluntarily a 5.0 per cent pay cut followed by a two-year wage freeze. Teachers complied without any organized protest. In addition, in the same year, the government passed Bill 19, the School Amendment Act, which strengthened the role of the education minister at the expense of local school boards by transferring their taxation power to cabinet. From then on, the government would collect the tax money and distribute it among the school boards on a per-student basis, thereby reducing the discrepancy between boards in richer urban centres and those in less affluent, rural areas.

In 2001 several events raised teachers' expectations for significant wage increases. First, in January, after accepting the province's offer of a 21.9 per cent fee increase, the Alberta doctors had become among the highest paid in Canada. Two months later, only nine days before the provincial elections, the United Nurses of Alberta (UNA) (representing some 18,000 registered nurses) and the Provincial Health Authorities of Alberta had reached an agreement that increased nurses' salaries by 17.0 per cent over two years. The nurses further received increases to overtime rates, vacation, and on-call premiums. Second, in April, members of the Legislative Assembly (MLAs) had voted themselves a salary increase of 3.3 per cent. Then, in August, they voted themselves a second increase of 11.0 per cent and launched a new transitional allowance that would reward MLAs three months' salary for every year served, based on their three highest years of income. In December they awarded themselves another salary increase of 4.0 per cent effective 1 April 2002. In total, over the last nine months of 2001, MLAs had approved themselves three salary increases resulting in an overall increase of 18.3 per cent.

Third, on 5 April, shortly after his third consecutive victory in the provincial elections, Premier Klein admitted that "there is no doubt Alberta teachers were part of the [economic] solution a few years ago ... We'll make sure that our teachers and instructors and professors are fairly compensated and given as good a work environment as they can have so that they know how much they are appreciated" (Thomson, 2001). To those asking for specific details, Klein would say only that they should wait for the next budget. Within less than a week it became publicly known just how much the province appreciated its teachers. In its new budget, the government took an exceptional step. It created Teacher Salary Enhancement Funding through which it set aside money for school boards to give teachers a 4.0 per cent raise in September 2001, and an additional 2.0 per cent increase the following year. Practically, the government abrogated collective bargaining over a major interest. It is noteworthy that the surplus for the previous fiscal year was pegged at $6.4 billion. In addition, in its original form, the 2001 budget had a surplus of $817 million (later that year, the economic repercussions of 9/11 forced the government to trim the richest budget in its history). In other words, the policy likely was not a response to a dire fiscal situation.

In 2003 an arbitration tribunal referred to the above three events as "factors which increased the teachers' expectations for higher increases" (*Edmonton Public School Board No. 7 and the Alberta Teachers' Association*, 2002: 38). The tribunal emphasized that "the introduction of the Teacher

Salary Enhancement Funding clearly set a *floor* of 4% for increase in teachers' salaries for 2001–02 and 2% for 2002–03" (ibid.: 39; emphasis in original). The claim was based on an argument then-Learning Minister Lyle Oberg had made to the legislature in November 2001:

> First of all, in the last budget there was 4 percent and 2 percent that was put in exclusively for teachers' salaries, which meant that the school boards could not touch that. It had to be for teachers' salaries. *This was a minimum.* They also had 3 and a half percent on their general grant rate that they can negotiate with the teachers, and that's exactly what they're doing. That's exactly what they're doing, for example, in Medicine Hat, where the school board and the ATA both voted to accept their contract ... The other point that I'll make is that the rationale behind the 4 percent and the 2 percent made them the highest paid teachers on average across the provinces in Canada. (*Hansard*, 2001: 1127; emphasis added

Originally, the above-mentioned 3.5 per cent allocation was earmarked for improving class conditions. Most local unions refused to ask the school boards to use it for salary-enhancement purposes. However, in three cases, local unions managed to secure respectable wage increases from school boards without dipping into the class- condition improvement fund. In early 2001, during the initial bargaining stages, the ATA demanded no less than a 30.0 per cent pay raise over two years. By the end of 2001, the ATA had reduced its demand to a less than 20.0 per cent increase over two years. It also demanded improved classroom and teaching conditions and financial help to address issues of teacher attraction and retention.

In Alberta, collective bargaining in the education industry was conducted locally between a local union and a school board. After learning about the government's 2&4 scheme, the ATA appointed bargaining agents to work with each bargaining unit, thereby laying the basis for coordinated bargaining. Then-ATA President Larry Booi explained that the ATA "has set standards. Nobody signs a contract below a certain level" (Hagan, 2001). By the end of January 2002, fourteen bargaining units had held strike votes resulting in overwhelming support for job actions; nine had applied to the Alberta Labour Relations Board for supervised strike votes; another twenty-eight were in mediation; and nine bargaining units had settled. From the ATA's perspective, the only way to avoid job action was by pressuring the government to improve its financial "offer."

The government, however, refused to budge from its original diktat. On 4 February, after a failed mediation process, the ATA managed an unprecedented feat. For the first time in its history, the union coordinated a series of strikes across nineteen of Alberta's sixty-two school districts. The walkout of 14,538 teachers kept 250,196 students at home. Two weeks later, as the strike activity spread to three more school districts, the number of striking teachers rose to 20,976. At that point, 356,845 students were affected. The strikes, which lasted thirteen working days for most participating locals, ended on 21 February, when the government, just two days after saying it did not have enough evidence to declare a public emergency and order the striking teachers back to work, did just that (Olsen, 2002; Holubitski, 2002). Order-in-Council 77/2002 declared that "on and after February 21, 2002 all further action and procedures in the dispute are hereby replaced by the procedures under section 112 [Emergencies] of the Labour Relations Code."

The teachers complied and returned to the classroom the following day. The learning minister gave the twenty-two affected school boards and local unions until 15 March to reach a contract settlement, either on their own or with the help of a government-appointed mediator. If a settlement could not be reached by then, the dispute would be referred to arbitration. The ATA did not agree that its thirteen-day (in three cases only three-day) action had created an emergency and, therefore, appealed the decision. Meanwhile, it advised its members that "until further notice ... members who have agreed to participate in or conduct extracurricular activities [should] continue with those arrangements. However, where no commitments have been made, teachers should not now be volunteering to take on new tasks" (Alberta Teachers' Association, 2002).

On 1 March, Court of Queen's Bench Chief Justice Allan Wachowich struck down government order 77/2002. He ruled that the government had failed to give consideration to each of the twenty-two disputes. Consequently, it had engaged "in the fallacious logic of either regarding hardship generally across Alberta as proof of specific hardship caused by each bargaining unit, or by attributing hardship caused by one bargaining unit as proof of hardship caused by another or all" (*Alberta Teachers' Assn. v. Alberta*, 2002). The government had thus failed to prove that there was an emergency causing an unreasonable hardship to a third party (i.e., students, families, and laid-off support staff) across the province. The chief justice added that "it must be borne in mind that the very purpose of a strike is to cause some hardship in order to raise the profile of the issues being contested, and to pressure the other side into making concessions. If a strike did not cause some degree of hardship, it would be pointless" (ibid.). Notwithstanding that ruling, the ATA decided not to resume the strike, and the teachers were back at work on Monday, 4 March.

During the dispute, the government made two controversial decisions. First, it imposed its own wage terms on what should have been a free bargaining process. Without any apparent reason or warning, and against the grain of the vital events outlined above, the government nullified bargaining over a key item. Second, for a long time, both Learning Minister Lyle Oberg and Premier Ralph Klein made it clear that, following the legal precedent established in Ontario, an emergency in education should occur only after twenty days of strike action. Yet the Calgary teachers had been ordered back to work almost immediately after they had gone on strike. At that time, the number of days missed by students within the Calgary Board of Education was no more than what they normally lost to the annual two-day teachers' convention. The rest of the local unions had been on strike for less than two weeks.

Quebec

On 14 April 2003 Jean Charest and his Liberal Party defeated the incumbent Parti Québécois in the provincial elections and won office for the first time since 1993. With 76 seats in the 125-seat legislature, Charest had the majority he needed to restructure, or in his words "to modernize," the public sector. According to then-Treasury Board President Monique Jérôme-Forget, "Quebec will gradually cut its public-sector workforce by 20 percent over the next 10 years. The move would save $700 million a year" (*Gazette*, 2004). The master plan was to hire one civil servant for every two that retired, so that, by December 2013, 16,000 jobs would have been eliminated (De Souza, 2004). To compensate for this loss, the government would test the markets for public-private partnerships in various sectors, such as roads, health care, and education.

The new Quebec government identified industrial-relations institutions as potential roadblocks and therefore targeted them for reform. For instance, in December 2003, the government passed Bill 31, an Act to Amend the Labour Code. The act amended section 45 of the Labour Code, which dealt with the transmission of collective- bargaining rights and obligations upon the transfer of ownership or operation of all, or part, of an undertaking. The amendment provided that section 45 would not apply in the case of "the transfer of part of the operation of an undertaking where such transfer does not entail the transfer to the transferee, in addition to functions or the right to operate, of most of the elements that characterize the part of the undertaking involved." Practically speaking, this amendment opened the door for the subcontracting of non-core functions (e.g., janitorial services, snow removal for municipalities). In such cases section 45 did not apply and, therefore, the union certification and collective agreement that was in force would not follow.

In the same month, the government also passed Bill 30, an Act Respecting Bargaining Units in the Social Affairs Sector and Amending the Act Respecting the Process of Negotiation of the Collective Agreements in the Public and Parapublic Sectors. The bill cut the number of health-care bargaining units from 3,671 to 1,320 by limiting to four the number of bargaining units in "any institution in the social affairs sector" (NUPGE, 2007). Consequently, it cleared the way for managers to transfer staff as they saw fit between departments and hospitals. Notwithstanding these legal developments, the upcoming collective bargaining with more than 500,000 public-sector workers posed a formidable challenge to government and unions.

On 30 June 2003 collective agreements for more than 500,000 public-sector workers in education (209,000), health (230,600), and other government agencies (96,500) expired (Dougherty, 2005a). The task of negotiating new agreements on behalf of the government fell to the Treasury Board, headed by Monique Jérôme-Forget. On the union side, things were complicated. The Quebec labour movement is characterized by high union density. In 2005, with 40.4 per cent unionization, Quebec was the most unionized jurisdiction in North America (*Gazette*, 2005). Public-sector union density reached 74.0 per cent, with education (74.2 per cent), public administration (74.0 per cent), and health (60.5 per cent) being the highest unionized sectors (*Perspectives on Labour and Income*, 2005).

But the labour movement in Quebec is also the most diversified and fragmented in Canada (Grant, 2003: 59). The unions affiliated with the two leading labour federations, the Quebec Federation of Labour and the Confédération des syndicats nationaux, represented about two-thirds of the unionized workforce (Boivin and Déom, 1995). Some 40.0 per cent of QFL members worked in the public sector, and the QFL had considerable strength in the municipal sector and significant representation in the parapublic sector (more than half of CSN's 300,000 members were in the parapublic sector, particularly in health care). The Centrale des syndicats du Québec (CSQ; Quebec House of Labour) was the third-largest labour federation. Of the almost 160,000 members, over 100,000 worked in education (http://www.csq.qc.net/). Among the many individual unions involved in the conflict, the Syndicat de la fonction publique du Québec (SFPQ) represented some 43,000 civil servants; the Syndicat de professionnelles et de professionnels du Québec (SPGQ) represented some 19,000 civil servants; and the Fédération des infirmières et infirmiers du Québec represented 56,000 nurses (in December 2006 it changed its name to the Fédération interprofessionnelle de la santé du Québec [FIQ]). The majority of the workers belonged in two ad hoc "common fronts" – QFL-CSN represented more than 200,000 workers, and CSQ-SPGQ-SFPQ advocated on behalf of about 235,000 workers.

The government offered 12.6 per cent over six years and nine months, including pay equity. The cost of this settlement was estimated at $3.25 billion. The unions demanded 12.5 per cent over three years, plus improvements in pensions and other benefits, at an estimated cost of $4.2 billion. In addition, the unions believed that pay equity should be settled through separate talks, as was called for under Quebec's pay-equity law. In October 2005 the unions began a series of short rotating strikes in education, health care, and some other services of the public sector. The government stepped in two months later. On 14 December 2005 the government adjourned the fall session of the National Assembly, a move that allowed it to limit debate on public-sector collective bargaining. The government then announced that it would convene a special sitting on 15 December to legislate salaries and working conditions for about half a million public-sector workers. Bill 142, an Act Respecting Conditions of Employment in the Public Sector, was introduced on 15 December, passed on the very same day, and became law the following day. It imposed contracts of six years and nine months that froze salaries for the first two years, beginning with the expiration of the old contracts in June 2003. The legislation provided wage increases of 2.0 per cent per year between 1 April 2006 and 31 March 2010. On average, the settlement provided a 1.2 per cent increase per year over the six-year, nine-month term of the contract. This was well below the predicted rate of inflation, which was set at 2.0 per cent per year for that period. The government also set aside about 4.6 per cent for pay equity that would be negotiated outside the collective agreement, an issue that was settled in June 2006. More than 300,000 workers in health and education saw an average retroactive pay increase of 6.25 per cent, with some receiving as much as an 11.0 per cent increase. The deal cost the government approximately $4.0 billion.

Looking Ahead

In the next four chapters we analyse texts gleaned from the seven cases to explore how the parties manipulated language to legitimate their behaviour. At this point, we would like to remind the reader of a few points. First, since our sample of cases was not drawn randomly, we do not know to what extent our data represent the totality of public-sector conflicts. Second, because of space limitations, we use only a small amount of the data we collected. However, we do believe that the data we present are powerful enough to illustrate and support our arguments. Whenever the evidence is unique to a single case, we state so. Third, unlike the research we have reviewed, this study deals with two protagonists rather than a single one. This allows us to compare how two parties participating in the same event used linguistic strategies to advance their interests.

Chapter Five

Authorization-Legitimation Strategy

Van Leeuwen (2008) and van Leeuwen and Wodak (1999) have outlined six types of authorization-legitimation strategy. As Tables 4 and 5 (see chapter 6) demonstrate, speakers in the cases selected for this study used three of them. Personal authorization, which is vested in the status of speakers, was practised in all cases. The most frequently interviewed union and government spokespersons were high-ranking executives and politicians. Union leaders, union executive directors, chief negotiators, premiers, and ministers expected to sway an audience by their arguments for several reasons, one likely being their position in the organizational hierarchy. Thus, it was thought that the audience would listen to them and embrace their messages because, at least in part, of who they were. There was some truth to this. As high-ranking politicians and union personnel, they should have been privy to the best available information and enjoyed a solid grasp on the situation, the history of the conflict, and the sentiments of their constituents, be they taxpayers or union members. This might have conferred an aura of credibility on the evidence they provided and on their arguments, explanations, analyses, and accusations.

Yet the fact that most speakers were vested with institutionalized authority that granted them access to privileged information does not mean that their arguments always enjoyed solid face value. For example, Nova Scotia Government and General Employees' Union President Joan Jessome provided the main source of authorization for the union's legitimation efforts. She made several controversial statements, such as:

> 5.1: This is going to drive nurses out of the province. I just can't believe they can say they value health-care providers and then turn around and take away every single right they have negotiated away [by passing Bill 68] from them. (*Trail Times*, "Nurses Protest 'Draconian' Bill," 15 June 2001)

5.2: This is about the survival of democracy in this province. That is what we are fighting for. (Kevin Cox, "Union Sets June 27 for Nova Scotia Health-Care Strike," *Globe and Mail*, 23 June 2001)

5.3: It's either do [something] or watch our rights to free bargaining be extinguished ... The labour movement in Nova Scotia should shut the province down, private and public, shut her down. (Michael Tutton, "Walkouts Play Havoc with N.S. Health Care," *Kingston Whig-Standard*, 26 June 2001)

Perhaps Jessome made these utterances for dramatic effect, hoping that they would render her arguments more convincing. However, she never grounded any of her hyperbolic statements in fact. Was it true that nurses would leave the province because of the government's behaviour? Was democracy in any real danger in Nova Scotia? What was the meaning of "shutting down the province?" Could the labour movement in Nova Scotia shut down the province? Making exaggerated statements was not only a union tactic. In Newfoundland and Labrador, Premier Danny Williams likened the province's situation to that of a mighty vessel facing the danger of sinking – or "drowning," to use his word – under the choppy waves of a turbulent future:

5.4: The time has come to turn the tide in Newfoundland and Labrador and chart a new course to prosperity and self-reliance ... Unless we significantly adjust our course, we are facing total deficits of 1 billion dollars or greater for the next four years at least ... We are in very real danger of drowning in our own debt. (Williams, 2004)

As in the 5.1–5.3 quotes, drowning signals an apocalyptic event that must be avoided by resorting to unorthodox measures, which the premier presented later in his speech. There was no middle way; a tough situation calls for tough measures and sacrifice. Williams made sure that the audience got the point by using the above bleak metaphor. The relationship between the factual and theatrical aspects of legitimation is intriguing. How convincing is a union leader when s/he makes ungrounded doomsday statements? Can attempts to undermine an opponent using melodramatic arguments backfire? How far can a speaker go before her/his arguments are considered farcical or empty? What happens to public opinion when the audience considers a speaker's arguments unfounded, or overly sensational?

Government (but not union) speakers used impersonal- and expert-authorization legitimation strategies on several occasions. As indicated in Table 4, the governments of New Brunswick, Alberta, and Newfoundland and Labrador cited budget and market forces as a source of impersonal authority to justify actions and policies. In New Brunswick, Premier Bernard Lord declared:

> 5.5: I sympathize with the poorly paid workers, but the cash-strapped government can't make up for 10 years of neglect in one contract [the PC government won the 1999 elections after a twelve-year Liberal administration]. The unions are asking for more money than we think is reasonable and fair to the taxpayers of New Brunswick. (Kelly Toughill, "N.B. Hospitals Hit by Massive Strike," *Toronto Star*, 3 March 2001)

The New Brunswick minister of finance, Norman Betts, added emphatically that a balanced budget was the ticket into the new century:

> 5.6: Last year I said: "The price of admission to a new century is a balanced budget." Deficits today are simply taxes tomorrow. Maintaining a competitive position in the "new century" requires continued fiscal prudence leading to balanced budgets with balanced results. It is only through this strong fiscal management that we will achieve the flexibility to invest in health care and education and to lower taxes for workers and families. (Betts, 2001: 7)

In Newfoundland and Labrador, on 30 March 2004, Finance Minister Loyola Sullivan delivered his first budget speech, "Protecting Our Future." He painted an ominous picture of the province's financial situation. Among other things, he explained that:

> 5.7: We must bring the deficit progressively and strategically lower each year in order to protect the province's credit rating ... The consequences of a rating decline would be higher interest rates, reduced access to capital markets and increased exposure to foreign exchange fluctuations. (Sullivan, 2004)

In Alberta, Learning Minister Lyle Oberg used his government budget to justify the highly controversial compensation scheme he forced upon the Alberta Teachers' Association and the Alberta school boards:

> 5.8: This money [the 6 per cent raise over two years] is final. This is the amount of money that is in the Learning budget for the upcoming year.

I think that is quite reasonable. (Allyson Jeffs, "Teachers Offered 6-Per-Cent Raise," *Edmonton Journal*, 25 April 2001)

In the 5.5–5.8 texts, speakers used the demands of the global capital markets and meagre provincial finances to justify the austerity measures they had inflicted – or were about to – upon public-sector employees. Thus, to the implicit question, "Why do you do this?" the implicit answer was, "I was forced to." The Alberta learning minister's move was especially interesting. He chose to present a man-made document as an independent entity that handcuffed the hands of stakeholders, including its own creators. When Oberg declared that "this money is final," his words sounded like an axiom that everyone must accept. There was no mention of the fact that the Teacher Salary Enhancement Funding, which was vested with the limited money earmarked for the teachers' pay raise, was his own creation, a unilateral and unusual act that sapped collective bargaining of its vitality. Perhaps, if Oberg had given the full budget to the various school boards and allowed them to allocate it among their various budget items, they might have found a better, less confrontational way to deal with the union demands.

In addition to impersonal authorization, we found one instance of a third-party, or expert-based, authorization-legitimation strategy. On 5 January 2004 the recently elected premier of Newfoundland and Labrador, Danny Williams, issued a warning about the province's dire financial situation in a dramatic live telecast. The trigger for the speech was the release, in late December, of an independent audit of the province's fiscal situation. The audit found that the projected deficit for the 2003–4 fiscal year had ballooned to $827 million (PricewaterhouseCoopers, 2003: 2). The province's debt was estimated at $11 billion. This audit was an important source of legitimation for the austerity plan to which he alluded in quote 5.4.

Besides personal, impersonal, and expert sources of authorization, the evidence reveals another type of authorization legitimation, which the literature we reviewed does not mention. Tables 4 and 5 indicate that union and government speakers used a strategy that we call public-authorization legitimation. Speakers called upon the general public as well as specific groups (e.g., teachers, nurses) and broadly defined ones (e.g., workers, taxpayers, students and their parents, the sick and their families) to legitimate arguments and behaviour. Legitimation, as noted, is the answer to "the spoken or unspoken 'why' question – 'Why should we do this?' or 'Why should we do this in this way?'" (van Leeuwen, 2008: 106). Here, most often, when a speaker used authorization-legitimation strategy, the answer was, "because I say so." The "I" was a figure in whom some authority is vested. In the case of public authorization, there is no "I." Instead there is "you," where the "you" is an entity whose collective wish is "the speaker's command." Now the answers to the above questions are, "because you say so," or "because you tell me so," or "because this is your wish." Because this variant is not mentioned in the literature and because it was used fairly often in our cases, we discuss it at length below.

Public Authorization

Public-based authorization-legitimation strategy is elusive. Unlike other authorization types, its potency is not necessarily a direct derivative of its putative source, the public. Rather, it is contingent upon the fundamental tenet of democracy that enables the public to raise its voice and expects the leaders of society to heed it, or at least not dismiss it out of hand. As such, part of its power derives from the inherent structure of society itself. A democratic society enables a government and a union to present itself not as forwarding its own agenda but as acting on behalf of the people. In this way, unions and governments can portray themselves as altruists, or unselfish guardians of the public interest. To disagree with a leader speaking on behalf of the public is to go against the people's wishes, and perhaps even to quarrel with the process of democracy itself. Since in our cases both governments and unions presented themselves as speaking on behalf of the people, thus having society's best interests at heart, it is not surprising to find similarities between their discourses, and also to witness a type of discursive stalemate wherein each side claimed to be the bona fide "custodian of the people's discontent."

We would expect to find government portraying itself as speaking on behalf of the people. Generally speaking, since the voters have put the government in place, it can logically argue that it represents the majority of the electorate. Such a view, however, blurs the fact that less than half of the voting population may have voted for the government party, and it may be unclear how many of those voters agree with the government's position on any one issue. Similarly, union leaders may speak as though all of their members comprise a single entity that speaks with one voice. Yet this may not reflect the reality of mandatory membership and divergent opinions held by the membership.

Further, speaking in terms of *the public, the taxpayers*, or *the working people* means a high degree of assumed unison, abstraction, and generalization. In the context examined here, this tactic enables both sides to present themselves as cohesive entities united in their opinions and goals. Public authorization of this kind can be a double-edged sword, however, for while it, at least rhetorically, places the collective authority of an entire group in the hands of the person speaking on its behalf, it can also render that person a mere "errand boy." If government pretends to march to the beat of the public's drum, or a union to that of its members, then their actions can be interpreted as those of a steward. Yet government and union executives are also keen to be regarded as providing leadership. Later we show that, in our case studies, elected officials often portrayed themselves as ready to make necessary changes, as ones who did not flinch in the face of "tough choices." As such, few, if any, wished to follow public opinion heedlessly. The evidence suggests that the discourse of stewardship can coexist "peacefully" with the discourse of leadership. Speakers were never asked to reconcile the two legitimation discourses – the one that emphasizes the group as a source of authorization legitimacy and the one that stresses the value of responsible decision makers who do not hesitate to make unpopular or illegal decisions, even if it may cost them their political future or land them in jail. Perhaps acting in accord with the public can be considered an expression of leadership.

Government Use of Public Authorization

As revealed in Table 4, with the exception of New Brunswick, all the governments resorted to public authorization. Perhaps this is to be expected. After all, democratic governments are elected by the people for the people. They may feel comfortable, even obligated, to represent their constituents' interests and use them as a source of legitimation. Government speakers did that in several ways, which were distinguished from one another mainly by the level of the argument's generalization. For example, in the case of Saskatchewan, Premier Roy Romanow vigorously stated:

> 5.9: I'm firmly of the view that the overwhelming majority of Saskatchewan people strongly disapproved of defiance of the law, on top of it, strongly disapproved of defiance of the court injunction. People of Saskatchewan said [that the] 22 percent [wage increase the union is demanding] is just not on. (David Roberts, "Saskatchewan Nurses Back on Job," *Globe and Mail*, 19 April 1999)

This authorization strategy rested on the "people of Saskatchewan," who were summoned to grant popular support and credibility to the speaker's rhetoric. When the people of Saskatchewan had made that argument, and how Romanow knew that "the overwhelming majority" of them had made it, remained unknown, but the message was obvious – the government was acting on behalf of the people. Thus, the premier used the public to provide additional clout to his texts, clout that supposedly was independent of his being the "first citizen" of the province. Even though the argument was not grounded in fact, the public, at least implicitly, was expected to trust the premier's message because of who he was. After all, the people of Saskatchewan would not readily confide their innermost thoughts about the union's wage demands to just anyone. Hence an important attribute of public authorization is that, when it is not grounded in fact, its credibility rests on the speaker's attributes.

Similarly, Quebec's premier, Jean Charest, baldly stated that he spoke on behalf of all Quebecers:

5.10: My responsibility is to make things clear and to [speak] ... in the name of the Quebec citizens who must bear the cost of these talks and eventual collective agreements ... and that's what I've done. (Sean Gordon, "Charest Faces a Raging Bull: Quebec Premier Attacks Public Sector Unions' Privileged Status," *Toronto Star*, 13 August 2005)

In the same vein, Premier Williams of Newfoundland and Labrador opened his televised *State of the Province Address* with the following words:

5.11: On October 21, the people of Newfoundland and Labrador elected a new government because you wanted a new approach that will see the true potential of our province fully realized in a meaningful way. (Williams, 2004)

Clearly, not everyone had voted for Williams, but he recast his recent victory as an expression of the collective doing of Newfoundlanders and Labradorians. He was thereby now authorized to pursue their collective wish for a new future, of which Bill 18 was an important component:

5.12: We were given a mandate from the people to run this province on their behalf. That is exactly what we are trying to do [by passing Bill 18, terminating the strike by government workers, and imposing the government's final

· offer]. (Deana Stokes Sullivan and Barb Sweet, "Tough New Bill Aimed at Ending Ugly Strike," *Leader Post*, 27 April 2004)

In stating that the people had elected a new government because they "wanted a new approach," Williams depicted himself and his government as the visible manifestation of that fresh approach. His actions, then, were authorized because they were in accordance with, and cogently represented, the expectations of all the citizens; or in his words, his government "was given a mandate from the people" to do what was best for the people of Newfoundland and Labrador. Entrusted with a broad-based mandate, he sought to implement the agenda that the people had handed over to him. In this way, Williams was not responsible for the bitter debate arising from Bill 18 or for the strike itself. Instead, he presented himself as a conscientious steward who was carrying out the wishes of his master, the people. Whether or not this was what the people wanted, and precisely how many people were in favour of these actions, we do not know.

Occasionally, speakers relying on public authorization attempted to personalize a faceless crowd by informing the audience that members of the authorizing group had communicated their concerns to the speakers. The latter capitalized on something that was unavailable to the average person, a perspective that allowed the speakers to figure out the opinions held by the public and determine which ones were dominant. Like the proverbial orator preaching from a hill, some modern leaders seem to enjoy a vantage point that enables them to see how many people have raised their hands in favour of a motion. Unlike the man on the hill, the crowd cannot see the forest for the trees. Therefore, recognizing the leader's superior vantage point, the crowd may accept the orator's subsequent message at face value.

In British Columbia, the minister of health services, Colin Hansen, defended his government's actions by saying:

> 5.13: I have certainly had lots of phone calls to my office. I've had lots of e-mails. In talking to other members of the chamber, I know that they also have been in receipt of a lot of phone calls and letters and e-mails. (*Hansard*, 28 April 2004, 10635–6)

Again, we do not know how many people actually contacted the government seeking its intervention, or how many demanded that it not intervene. However, Hansen legitimated his government's actions by portraying them as faithfully representing the people's collective will.

A private case of public authorization occurred when a speaker from one side referred to members of the opponent camp to legitimate his group's actions. In Nova Scotia, Premier John Hamm called upon anonymous health-care workers to substantiate the argument that money was not the main issue of contention:

> 5.14: I had an opportunity to discuss the matter with a number of health care workers who came to visit here in Province House over the last number of days. Many of them were far more upset with working conditions, unacceptable call-back conditions, unacceptable workloads because of inadequate staffing, than they were with the offer that was put forward by the government. (*Hansard*, 26 June 2001, 5784)

Similarly, in Alberta, Premier Ralph Klein talked to reporters about the option of designating teaching an essential service:

> 5.15: My sense is that it is a priority – the whole issue of governance, the whole issue of whether teachers are an essential service. I have received many, many letters from teachers – even today, I received another stack of letters from teachers – indicating how important and essential they are to the future of our children in the province. (Dennis Hryciuk and Tom Barrett, "Klein to Teachers: You Can't Win: Gov't Vows to Remove Their Right to Strike if Court Rules in the Union's Favor Today," *Edmonton Journal*, 1 March 2002)

Although Hamm and Klein never mentioned how many workers communicated with them and made the purported arguments, or who they were, that such things occurred at all might have carried some weight with the public and undercut the union's position. The technique in which one side legitimates itself by drawing on supportive utterances from the other side is a powerful instance of public authorization. It has some interesting qualities. First, it is a great comfort to have representatives of one's opponent on one's side. This might add a layer of reassurance to one's own arguments. Second, usually, and this case is no exception, the sources of the legitimation – here "a number of health care workers" and "many, many letters from teachers" – remain suspiciously amorphous. Other stakeholders do not know who exactly they are, how many of them are involved, how many actually have made the arguments attributed to them, and how many actually support the union's positions. Finally, the public may embrace such arguments only because they are used by a prominent political figure. In other words, lacking concrete shape and form, this argument may not be able to stand on its own feet. Its utility likely depends on the status and credibility of the speaker.

In the above cases, the speakers implied that they were the trustworthy custodians of the public's sentiments, concerns, and preferences. As managers of the public well-being, they were confident enough to define categorically what the public interest was. Sometimes they simply knew what the people wanted, whereas on other occasions people had communicated their wishes and concerns to them. The upshot of this strategic tack is that one should listen to the speakers because they express the will of the people. Such an assumption is critical to the success of this legitimation strategy, since it appears that governments were not likely to support their public-authorization claims with concrete evidence. Veracity hinges on the speakers' attributes, such as status, bearing, and integrity. Implicit in public authorization is the notion that leaders should be in the privileged position of knowing what it is that the people want. They are the ones standing on the hilltop looking at the sea of raised hands. By contrast, ordinary people would not know what the majority want because they do not have access to that perspective.

Without hard evidence, public authorization would seem secondary to personal authorization. Nonetheless, it can be a powerful legitimation strategy. By deriving authorization for action from its constituencies, the government implies, if not directly declares, that "we are giving you, the public, what you have asked for." Then, an argument with the government becomes an argument with the people for whom the government speaks. This can paint the dissenting party as an interest group that is selfishly pursuing a narrow agenda at the expense of the public well-being. If successful, public authorization can render the union protests as nothing more than the grumblings of a disgruntled, and often unduly powerful, minority. Without it, unions can portray the government as the powerful Goliath bullying the weaker David.

Union Use of Public Authorization

Naturally, union speakers also employed the public-authorization legitimation strategy. As Table 5 shows, in five cases, leaders drew legitimacy to act from their union members. In the case of Saskatchewan, for instance, Rosalee Longmoore, the president of the Saskatchewan

Association of Health Organizations, legitimated an illegal strike by arguing:

> 5.16: The union will not direct people to go back to work. People have made a personal choice to stay out and we can't tell them to go back. Anger has been building for a decade because employers and administrators and this government have not listened to the issues that nurses have addressed in their workplaces. (Martin O'Hanlon, "Saskatchewan Nurses Vow to Defy Any Court Injunction," *Calgary Herald*, 10 April 1999)

In other words, the members had made a decision to defy the government back-to-work order. The union not only supported this decision but likely also provided the leadership and organizational infrastructure to sustain the illegal strike. Presumably, it would be well within the union leaders' scope to tell the members to obey the law and return to work. And yet, like her government counterparts, Longmoore presented herself as someone who was merely acting on the members' behalf in giving voice to their collective will. Since the union members had "made a personal choice," the union leaders could not "tell them to go back." Longmoore informed the public of what union members had decided, and then she provided an assessment of how this stage had been reached, which essentially placed her in the position of interpreter or commentator. Thus, not only did she relay the message but also she provided a meaningful context for understanding why that message had been given. In New Brunswick, the Canadian Union of Public Employees negotiator, Daniel Bernatchez, stated:

> 5.17: [The members] are very, very angry, they're disgusted, they're frustrated, they're everything you could imagine. We've tried to keep everything legal and now if the membership says to hell with the legal [strike], we want the illegal, that's the choice they're going to call for, and if that's what they call for we'll be there for them. (Kevin Cox, "Angry N.B. Workers Vote on Ending Strike," *Globe and Mail*, 6 March 2001)

Bernatchez positioned himself as the veritable custodian of the workers' anger and disgust with the government. It was the members who were angry and who might pursue illegal action, not Bernatchez and the union brass. In fact, Bernatchez presented himself, and presumably other union leaders, as the voice of reason and moderation as he tried to restrain the membership from acting illegally. By separating the members from the union administration, Bernatchez portrayed himself as an intermediary between the angry members and the government and public. But in the end, if the members chose illegal activity, the union leaders had no other choice than to "be there for them." This is a necessary consequence of public authorization. By arguing that they receive their marching orders from the public, leaders become guardians of the public will and managers of their discontent.

Unlike government, when unions used public authorization, the "public" was often tantamount to their members. This, in turn, could have saddled them with the status of a special interest group, an entity that might be oblivious to the needs and wishes of the general public. We will show in a later chapter how unions used moralization- legitimation strategy to blunt the edge of this image.

The Speaker Is One of the Group

We have argued that the use of public authorization often portrayed union and government leaders as stewards and managers of public disagreements, expectations, and interests. As such, they tried to heed the public's preferences by articulating them as a single cogent voice and converting them into policies (government) or collective action (unions). From this perspective, these organizations managed constituents' portfolio of grievances. Premiers, ministers, and union leaders listened carefully to the rank and file and then tried to act upon their messages. In short, they were executors of the public's will. Yet, occasionally, speakers using public authorization played a different role vis-à-vis the group they wished to promote.

With public authorization, speakers sometimes appeared to be intimately aware of what it was that stakeholders wanted, and also why they wanted what they did. Such intimacy may often manifest itself as strong identification between the speaker and the group members. Unlike the previous instances where the speaker stated boldly what members wanted but remained an independent envoy, the speaker now identified completely with the message. It was no longer a matter simply of what the members had said; rather, the speaker, too, held those views. For instance, in replying to the Newfoundland/Labrador government's proposed Bill 18, the president of the Newfoundland and

Labrador Association of Public and Private Employees, Leo Puddister, declared:

> 5.18: I'm really angry. I'm really mad ... We will gladly go to any bargaining table, but we've stated our position quite clearly for 20 days: we will not talk concessions. ("Newfoundland Tories Legislating End to Public Sector Strike," National Union of Public and General Employees, 21 April 2004)

Puddister was not just relaying a message from the members – he was himself one of them. Authorized to speak on behalf of the members, he now presented himself as being so intimate with their sentiment that it was his own. In truth, it was Puddister who had been stating the union's position "for 20 days." Yet his use of "we" suggests that his voice and actions were but the visible manifestation of the members' collective will. This fusion implies that he was keenly aware of what it was that the members wanted, since it was not only the members' cause but also his own. He was part and parcel of a specific in-group.

As noted earlier, public authorization tacitly assumes that the group has spoken as one, with no dissenting voices. Similarly, Puddister's identification with the members that he represented ("we") implied that this was a single group in wholehearted agreement. To say that "we will not talk concessions" portrayed the group as singular in their purpose, with no "me's" willing to offer concessions. In reality, one may never know how many are for or against a specific course of action. "We" is a key word in public authorization since it presumes that the speaker stands before us with the full force of the people behind him. "We" implies that there is a coherent and well-defined group that has rallied around a cause in opposition to another group. It should not surprise us, then, to find that "we" was used by all of the union leaders when defending their actions and asserting the solidarity of their unions.

Given that "we" is such a powerful word, it is also, naturally, a favourite among government leaders. The case of Saskatchewan represents its general use and rhetorical potency. When Finance Minister Ed Tchorzewski tabled his first budget, in 1992, he said:

> 5.19: Saskatchewan faces a finance crisis of immense proportion ... Let us look forward to the day when we can tell our children that, though we entered the 1990s plagued by financial crisis, we made the difficult decisions. We turned a new page in our history and put this Province firmly on the path to prosperity. (George Oake, "Saskatchewan Gets Tax Hikes in NDP

Budget," *Toronto Star*, 8 May 1992; Eric Cline, minister of finance, *Budget Address: Moving Forward Together, Saskatchewan Finance*, March 1999: 2)

The plural "us" and "we" of which Tchorzewski spoke likely referred not just to the newly elected New Democratic Party but to the wider community of Saskatchewan. Such usage presented the entire province as a single, cohesive entity that must now confront difficult choices to "turn the page" and return to "the path to prosperity." The minister's identification with the people (he is one of "us"), and the fact that a province of diverse people could be referred to as a single entity ("we"), demonstrated that government and citizens formed one united front.

Tchorzewski's use of the plural "we" and "us" deliberately diminished, or ignored, possible fissures within the group. At least on the surface, "we" painted a picture of a group that shared something important in common, and by contrast suggested that those who might speak out against "us" must belong to another group outside "our" own. "Difficult choices" would likely entail cutbacks and austere negotiations with the union. Yet "we" would work doggedly and persistently along the course of action "we" had chosen for restoring "our" province to "the path to prosperity." Those who opposed such measures were not part of "us." And, though it was not clear what to do with those outsiders, probably "we" should not let them derail "our" plan. Thus, "we" and "us" statements were inclusive and exclusive at the same time. The use of "we" created both an in-group and an out-group.

Another instance of this plural usage was illustrated when Newfoundland and Labrador Premier Danny Williams addressed citizens in his televised address. In this broadcast, as mentioned before, the central metaphor used by Williams to describe the province's situation was that of a mighty vessel forced to chart its way through the choppy waves of a turbulent future:

5.20: The time has come to turn the tide in Newfoundland and Labrador and chart a new course to prosperity and self-reliance ... Unless we significantly adjust our course, we are facing total deficits of 1 billion dollars or greater for the next four years at least ... We are in very real danger of drowning in our own debt ... My government and I were elected to help turn this situation around, and together we can do it ... It is not about shifting around the chairs on the deck of a sinking ship. It is about restoring the seaworthiness of the vessel so we can launch out into the deep with confidence and success ... The decisions that need to be made will not be easy, but with your participation, support and understanding, your government will lead you through it in a planned and progressive manner. (Williams, 2004)

Williams's metaphor depicted all the citizens of Newfoundland and Labrador as aboard a single vessel undertaking a voyage to the promised land of "prosperity and self-reliance." While such a metaphor allowed for dissension (mutiny), it did not allow anyone to not be on-board, and it assumed that it was government at the helm, carefully guiding the vessel of state. Though Williams could have presented the fiscal challenges as choppy seas ahead, he chose instead to present the problem as the ship itself. It was sinking because of an internal malfunction, and the solution lay not in seeking a safe harbour but in restoring the troubled vessel to seaworthiness. Yet, while captains have full control over their vessels, the present government had now assumed the wheel based on the "participation, support and understanding" of all its crewmembers and passengers. Together, they would go from drowning in debt to launching "into the deep with confidence and success."

On the one hand, Williams's metaphor presented all of the citizens as working together to restore the vessel, and, on the other hand, it tacitly assumed that those who were not on-board were not part of that great effort. While such terms as "we," "us," and "our" can be used to cement together a diverse group of people, they are also terms of exclusion since they distinguish "us" from "them." In this way the conflict was presented clearly. The details that necessarily muddy the waters in any conflict, like some members disagreeing with the official stance or agreeing with proposals from the other side, could be minimized and the conflict expressed in unequivocal terms. In addition, given that reports submitted via the media are a way to communicate with in-group members and the opposition, leaders' use of "we" can present a unified and defined group that has mobilized whatever means at their disposal to fight for what they believe. While government offers and union counter-offers are typically intricate, involving concessions in one area while demanding compliance in another, public authorization crystallizes the conflict into a defined and easy to comprehend battle between two forces clashing over a single point. The audience is left with one very clear, if simplistic, choice – do you wish to join "us" or "them?" Are you a member of the in-group or not?

And so, along the familiar dimensions of the in-group ("us") and out-group ("them") expression, we find that the in-group represented the will of the public; acted to promote the public interest; showed consideration and understanding towards others; and bargained diligently with the genuine aim of reaching a negotiated settlement. The opposite holds for the out-group, which, in a nutshell, was responsible for the current crisis because it had bullied the in-group; avoided bona fide negotiations; taken advantage of weaker groups; and acted to promote its own narrow interests.

The Effectiveness of Public Authorization

Given our data, we can only speculate that the success of this legitimation strategy rests upon its credibility and veracity. How can speakers' statements attain such status? First, if leaders speak on behalf of others, their arguments may carry more weight if grounded in concrete, unequivocal evidence. Our cases offer little such evidence. By and large, public-authorization statements were general; perhaps they were expected to be accepted at face value. Second, theoretically speaking, the success of this legitimation strategy also depends on the speaker's status, bearing, and reputation. To a certain extent (possibly a large one), the usefulness of public authorization is a derivative of personal authorization. In the absence of arguments firmly grounded in fact, this factor is liable to become all the more critical.

Third, we believe that, in an ideal world, speakers should maintain a delicate balance between the abstract entity that, supposedly, has authorized their actions and the actual individuals constituting that entity. It may indeed be difficult to arouse sympathy for a faceless body of people. Therefore, speakers should try to concretize their arguments by appealing to specific experiences, characteristics, and conditions of individuals within the group. For example, government speakers can draw attention to individual sick people and their family members who were directly affected by a strike in health care; to specific students who missed important examinations; or to working parents who had to stay home with their children as a result of a teacher strike. Union speakers, too, besides mentioning unacceptable working conditions, could point out the plight of a single parent who was forced to go on strike to improve her living conditions, or a young teacher with small children who felt compelled to go on strike to improve his classroom conditions. Such personal stories might help visualize, personalize, and concretize the predicament of an otherwise abstract group. By invoking familiar emotive scenarios, speakers might help ground elements that are less familiar to, and hence more difficult to grasp by, the general public.

In any government-union conflict, both sides are likely to appeal to the general public – those who are not in the eye of the storm (e.g., union members, students and their parents, the sick and their immediate families) – in order to elicit support for their positions and legitimate their actions. To reach those on behalf of whom one speaks as well as those who are not direct stakeholders, one must find something that is held in common, the reason being that "when people can locate themselves in the story, their sense of commitment and involvement is enhanced" (Shaw, Brown, and Bromiley, 1998: 50). But the story can collapse "if the audience is not interested or does not have the time to listen, if the narrative does not deliver verisimilitude by failing to 'resonate,' i.e., to touch those important wishes and desires that give it vibrancy and meaning, if the trust in the storyteller's ability, integrity or authority are undermined" (Gabriel, 2004: 69). Yet, surprisingly, in our study, we found only one anecdote where a speaker tried to concretize a situation. It was Alberta Premier Ralph Klein's story, told on CBC Radio, about the comparatively hard life of a Japanese teacher:

> 5.21: Speaking at a Tokyo luncheon, Premier Klein told an audience he had spoken to the husband of a Japanese teacher who said that his wife "makes about the same" as a Canadian teacher. The difference being, instead of working four or five hours a day, she works eight hours a day. And she only gets one-month holiday instead of two. And only one week at Christmas and one week in the spring instead of two weeks. And she has to work two Saturdays a month ... and she doesn't go on strike. (Jeff Holubitsky and Allyson Jeffs, "Teachers Outraged by Klein Criticism," *Edmonton Journal*, 9 February 2002)

The story was relayed to the public in an attempt to undermine the ATA's legitimacy. It was expected to concretize the greed and ingratitude of the union by contrasting its discourse about poor working conditions with the ethos of hard-working people who were satisfied with much less. Theoretically, we assume that, like a circus performer, speakers using public-authorization arguments should attempt to maintain their credibility by walking a tightrope that is stretched between the highly concrete (individual experiences) and the more abstract (group-based claims) aspects of the public-authorization strategy. Specific stories might give a certain shape to a faceless crowd.

Counteracting Public Authorization

Public authorization is predicated upon an assumed congruity between the interests of an in-group and those of the speaker who articulates them. Theoretically, to be credible, whenever speakers purport to speak on behalf of a group, they should use concrete evidence to justify their rhetoric as accurately reflecting the wishes of the group. And yet our evidence suggests that usually this does not happen. In our case studies, the government and union leaders presented themselves as speaking on behalf of cohesive entities whose members had confronted a well-defined adversary or predicament. Generally, a rather simplistic and ungrounded presentation likely rendered a complex situation meaningful and easy to digest. What this might have glossed over was how broad, or narrow, the group consensus was. After all, there will always be those who hold divergent views. The Achilles heel of the public-authorization legitimation strategy is therefore the counter-argument that the speakers have been selective in their hearing, or that they are only speaking on behalf of a few people or, worse, on their own behalf.

Initially, it may be assumed that, if government has spoken on behalf of the people, then speaking against the government is tantamount to subverting the will of the people. The case of Nova Scotia, however, demonstrates how the strategy of public authorization can be thwarted by giving speakers a taste of their own medicine. For, while the government claimed to express the will of the people, Opposition members countered that the government had actually ignored the people, that public voices had fallen on deaf ears. Unlike the government, the Opposition backed up its claims with hard evidence. The Nova Scotia health minister, Jamie Muir, proclaimed that the offer made to nurses would not only make them

> 5.22: the best paid in Atlantic Canada, but also it had been deemed by most people as being very fair. (*Hansard*, 26 June 2001: 4578)

The government's offer to the nurses thus represented what "most people" believed was fair. While it is not clear who "most people" referred to, or how Muir learned that they had "deemed" the offer "very fair," it is probably safe to assume that "most people" did not include the majority of the nurses. Muir continued with this theme when he justified the introduction of Bill 68, which, according to him, was something that "Nova Scotians I believe would support" (ibid.: 4579). Thus, he concretized the scope of "most people" by using the term "Nova Scotians." Muir's sentiment was echoed by Premier Hamm, who declared:

> 5.23: Nova Scotians understand fully that when you have revenues of the province growing at approximately 3 percent a year, and if, in fact, wage

settlements are exceeding that, we will continue to always be in a deficit position. (Ibid.: 5784)

The phrase "Nova Scotians understand fully" implies that the premier had a finger on the pulse of Nova Scotians, and therefore his actions likely had not alienated them. Precisely how many Nova Scotians supported the government's position was nebulous. Probably, the phrase was invoked to refute the discussion occurring previous to this speech in which the leader of the Liberal Party, Wayne Gaudet, had asked the Speaker's permission to table a petition circulated by residents of Nova Scotia. The petition said:

> 5.24: Whereas the Premier and Minister of Health have continually shown their disrespect for health care workers, especially with the introduction of Bill 68, therefore be it resolved that we, the undersigned, call on this government to demonstrate their trust in, and respect for, health care workers in Nova Scotia by immediately withdrawing Bill 68. (Ibid.: 5715)

This was but one of many petitions brought before the House of Assembly. In total, 100 petitions asking that Bill 68 be withdrawn were presented to the legislature. The petitions had as few as three and as many as 300 names affixed, collectively totalling 3,967 signatures. Submitting these petitions consumed a great deal of time and was meant to show the magnitude of the public's disaffection with Bill 68. The petitions challenged the government's claim of public authorization by questioning who was speaking on behalf of the people, the government holding the parliamentary votes or those MLAs holding the signatures of so many disenchanted citizens.

Of the seven cases selected for this study, this was the one and only occasion where a party used concrete data to defy its opponent's public-authorization claims. Surprisingly, for some reason, most such claims went unchallenged. Reporters, parliamentarians, leaders on both sides of the conflict, and the public did not ask simple questions, such as: How many people did approach the speaker? How did they communicate their concerns? What exactly did they say? If anything, the challenging of public authorization followed the same sweeping pattern as that of the initial claims. For example, at 4:30 a.m., Opposition member David Wilson contended that:

> 5.25: the overwhelming majority of Nova Scotians are saying that this bill is wrong and should not be passed. (*Hansard*, 26 June 2001: 5811)

Graham Steele added that the

> 5.26: government refused to hear the people of Nova Scotia ... There is no precedent for that, Mr. Speaker, in Nova Scotia. This government will not listen to the people of Nova Scotia. (Ibid.: 5821)

The image of a government that had appropriated the voice of the people and now turned a deaf ear, and a blind eye, to their genuine and impassioned cries was presented poignantly by Opposition member Frank Corbett:

> 5.27: Mr. Speaker, that noise outside the House is going to build. I said, if it triples in decibels, the Premier won't hear it, because he is blinded by an ideology that says let them eat cake. He doesn't care. I appeal to the less strident members of that Party on the other side, hear the noise, hear what that [the noise outside] is saying, hear what it is telling you. It is telling you Nova Scotians don't do business this way. Nova Scotians are fair; they are fair from Yarmouth to Glace Bay ... They are here to be heard. I want the backbenchers to hear them. If your strident, hard-core, heartless, government Leader won't hear you, let the backbenchers hear you. (Ibid.: 6037)

In a similar vein, Darrell Dexter, the leader of the Opposition, contested Hamm's assumption that he was speaking on behalf of Nova Scotians, stating:

> 5.28: Voters thought they were getting a mild country doctor but, instead, they have gotten a Premier who [pursues his personal wishes] not the wishes of Nova Scotians. (Ibid.: 5772)

Opposition member Robert Chisholm criticized the premier for allegedly ignoring the public will:

> 5.29: Nova Scotian after Nova Scotian came forward to that Law Amendments Committee and recommended binding arbitration as a way out, that is what should have been proposed in the first place. (Ibid.: 5823)

Overall, the Nova Scotia government was portrayed as having callously disregarded what it had claimed to be its own source of legitimacy, namely the people who, according to the government, considered the offer to the nurses fair. The technique used by the speakers, typical to public-authorization legitimation, was comprised of eloquent, dramatic, and yet unsubstantiated sweeping arguments.

Unions, too, can find themselves charged with not listening to their members. In example 5.14, Premier Hamm of Nova Scotia articulated such a criticism. He implied that those who were speaking on behalf of union members had not accurately expressed their sentiments. When given the opportunity to say what they really thought, at least some members told the premier that they in fact agreed with the government's offer; they might have tried to make their voices heard within the union, but for whatever reason they had been shunted aside. Hamm portrayed the government as open-minded and warm-hearted, willing to sit and "visit" with those on the other side of the issue. Such a statement is to be expected since, for those holding political office, public authorization is based on the premise that government is there to listen to all citizens. Another implication of Hamm's remarks was that these union members might have been disenfranchised. Their voices had fallen on deaf ears, which meant that perhaps the union leaders had selective hearing in pursuing their agenda.

This argument cuts to the heart of leaders' use of "we" since it suggests that there might be fissures within the in-group, that "we" might be a fiction conveniently used for strategic reasons. The metaphorical line separating the in-group from the out-group likely depends on the speaker. This is better illustrated in example 5.15, where Alberta Premier Ralph Klein reported what he had heard from teachers themselves regarding the essential character of their profession. Again, as we have seen throughout, Klein mentioned that he had received "many, many letters" rather than a particular number (how many is "many, many?"). And the blizzard of paper continued with the current receipt of "another stack of letters." The rhetoric suggested that teachers themselves, regardless of their union's official position, had made their views known to the premier, who had listened attentively and sympathetically. The receipt of so "many" letters represented the high level of trust that these teachers had for the premier, and perhaps frustration with their own union's hard line.

Conclusion

In summary, if challenged, public authorization can be a slippery legitimation strategy since, at least according to our data, it contains a built-in flaw. This weakness lies in the reduction of a large number of individuals to an abstract entity, such as "taxpayers," "the public," or "Albertans," that had allegedly responded in unison to a particular exigency, policy, or argument. To be a credible source of legitimacy, the audience should accept that the core collective identity is not a figment of the speaker's imagination or opportunism. Yet, as we have argued above, rarely were public-authorization claims contested because of a lack of supporting evidence. Audiences might have believed the speakers because of who, and what, they were. In such cases, public authorization was a derivative of personal-authorization legitimation. Speakers, however, can substantiate public authorization as an independent source of legitimation. First, they can concretize their arguments by grounding them in fact. Second, they can personalize a faceless group by offering testimonials of individuals who are caught in the "line of fire" between unions and governments. Naturally, the weakness of this move is the speaker's inability to indicate how representative the examples are.

Our seven cases offer little evidence of attempts to concretize public-authorization statements. Except for the cases of the Nova Scotia Opposition and Klein's story, both union and government speakers did not bother to ground their legitimation utterances in fact. It would therefore appear that, although government and union personnel relied on public authorization to legitimate their behaviour, decisions, and arguments, they did not substantiate the sweeping statements that underpinned this strategy. Perhaps this was because of the lack of any serious attempt to undermine public-authorization claims. For some reason, despite their vulnerability, these claims – and the strategy underlying them – were left unchallenged.

Chapter Six

Rationalization-Legitimation Strategy

Nearly one hundred years ago, Max Weber (1977: 325) argued that "every system of authority attempts to establish and cultivate the belief in its legitimacy." As explained before, this process is multifaceted. In our case studies, besides resorting to authorization-legitimation strategy, unions and governments cultivated belief in their legitimacy through rationalization, of both the instrumental and theoretical variety. As shown in Tables 4 and 5, instrumental rationalization was widely used by unions and governments alike. In contrast, we could find only a few examples of theoretical-rationalization efforts.

Van Leeuwen (2008: 113) defines instrumental rationalization as occurring when practices are legitimated "by reference to their goals, uses, and effects." When actions are rationalized in terms of a clear utility, concrete and well-defined results are linked to the current action. In the government texts analysed here, such results were frequently presented as fiscal gain and/or protection of society's more vulnerable members. For example, wage freezes/rollbacks and/or job cuts would bring much-needed financial relief in the short term, and prosperity in the long term. Conversely, government texts might attribute stark monetary consequences to union demands so that, for instance, a 1 per cent increase in salaries would cost $x million a year to taxpayers, and sink the province deeper in debt. In the hands of unions, instrumental rationalization often emphasized service quality, people's well-being, working conditions, and labour rights. For example, union texts presented the cost of spurning labour's demands in terms of decreased service availability and quality. Government-imposed austerity measures would result in longer lines, reduced access, and poorer service quality related to unreasonable working conditions and the exodus of valuable workers.

Table 4 Main Findings: Government

	Saskatchewan	New Brunswick	Newfoundland	Nova Scotia	British Columbia	Alberta	Quebec
Authorization	Personal Public	Personal Impersonal – Fiscal exigency	Personal Public Impersonal – Fiscal exigency; Expert third party	Personal Public	Personal Public	Personal Public Impersonal – Budget	Personal Public
Rational-ization — Instr.	Fiscal Patient Safety	Fiscal Patient safety Avoid arbitration	Fiscal Public safety Protecting the next generation	Fiscal Public safety Restart the stalled bargaining process	Fiscal Patient safety Restart the stalled bargaining process	Fiscal Bargaining is a local matter. Government should not intervene	Fiscal Government's actions will result in more services. Bill 142 was an option of last resort for getting a contract
Rational-ization — Theor.	Government ought to act in the interest of patients	– – –	– – –	– – –	Government ought to act in the interest of patients. One can't stop layoffs in a multi-billion-dollar industry	Teachers and students belong in the classroom	
Moralization	Public interest Leadership Collective bargaining	Public interest Leadership Collective bargaining	Public interest Leadership Collective bargaining	Public interest Leadership Collective bargaining	Public interest Leadership Collective bargaining	Public interest Leadership Collective bargaining	Public interest Leadership Collective bargaining

(Continued)

Table 4 (Continued)

	Saskatchewan	New Brunswick	Newfoundland	Nova Scotia	British Columbia	Alberta	Quebec
Mythopoesis	Government chose to act responsibly to protect public safety rather than court labour support in next elections.	A government found itself trapped in a crisis created by its inept predecessor. Yet it did not shirk its responsibility to the public. Facing a strike in an essential service, the cash-strapped government was left with little choice. It acted fast and decisively in the interest of the public.	A cautionary tale of an irresponsible Liberal government that brought the province to the brink of a fiscal catastrophe. This government was punished by the electorate. The new government was at the centre of a moral tale. It was the more responsible and honest protagonist, engaged in legitimate, if somewhat unpopular, practices.	The government was convinced it was fair, generous, and responsible; it did not hesitate to take a tough step for the collective good of Nova Scotians. This government was not bullying the workers. It respected organized labour and collective bargaining. However, because of the province's fiscal situation, it could not accept the union demands.	The story mixed cautionary and moral elements. The cautionary part highlighted the previous NDP government. Its close relationship with unions and general mismanagement undermined the health-care system in B.C. The government then added a moral aspect to its story by recounting its own efforts to rectify the situation.	The government was fiscally responsible and generous in its treatment of the teachers. Not only did it offer teachers very generous wage increases, it also offered to assume responsibility for the unfunded portion of their pension. In addition, the government showed respect for collective bargaining and preferred negotiated to legislated settlements. The teachers' greed and lack of flexibility forced it to use legislation to end the strike.	A moral tale of a responsible and reasonable government that went to great lengths to negotiate a fair agreement with the unions. A cautionary tale featured greedy and irresponsible unions that presented the government with unreasonable demands. It is a story about a government that chose to defend some seven million Quebecers against greedy unions representing about half a million workers.

Table 5 Main Findings: Unions

Saskatchewan	New Brunswick	Newfoundland	Nova Scotia	British Columbia	Alberta	Quebec
Personal Public – Members	Personal Public – Members	Personal	Personal	Personal Public – Members	Personal Public – Members	Personal Public – Members
Service quality Patient safety	Members' low wages	– – –	Democracy Labour rights	Restoring order to a chaotic system Labour rights	Service quality Internal solidarity Prepare others for strikes Pressuring government to provide more money to school boards	Protecting the public and union members from the government modernization plan. Getting a fair deal at the bargaining table.
– – –	Union leaders support the members' wishes	– – –		Workers will not respect a law that does not respect them. Angry workers are likely to strike	Regarding the withdrawal of extracurricular services, the union did not have any other choice. The ATA was obliged to fight Minister Oberg, who had resolved to break the union.	The government was stubborn and unrealistic. It was unwilling to reciprocate the union concessions. Consequently, the unions could not pull their punches.
Labour rights Public interest	Labour rights Living wage	Labour rights	Labour rights Democracy Respect	Labour rights Public interest Respect	Labour rights Public interest Equity	Public interest Representation

(Continued)

Table 5 (Continued)

Saskatchewan	New Brunswick	Newfoundland	Nova Scotia	British Columbia	Alberta	Quebec
The government was unable, or unwilling, to address the nurses' deteriorating working conditions and the failing health-care system in the province. SUN was acting to redress the situation.	A powerful, inconsiderate government declared war on organized labour. Its behaviour forced the workers to, first, walk off the job and, then, launch an illegal action to defy Bill 30.	A cautionary tale of a government that was engaged in socially unacceptable behaviour that might result in chaos in the province. A heavy-handed government tried to break the unions by turning a legal job action into an illegal one with a stroke of a pen.	The introduction of Bill 68 was an immoral step with dire potential consequences to Nova Scotians. To avoid such catastrophes as the loss of democracy and the chasing of nurses out of the province, organized labour had to face up to the hostile regime.	A newly elected government shook up the health-care system by shredding existing collective agreements and terminating workers. The unions decided to call a province-wide strike that would restore order and stability to the health-care system.	The moral tale involves a union that fought to restore proper funding to an underfunded education system. One cautionary tale explains that, by being careless, irresponsible, and vindictive, the government was responsible for the conflict. A second cautionary tale painted Oberg as a villain who was out to punish the ATA and teachers.	A moral tale of unions that were in the vanguard of a campaign to protect all Quebecers from their government. Accordingly, they should be praised rather than condemned as greedy. And the government should be denounced for being an inept bully rather than prudent and responsible, as it presented itself.

In contrast to instrumental rationalization, which pertains to a clear utility, van Leeuwen (2008: 113) defines theoretical rationalization as legitimating practices "by reference to a natural order of things." While implying that there is an immutable "natural order of things," it also invokes general accepted wisdom and presents a context wherein unavoidable events might lead to a particular outcome. Government theoretical rationalization may take the form of its inherent function or duty to protect citizens, and especially weaker groups. For example, government had to order teachers back to work. Why? Because it was government's duty to protect students. This is obvious to anybody, a well-known truism. From the union perspective, however, government can be portrayed as oblivious to the teachers' poor, and deteriorating, working conditions. The union may have tried to reason with the government, but the government does not listen – this is how governments are. Hence the only way to gain the government's attention is with strike action.

At first glance, instrumental rationalization appears as the straightforward justification of practices by reference to the function they serve, or the needs they fill, or the positive effect they will have. Yet rationalization, as practised here, does not stand on its own. To function properly, it maintains a symbiotic relationship with moralization. Thus, it would be morally wrong to keep students out of the classroom for a long period because their teachers were on strike. In other words, it may not be enough to justify an action on the basis of the clear-cut result it is likely to achieve. Frequently, the action should also be morally right; the utility the action seeks to attain should have an acceptable ethical standard. However, the relationship is not straightforward: "Moralization and rationalization keep each other at arm's length ... in the case of rationalization, morality remains oblique and submerged, even though no rationalization can function as legitimation without it" (van Leeuwen, 2008: 113). In our case studies, the rationalization purposes, functions, and utilities take the form of "moralized activities," that is, activities that have a moral dimension to them (e.g., they are the right things to do). For example, a government may rationalize its refusal to increase worker wages, or to roll back wages, by reference to utilities such as deficit reduction, debt control, and a desire to avoid additional taxation. The moral underpinnings of these utilities are not explicitly discussed. But, nowadays, they are likely to have positive moral connotations and receive popular support as the right things to do.

Union rationalization, too, may evoke a submerged moralization. Often, union texts depicted the consequences of government actions as deteriorating working conditions and service quality. It was not unusual for the union speakers to declare that they would do whatever it took to counteract such actions, even if it involved illegal practices. It was also common for speakers to invoke the protection of public welfare as a pretext for their behaviour. Fighting on behalf of the public to preserve the integrity of a public service may implicitly connote moral values, such as the union being a responsible organization advancing a broad social agenda.

According to the above, on the surface, instrumental rationalization is based on explicit and reasonable arguments that link actions and decisions to specific results. However, rationalization arguments also embody moral values, which should imbue utilities with an "ought to" quality. This, in turn, should help decision makers secure popular support for actions taken or avoided. Yet, at the same time, these values might be detached from the moral discourse from which they are derived. Often what remain are clearly expressed utilities and a set of functional justifications for their pursuit, associated with moral connotations that are expected to generate public endorsement. Therefore, in this chapter, as long as they are not explicitly moralized, we consider those justifications that unambiguously rest on utilities, or "such is life" notions, to be rationalization-legitimation strategies.

Frequently, the decision to seek specific utilities represents a choice. To understand why governments and unions choose to seek certain utilities over others, we have to extend the discussion to the contexts that have made it practical to promote these utilities. Context plays a fundamental role in the description, explanation, and interpretation of a situation. It is "the structure of all properties of the social situation that are relevant for the production or the reception of discourse" (van Dijk, 1997: 19). Contexts are a product of both the wills and the choices of the parties, and conditions not wholly within their grasp. The following presents each party's instrumental- rationalization techniques followed by a discussion of their contexts. Then we discuss the few texts expressing a theoretical-rationalization strategy that were produced by speakers from both parties.

Government Instrumental Rationalization

Instrumental rationalization is marshalled to legitimate practices vis-à-vis concrete goals, uses, and effects. Demonstrating how instrumental rationalization is manifested in the texts can be a straightforward exercise in that actors are often clear about how their actions will lead to specific outcomes. Therefore, we present only a few of the many available semantic instances. In the case of Alberta, Learning Minister Lyle Oberg rationalized his government's tough stance with the Alberta Teachers' Association by linking it to the need to restrain government spending:

> 6.1: Every decision I make on my budget affects every other budget and because my budget is so large, a one-per-cent increase in my budget is probably more than the rest of the government combined apart from health care. I'm exaggerating, but not by much. (Jeff Holubitsky, "Demands Tough on Teachers," *Edmonton Journal*, 3 January 2002)

He reiterated the gist of the argument a month later in the Alberta legislature:

> 6.2: A one-per-cent increase to all teachers' salaries costs the province about $23 million annually. (Dennis Hryciuk and Kelly Cryderman, "Province Challenges Union Estimate of Cost of Settling Dispute," *Edmonton Journal*, 7 February 2002)

Oberg thus rationalized his government's actions by reference to the likely financial consequences of straying from the 2&4 scheme set for the teachers in his budget.

Another example of instrumental rationalization appears in the case of Saskatchewan. In introducing back-to-work legislation, Justice Minister John Nilson and Premier Roy Romanow rationalized their government's actions by calling attention to patient safety. As leaders of the NDP, an allegedly pro-labour government party, they were prudent to create an appropriate context for the unusually quick back-to-work legislation, one that would show that they had not betrayed organized labour; simply, they had no other choice: To quote Nilson:

> 6.3: Today this government finds itself in the position [that] it must take the step of introducing back-to-work legislation. Our commitment to collective bargaining makes this a difficult step but one that is essential to safeguard the lives and health of Saskatchewan citizens. (Martin O'Hanlon, "Saskatchewan Nurses Vow to Defy NDP's Back-to-Work Order," *Globe and Mail*, 9 April 1999)

102   Bad Time Stories

And Romanow:

> 6.4: In the circumstances, the government has no alternative but to act. (Ibid.)

On 26 June, a day before the NSGEU began its legal strike, Nova Scotia Premier Hamm spoke in the House. He explained and justified the decision to pass Bill 68, which would render the looming strike illegal:

> 6.5: I think Nova Scotians understand fully that when you have revenues of the province growing at approximately 3 percent a year, and if, in fact, wage settlements are exceeding that, we will continue to always be in a deficit position. ... this is the single biggest offer that was made to any public sector group, as a reflection of the importance we put on health care workers. (*Hansard*, 26 June 2001: 5784)

In the same province, Health Minister Jamie Muir and Public Service Commissioner Minister and House Leader Ronald Russell provided another rationalization for Bill 68:

> 6.6: [Muir:] We are acting responsibly and decisively to protect the health and safety of Nova Scotians ... (*Daily News*, "N.S. Government Will Nix Nurses' Right to Strike," 15 June 2001)

> [Russell:] I think it's unfortunate but necessary. I think under the circumstances we have to protect the welfare of the people of Nova Scotia, who expect to receive a standard of health care that unfortunately cannot be continued under a strike situation. (Ibid.)

In Newfoundland and Labrador, Premier Williams stressed the need to live within the province's means for two reasons: first, there was no extra money available; and second, the welfare of future generations was at stake:

> 6.7: Our government may have inherited this serious fiscal situation but we have absolutely no intention of letting our children and grandchildren inherit it from us. There is no money available for salary increases at this time ... We can only conduct collective bargaining based upon the fiscal realities we all face, and we should only reach agreements that we can afford. Otherwise we only postpone the inevitable. (Williams, 2004)

In Quebec, Treasury Board President Monique Jérôme-Forget promised that savings were not the only reason for the upcoming budget cuts. The government's ultimate goal was more and better public services:

> 6.8: I promise that four years from now, there will be a hell of a lot more [services] than there are today. We have to go progressively like "the little train that could." That's my philosophy. It's clear that we want savings, but that's not the main goal. The objective is, more importantly, to give better services to people. (Mike De Souza, "16,000 Quebec Government Jobs to Disappear by 2013 under Plan," *Gazette*, 6 May 2004)

More than a year later, Quebec's Premier Jean Charest defended Bill 142, which imposed a collective agreement on about five hundred thousand public-sector workers, by saying:

> 6.9: We've negotiated everything we could. We are now left with one conclusion: We will not be able to have an agreement on salaries and therefore the National Assembly will be called back tomorrow so that we legislate on this issue. (Rhéal Séguin, "Quebec Set to Impose Public-Sector Contract," *Globe and Mail*, 15 December 2005)

> As we look ahead, given the public finances we have in Quebec, there's probably a number of people who, like us, believe that the approach and the negotiations in the future should be based less on some sort of artificial game played [but more] on whether there is or not money. (Kevin Dougherty, "Charest Calls Wage Negotiations an 'Artificial Game," *Gazette*, 17 December 2005)

The above speakers created a context wherein the government had to take painful steps to protect and improve the public's welfare, and the future of succeeding generations. The various messages also implied that legislation was not intended as an assault on collective bargaining. Rather, it was a measure of last resort. Thus, the government speakers implicitly, and occasionally explicitly, blamed the unions for being less than forthcoming bargaining partners.

In each of our seven cases, the government texts share all or some of the elements of the above examples. First, the government made it clear that it must act to protect the public against union collective action and/or excessive wage demands. The utility was explicit. In addition, it was implicitly moralized as something a responsible government ought to

104 Bad Time Stories

do. Second, the government took tough, yet necessary, steps to maintain order and keep public expenditure in check. Third, the government was not acting opportunistically; it was not taking advantage of the situation to undercut unions. On the contrary, the government had the utmost respect for organized labour, and its rights and institutions. However, the times were tough and they called for equally tough measures.

All of these government decisions also involved a choice. In the case of Alberta, the explicit choice was between transferring money from other ministries to finance the union's financial demands and choosing to reject those demands (more implicit government choices were raising taxes and/or tabling a deficit budget to meet the union demands). In Saskatchewan, the choice was between allowing collective bargaining to take its course and using back-to-work legislation to protect the sick and their families. Another choice concerned the timing of the legislation. The Alberta government ended the teachers' strikes three to thirteen days after they had started, and shortly after it had announced that it would not issue back-to-work legislation. The Saskatchewan government chose to order the workers back to work a mere six hours after they had gone on strike. Assuming that the ultimate decision was not made mechanically, it probably reflected its makers' values and preferences. Yet the logic that informed the actions of Alberta and Saskatchewan politicians remained hidden. In the cases of Nova Scotia and Newfoundland/Labrador, the government chose to terminate a legal strike (Nova Scotia) and cut jobs and impose a collective agreement (Newfoundland/Labrador) to protect patients and future generations. Here, the underlying logic was more explicit. Protecting the weak was likely perceived by many as something warranted – it was the "right" thing to do.

The above analysis emphasizes straightforward utilities (e.g., public safety, protecting future generations, prudent fiscal management) that were embedded within a context (e.g., political – government must stand up to unions; fiscal – it cannot afford giving in to union demands; social – the measures taken are painful yet essential) that was socially constructed to render inevitable, and morally correct, actions geared to securing those utilities.

The Context of Government Instrumental Rationalization

There are many instances of instrumental rationalization roughly similar to the ones discussed above. Further citation and examination of these instances would risk tedium and repetition. It might also miss more probing and provocative questions regarding why an actor has chosen a specific rationalization. As we have mentioned earlier, rationalization occurs within a specific context. Context is crafted to rationalize a chosen instrumental-rationalization legitimation, and in some important ways prescribes its outcomes. Context is like train-rails in that it provides rationalization with the means to operate while demonstrating how various points are connected; thus, it also determines the destination. While context provides rationalization with a coherent and meaningful medium for expression, it also prescribes its scope and may conceal the often arbitrary route of the fictional rails on which it runs. Recall that context is the structure of the social situation that is relevant for the production and the reception of discourse. If a discourse represents events and makes them known to us, a context provides filters that emphasize and dim objects in our view. Features of context therefore influence, and perhaps even condition, discourse, but the reverse is also true: characteristics of context may be defined by the preferred discourse.

It may be helpful to illustrate the importance of context by drawing upon a concrete example, and so we return to the case of Alberta. In the discursive context created by Learning Minister Oberg (see texts 6.1 and 6.2), a wage raise to teachers would negatively affect the allocation of finances to other ministries. While emphasizing this zero-sum constraint, he chose to ignore the handsome raises he himself, like other MLAs, doctors, and nurses, had received a few months earlier. In this instance, Oberg depicted the government as having a fixed amount of money that it could spend. Within such a context, spending in one area would result in less money elsewhere. Oberg thereby set a boundary condition that appeared to be both commonsensical and indisputable. There was, however, nothing that prevented his government from simply running a larger deficit, raising additional monies through taxation, seeking to justify a larger portion of spending for education within the budget limits, or adjusting the budget in any other way. In 2012, for example, the government of Alberta went through a "budget update" process. Facing falling oil revenues that might leave Albertans with an unpredictable deficit of between $2 and $3 billion (the original projected deficit was $866 million), all government departments were asked to find efficiencies to save at least $500 million in total (Bennett, 2012). While Oberg rationalized his government's position by outlining how a small increase in education spending would have dramatic consequences for other sectors, he could have similarly rationalized such an increase by appealing to the size and importance of his ministry, as ministers often do. The narrated context might have been a product of the neo-liberal discourse that pervaded the province during the 1990s

(Reshef and Rastin, 2003), or perhaps of Oberg's personal feud with the ATA. What we do know is that he tried hard to couch his decision in fairness to his fellow ministers and all Albertans, thus giving it a positive value connotation.

The importance of context may be further seen in the case of Saskatchewan. Premier Romanow invoked instrumental rationalization when he stated:

> 6.10: The province simply can't afford to meet the nurses' wage demands. (Martin O'Hanlon, "Saskatchewan Nurses Vow to Defy Any Court Injunction," *Calgary Herald*, 10 April 1999)

The Saskatchewan government had implemented a wage policy for all public-sector employees. Romanow argued that violation of this policy could open the floodgates for additional demands from other employee groups. A further rationalization highlighted public safety, which was a key interest the government wished to protect. According to Justice Minister Nilson:

> 6.11: It is our duty to ensure health care services for the people of Saskatchewan. It is a duty we take very seriously. (David Roberts, "Saskatchewan Nurses Back on Job," *Globe and Mail*, 19 April 1999)

Premier Romanow echoed the sentiment:

> 6.12 ... public interest in this case meant public safety. Patient care, that's number one. (Ibid.)

The context created by Nilson and Romanow implied that the only way to ensure public safety and keep the budget under control was to pass back-to-work legislation, and to do that summarily. The two politicians stressed that patient care was the government's number one concern. However, money was used as a supreme boundary condition as they put a premium on maintaining the integrity of the provincial budget. Safety had to be guaranteed within the limits of the budget. Back-to-work legislation and the imposition of a collective agreement were rationalized as the logical implementation tools. Interestingly, the speakers did not ground their arguments in evidence. They could have argued that, in the interest of public safety, government needed to reach an agreement with the union immediately, even if such an agreement resulted in more money for health care, which indeed happened later. But at the time, the financial imperative rendered such an argument inconceivable.

It should be noted that government can craft a context justifying a *lack* of involvement in an industrial dispute. In Alberta, this instance occurred when speakers tried to justify the government's (temporary) nonintervention in the teacher strikes. During the first days of the strikes, Clint Dunford, the minister of human resources and employment, explained:

> 6.13: The teachers aren't doing anything illegal ... Strikes are meant to be inconvenience. The government will only step in if job action by the teachers causes unreasonable hardship to third parties ... When these strikes end, I want school boards to be able to say they found local solutions to the issues in dispute. ("No End in Sight for Strike," *Edmonton Journal*, 20 February 2002)

Jerry Belikka, the Alberta Learning spokesperson, added:

> 6.14: Our stance is that bargaining is a local issue. Local trustees are elected to run the affairs of the local school board and make decisions based on what their communities want. (Wendy-Anne Thompson, "Union Wants Provincewide Bargaining," *Calgary Herald*, 17 February 2002)

Similarly, Learning Minister Oberg stressed the importance of not jumping the gun:

> 6.15: If we don't demonstrate it as a public emergency, the Alberta Teachers' Association can take us to court and have the arbitration ruling overturned. (Jeff Holubitsky, "Where's the Government?" *Edmonton Journal*, 8 February 2002)

In short, when the circumstances suited them, Oberg, Belikka, and Dunford announced that they would avoid legal intervention until they were convinced that a prolonged strike had created an emergency. Their twofold argument emphasized the importance of letting local unions and school boards find local solutions on their own, and the fact that the teachers were not doing anything illegal by walking off the job. This discourse would change dramatically within a few days.

A hazard of studying the instrumental-rationalization strategies of governments and unions is that it may become easy to overlook the socially constructed context in which they occur, or be aware of but accept it as a natural given. Our reading of the government texts serves to underscore ways in which instrumental rationalization functions within a pre-conceived context. In some ways, a study of rationalization can be like studying a key aspect of how trains transport passengers. It is easy to forget that the tracks on which the trains run could have been placed differently. Within the context of our study, the tracks between point A and point B may appear inevitable, but where the tracks have been laid might well be arbitrary. If designed differently, point A could have led to point C rather than to point B.

Union Instrumental Rationalization

As recorded in Table 5, unions, like governments, often used instrumental rationalization, with speakers framing it within a context that demanded immediate action to address burning issues and to right a wrong. But, while governments created contexts in which public safety and/or fiscal contingencies figured prominently, unions crafted contexts emphasizing government neglect, deteriorating service quality, endangered labour rights, and growing safety issues. In the case of Saskatchewan, Rosalee Longmoore, the Saskatchewan Union of Nurses president, justified the nurses' illegal strike by saying:

> 6.16: Nurses can no longer cope with staff shortages that have resulted in poor patient care and forced overtime. Anger has been building for a decade because employers and administrators and this government have not listened to the issues that nurses have addressed in their workplaces. (Martin O'Hanlon, "Saskatchewan Nurses Vow to Defy Any Court Injunction," *Calgary Herald*, 10 April 1999)

It had taken a decade to reach that tipping point where the union issues had to be addressed immediately. A Saskatchewan nurse emphasized:

> 6.17: We have to take a stand and now it's not only for ourselves but it's for our patients' safety and for all of Saskatchewan. (Ibid.)

Thus, the speakers established that the union and its members had arrived at a crossroads. After years of witnessing service deterioration, the nurses had to act to save the system, and they had to act now. In other words, the union was defying the law not to promote self-serving economic interests but rather to address an emergency situation that threatened an essential collective good.

In Nova Scotia, John McCraken, CUPE spokesperson, rationalized the union's actions by arguing that they were necessary to preserve the integrity of free bargaining:

> 6.18: It's either do [something] or watch our rights to free bargaining be extinguished. (Michael Tutton, "Walkouts Play Havoc with N.S. Health Care," *Kingston Whig-Standard*, 26 June 2001)

Joan Jessome, president of Nova Scotia Government and General Employees' Union, extended the argument by presenting the union members' decision to walk off the job as a protest against Bill 68, which suspended the right of the members to strike:

> 6.19: This is about the survival of democracy in this province. That is what we are fighting for. (Kevin Cox, "Union Sets June 27 for Nova Scotia Health-Care Strike," *Globe and Mail*, 23 June 2001)

Jessome used instrumental rationalization to pitch union actions as safeguarding the institution of democracy, a concern that should be close to the hearts of all citizens and that probably was used also to moralize the aggressive behaviour of calling an illegal strike (remember that the government made the strike illegal by applying Bill 68 to the strikers only hours after the strike had been called).

Like governments, unions used instrumental rationalization to create a sense of urgency and inevitability that required an immediate remedy to prevent the demise of a public service. However, unlike governments, unions faced two idiosyncratic challenges. First, at times, they had to defend an illegal action that interfered with the delivery of an essential service. They had to explain why they defied back-to-work legislation by not declaring an immediate end to strikes. They did so by emphasizing broad, public utilities as the pretext for their actions. This logic indicates the unions' second challenge, which compelled them to walk a fine line between pursuing their members' interests and championing the broader public well-being. Perhaps not surprisingly, only in three instances did speakers use wages to justify the union's actions. In the case of Quebec, Brent Tweddell, chief negotiator for the Centrale des syndicats du Québec, argued that the government offer was not acceptable:

> 6.20: What is on the table is basically going to impoverish people. (Kevin Dougherty, "Thorny Negotiations Ahead as Quebec Proposes Six-Year Contract to Unions," *Gazette*, 19 June 2004)

In New Brunswick, Marlene Ryan, president of CUPE Local 908, declared:

> 6.21: We don't even make above the poverty line. Many hospital workers are forced to take two jobs to make ends meet. (Kelly Toughill, "N.B. Hospitals Hit by Massive Strike," *Toronto Star*, 3 March 2001)

In Alberta, the ATA president stated clearly that an offer by the minister of education was a step in the right direction, but he expected more:

> 6.22: We are a step closer to a settlement but this is absolutely not a deal-maker. (Rick Pedersen, "Oberg's Pension Proposal Not Enough, Teachers' Union Says," *Edmonton Journal*, 12 January 2002)

In the cases that we have examined, these are the only occasions where union speakers acknowledged that insufficient wage increases were, at least somewhat, responsible for workers' discontent. It was more common to rationalize union actions by referring to the imperative of labour rights and/or a collective good, such as education or health care. As we have argued before, this approach might have helped the unions to present themselves as fighting on behalf of society at large, thereby escaping the label of interest group.

Given that interest-group dynamics are a part, perhaps even the essence, of the normal political process in Canada, it might be surprising that unions shied away from being considered an interest group. Likely, union leaders were concerned that the public would condemn them for pursuing better working conditions through strikes, let alone illegal ones, that denied ordinary citizens an essential service, and doing that at a time of restraint and restructuring. This might have shown the unions to be not just another interest group, but a callous one too. Perhaps speakers believed that, by avoiding the appearance of pursuing narrow selfish goals in favour of appealing broadly to collective goods, they would attract public support for their cause. Almost invariably, their rhetoric emphasized how unions were in the vanguard of campaigns on behalf of the public, fighting obstinate governments that stood in the way of service improvement.

Rationalization-Legitimation Strategy   111

The Context of Union Instrumental Rationalization

Union texts, like government ones, offer ample opportunity for exploring instrumental rationalization. As with our investigation of government texts, however, analysing the context in which instrumental rationalization is operationalized opens the door to a more provocative and illuminating discussion. The context created by union speakers enabled their rationalization efforts to appear straightforward and logical, but this was only because their context was constructed in a specific way. In other words, the context was crafted for a specific purpose, and should not be taken as the only possible representation of the way things were.

Let us briefly reconsider the previously mentioned case of Nova Scotia. Not only did the contextualization constructed by union president Jessome create a sense of urgency, it also invoked the very serious issue of a governmental assault on the fundamental institution of democracy (see text 6.19). Presumably, any measure, even if illegal, applied to the "fight" for democracy would be embraced by citizens living in that democracy. Yet was democracy in Nova Scotia facing a serious threat? How did an illegal strike by health-care workers serve to preserve democracy? Was the sovereignty, or the ability to pass legislation, of a democratically elected government not a cornerstone of democracy? Did the union not undermine democracy by supporting an illegal strike?

In the case of Quebec, CSN President Claudette Carbonneau outlined clearly what she believed would happen if the government proceeded unchallenged:

> 6.23: We won't let the government transform public-sector jobs into cheap labour and weaken the quality of services offered to the Quebec population. (Mike King, "Charest 'Swimming' in Troubled Water," *National Post*, 30 December 2004)

Carbonneau contextualized the union's actions as ensuring the health, safety, and convenience of Quebecers. What was not made explicit, however, was how the government's actions would transform public-sector jobs into cheap labour. The government had not, for instance, outlined a plan for privatizing or outsourcing the work. Neither is it clear how cheap labour would necessarily weaken the services provided to Quebecers. Perhaps most important is that the union president created a context in which the supposed consequences of government action would be felt acutely not only by the union workers but by all citizens. In this way, Carbonneau recontextualized the government's actions to demonstrate how they would affect the public. It follows that the union was fighting to protect the public rather than only its members' interests.

That the government actions would hurt the public, not just the union and its members, was again played out in the case of Saskatchewan. Though the government's measures appeared to affect directly and adversely the province's nurses, union texts portrayed patients as those who would suffer the most. A nurse contextualized the union's strike as being motivated by a concern for public safety and well-being:

> 6.24: We are striking for the safety of our patients because they're not being ensured safe care right now. There's not enough nurses and it's a dire, dire situation right now ... it's for our patients' safety and for all of Saskatchewan. (Martin O'Hanlon, "Nurses Defy Back-to-Work Order," *Calgary Herald*, 9 April 1999)

Within the context of this statement, the union's actions were rationalized by reference to its concern for the public. This is another example of how speakers rationalized union action by portraying it within a context where the public would bear the brunt of government (in)action, and where only the union was willing and able to confront the government head-on. In Alberta, ATA President Larry Booi expressed this theme succinctly:

> 6.25: Teachers are the only ones who are standing up for proper funding for education. (Jeff Holubitsky, "Huge Gap between Teacher Demands, Board Budgets," *Edmonton Journal*, 3 January 2002)

Generally, when constructing a context for instrumental rationalization, union speakers tried to avoid narrow interests that might portray their unions as interest groups pursuing a sectarian agenda at the expense of public well-being. As we stated before, although wage demands were often at the centre of the government-union conflict, union speakers mentioned them rarely, and then only to minimize their importance. Instead, they presented their unions as responsible social movements. According to McAdam (1982: 37), a social movement embodies "rational attempts by excluded groups to mobilize sufficient political leverage to advance collective interests through noninstitutionalized means." We suggest that this is the image union speakers tried to cultivate when they stressed, in their instrumental-rationalization arguments, how they were pursuing a collective good on behalf of everyone. As a result, they amplified the protection and promotion of public goods as the pretext for their actions, and downplayed wage issues. Often, they declared that they were fighting government to improve service quality, stop service deterioration, defend weaker groups, or protect democracy. In addition, they emphasized that they were the main, if not the only, group willing to do that. A context thus emerged where the union was the one group willing to take on a negligent and intransigent government to ensure the well-being of an essential public service (e.g., education, health care) or a fundamental institution (e.g., democracy). We note again that the unions did not use concrete evidence-based arguments. Instead, they opted for more sweeping, accessible arguments that required less complexity and elaboration, and that might have been more suitable for the mass media we use here as one of our main sources.

Government Use of Theoretical Rationalization

As noted earlier, theoretical rationalization invokes a supposed natural order of things, the way things are expected to be, as an answer to the implicit, or explicit, "why" question that underlies every case of legitimation. Where instrumental rationalization functions largely on the basis of a utility or purposeful action, theoretical rationalization is founded on some kind of accepted truth that requires little explanation. Practically, what this means is that speakers spend little time justifying their actions. Instead, they explain their action or decision by, for example, simply asserting, or implying, that "this is how things are," or, "this is what people do," or "this is life." Perhaps it is because of the apparent matter-of-fact nature of this rationalization that we found few explicit government statements of it in our research. Accordingly, compared with instrumental rationalization, a discussion of theoretical rationalization is often far less rhetorically intricate, which should not surprise us given that self-evident truths need not be explained – they are self-evident!

As indicated in Table 4, governments used theoretical rationalization on three occasions. In British Columbia, the president and CEO of the Health Employers Association of British Columbia, Louise Simard, argued:

6.26: The employers cannot put contracting-out on hold [during negotiations, as the unions demand]. This is a multi-billion dollar industry ... you can't just stop it and say everything's on hold. (James Vassallo, "Health Unions, Employers Deadlocked," *Daily News*, 5 April 2004)

The argument was presented as a maxim, a universal natural law that did not need any further elaboration. In addition, the B.C. premier, Gordon Campbell, explained:

> 6.27: Government has an obligation to act in the best interest of patients throughout the province. (Office of the Premier, "Agreement Reached to End HEU Dispute," 2 May 2004)

The premier made it clear that the natural obligation of government is to act in the interests of the people; this is what governments do. Similarly, in Saskatchewan, Justice Minister Nilson stated:

> 6.28: It is our duty to ensure health care services for the people of Saskatchewan. It is a duty we take very seriously. (*Hansard*, 8 April 1999: 457)

This is probably why the government ended the nurses' legal strike six hours after it had commenced. Although the government did not provide any concrete evidence for the actual impact of the six-hour-long strike, it invoked a truism as the pretext for its very quick action. Note that these statements are not the same as, "We act to protect people who might be at risk because of a strike." Rather, they rationalized the government actions (i.e., passing legislation to end legal strikes) without having to explain why those actions were preferable or in the citizens' best interests. It also implied that government had nothing against the unions and their right to strike. Simply, a government's duty to protect its citizens came first, outweighing its obligation to free collective bargaining and the right to strike.

In the case of Alberta we find another application of theoretical rationalization when Learning Minister Oberg stated plainly:

> 6.29: There is absolutely no way the public, the government or anybody else would tolerate kids missing six months of the year, half a year of schooling, because someone is on strike. I think that teachers belong in the classroom, I think that students belong in the classroom and anything we can do to ensure that happens I think is critical. (Kerry Williamson, "Oberg Fears Strike Can't Be Averted," *Calgary Herald*, 12 January 2002)

In Oberg's formulaic world, teachers teach and students study. This is a supposedly well-known truth to which much of Oberg's audience might readily subscribe. It follows that a teachers' strike was an unacceptable event. Thus, government action to preserve the integrity of this order needed no further explanation or justification. Teachers should be teaching and students should be studying, and governments should ensure that they continue to do so. With little intellectual effort one can extend this aphorism by substituting workers for teachers and working for teaching, thereby, theoretically, obliterating the notion of strikes altogether.

Theoretical-rationalization statements seem to be commonsensical. After all, they are supposed to be based on widely shared conventions. However, van Leeuwen and Wodak (1999: 107–8) have nuanced this observation by adding that "theoretical rationalization legitimations have the surface of explicit and reasonable arguments." They explain further that these legitimations "invariably embody values (and social prejudices) which are detached from the moral logic from which they stem, and presented as common-sense fact" (ibid.: 108). In other words, theoretical-rationalization utterances may be marked by subtext. The governments of British Columbia, Saskatchewan, and Alberta justified their actions (back-to-work legislation in all three cases) by referring to conventional wisdom – governments exist to protect their citizens, especially the weaker groups in society (in the first two cases), and teachers should teach and students should study (in the case of Alberta). These explanations, however, might have been a convenient excuse for engaging in ideologically driven behaviour. By the late 1990s and early 2000s, at least in Alberta and British Columbia, neo-liberal philosophy had matured and specific strategies (e.g., cutting budgets, privatizing public services, laying off public-sector workers, wage rollbacks) for its implementation in the public sector had been refined. For many politicians, that philosophy and its associated policy tools acquired moral connotations (Adams, 2001: 222; Reshef and Rastin, 2003: 228). So, perhaps, neo-liberal actions were moralized in ways that made those actions more "palatable."

There is little indication that, in Saskatchewan, the pro-labour NDP government was similarly influenced by the ideology of neo-liberalism. Its reaction to union demands, which were made in a context of a rising deficit and accumulating debt, appears to have been entirely pragmatic. What is harder to explain is the government's rush to end a legal strike merely six hours after it had started. Perhaps it wished to signal that its commitment to the welfare of all Saskatchewanians outstripped its loyalty to organized labour. Put differently, perhaps the Saskatchewan government wanted to demonstrate that it was not beholden to the interests of unions.

Union Use of Theoretical Rationalization

Like the governments, union speakers linked theoretical-rationalization legitimation to the unions' raison d'être. Unlike the governments, these speakers did not pull any punches when attributing union and rank-and-file frustration to government actions. In the case of New Brunswick, for instance, union negotiator Daniel Bernatchez stated:

> 6.30: [The union] tried to keep everything legal and now if the membership says to hell with the legal [strike], we want the illegal, that's the choice they're going to call for, and if that's what they call for we'll be there for them. (Kevin Cox, "Angry N.B. Workers Vote on Ending Strike," *Globe and Mail*, 6 March 2001)

Union action was rationalized via the nature of the union itself, which required it to stand up for its members and "be there for them." If members had decided to pursue illegal strike action, then the union must support their decision because unions were democratic organizations that listened to their members and acted upon their wishes. Not only had the action been rationalized, but it had also rendered inaction unacceptable. In a similar vein, in British Columbia, Jim Sinclair, president of the B.C. Federation of Labour, explained why workers defied Bill 37:

> 6.31: That's why workers throughout B.C. are angry today. They feel the government refuses to listen and doesn't care about working people. They see ordinary workers being hammered – they know they could be next. They see the unfairness when the government cuts wages for workers, but gives huge increases to those who are already the top paid. The vast majority of British Columbians recognize that Bill 37 went too far ... I expect there will be more disruptions and more people saying no to this government and its bully tactics. (Michael McCullough and Maurice Bridge, "Deal Ends HEU Strike," *Vancouver Sun*, 3 May 2004)

According to Sinclair, B.C. workers defied the law because that was how angry workers behaved towards an unfair government that had bullied them. Government had only itself to blame for the situation, given the way it had treated these workers.

In Alberta, ATA President Larry Booi crafted a similar context for the theoretical rationalization he used to explain the teachers' strike:

> 6.32: Teachers are so angry with Dr. Oberg. Dr. Oberg has wanted punitive legislation and union busting since the beginning. (Graham Thomson and Jeff Holubitsky, "Oberg Won't Tolerate 2nd Walk," *Edmonton Journal*, 23 February 2002)

Within this context, the union's implied sincere efforts to negotiate were presented as having been unheeded. Rather, Oberg was driven by an agenda that sought to bust the union. The decision to use power against power was only natural. Moreover, while the union had negotiated with the government in good faith, it now presented government in general and Oberg in particular as assaulting the union itself. In this way, Booi rationalized the union's actions within the context of fighting for survival. Implicitly, within such a context, further negotiation and bargaining talks were rendered moot, since a larger and more serious battle was under way. After the Alberta teachers returned to work, they continued their fight by withdrawing from extracurricular activities. The ATA president justified this controversial move by portraying it as the only thing the teachers could do under the circumstances:

> 6.33: Nobody's minimizing the loss of extracurricular activities for kids. But tell me what other choices teachers have that aren't simply a meek acceptance of a really vile process. (Tom Olsen, "Teachers Outline Next Step in Fight," *Calgary Herald*, 19 March 2002)

The message embodied in the above texts was straightforward – the governments had treated the rank and file unfairly and disrespectfully; not surprisingly, the union members were very angry; angry members would likely take their frustration to the street; and if they decided to act collectively, the union leadership would support them regardless of the action's legal status, or its inconvenience to the public. Unions would not allow governments to ride roughshod over their members without retaliation. They would not hesitate to disrupt the social order to counteract the bullying tactics of government, regardless of the legality of their actions. After all, this is why unions exist. As Bob White, former president of the Canadian Auto Workers and the Canadian Labour Congress, has succinctly explained: "Workers don't need a union to walk them backwards. They can do that on their own" (White, 1987: 182).

Generally, justification of actions and decisions within the framework of theoretical rationalization is essentially self-explanatory. It is based on the innate logic of a situation, as set out by specific speakers through the use of, usually, a short formulaic expression. It is underlain by conventional wisdom, or rather by that which speakers consider as such. This quality is the theoretical-legitimation strategy's main source of power. Supposedly, it requires little elaboration and should be immune to any counter-arguments. Its weakness surfaces when another party refuses to accept it or produces a different version of the truth, an alternative natural order. As we show in the next chapter, theoretical rationalization comes close to moralization-legitimation strategy, since both appeal to broadly shared conventions. The difference is that, when one uses theoretical rationalization, one implicitly argues that a decision/action has been taken because "such is life," "this is the way things are," "this is how people/governments/unions behave," or "what other choice do we have?" When one moralizes an action or decision, one is more likely to state that this is what ought to be done, and that anyone in the same situation might reasonably have done the same. Thus, when moralizing, speakers try to identify motives that are publicly endorsed. When using theoretical rationalization, the audience is expected to yield to force majeure.

Chapter Seven

Moralization-Legitimation Strategy

Moral evaluation is legitimation by reference to specific value systems that provide the moral basis for legitimation. Explaining actions in terms of public values identifies, or implies, motives that are expected to be publicly endorsed. It suggests that anyone in a similar situation might reasonably have adopted a similar course of action (Provis, 1996: 473–4). Sometimes, moral value is simply and clearly asserted using well-established yardsticks such as "bad" or "good," "right" or "wrong," "true" or "false." In many cases, it is true, "moral evaluation is linked to specific discourses of moral values," but "often, these discourses are not made explicit and debatable. They are only hinted at, by means of adjectives such as 'healthy,' 'normal,' 'natural, 'useful,' and so on" (van Leeuwen, 2008: 110). These linchpins evoke a moral concept but are not directly linked to the system of interpretation from which they derive. Sometimes we can recognize them only on the basis of our knowledge of the relevant culture (e.g., the moral connotation of "efficiency" or "streamlining" in North America). In more complex cases, an activity (*back-to-work legislation*) is referred to by means of several expressions (*government is committed to the well-being of all citizens, and especially to that of vulnerable groups; health care is an essential service; the union refuses to negotiate in good faith*) that extract from it a quality (*legislation is needed to protect patient safety*) which links it to a discourse of values (*a negotiated settlement is preferred to legislation, but patient safety is more important than a negotiated settlement; hence, given the current circumstances, back-to-work legislation to end a strike in health care is the right thing to do*).

Moralization can be a powerful legitimation strategy, since it "attacks" the innermost core of human existence – its value system. This, however, may also be a source of weakness. Moralization differs from the other three legitimation strategies in a fundamental way. To be effective, each strategy relies on a specific yardstick. Authorization rests heavily on the status of the speakers. Rationalization, at least its instrumental version, highlights concrete utilities and uses evidence to justify action to promote or protect them. Mythopoesis, as we show later, weaves stories that differentiate between those who are rewarded for engaging in acceptable social practices and those who are punished for deviating from them. Moralization, on the other hand, confronts one set of values with another and asks the audience to embrace one and reject the other. In the absence of a widely accepted yardstick, which often might be the case here (e.g., efficiency vs. job security, investment vs. sacrifice), the audience's response depends on the speakers' rhetorical prowess. Speakers have to persuade stakeholders that they are ethical and moral or, more accurately, more ethical and moral than their opponents.

When using moral-legitimation strategies, speakers are likely to rely on several value domains. Following are the domains from which the government speakers in our case studies borrowed the values they used to legitimate their government policies and actions. Note that several of the previously mentioned rationalization strategies focused on kinds of behaviour that were actually moralized activities, and hence reappear below. In other words, in addition to the fact that they were expected to generate specific utilities, these types of behaviour were also presented as "the right thing to do" or things that "you would also do had you been in our shoes." This is of utmost importance given the provocative nature of some of the behaviour concerned.

Government Moralization Strategy

Moral legitimacy, it will be recalled, reflects a positive normative evaluation of the organization – here the government – and its activities (Suchman, 1995: 579). How did the government speakers impress upon the public the notion that their collective good was promoted by its actions, and that these actions were the right ones? As revealed in Table 4, all seven governments used three core values to moralize their behaviour – public interest, leadership, and collective bargaining. Below, we offer a few examples to illustrate how speakers used each value to moralize their behaviour, plans, and positions.

Value of Public Interest

A key value that government speakers used to legitimate their policies and actions was the public interest, or well-being. We distinguish between two uses of this value. First, speakers argued that the public at large might suffer if the government did not act decisively and summarily. Second, speakers might focus on the plight of a specific group that was directly and adversely influenced by workers' job action or unacceptable union demands. In Saskatchewan, for example, the striking nurses were portrayed as robbing the public of an essential service that bore directly on people's safety. The nurses thus left the government little choice. Reluctantly, but acutely aware of the gravity of the situation, the government stepped in quickly to save the day, thereby performing its duty. According to Premier Romanow and Justice Minister Nilson:

> 7.1: [Romanow:] In the circumstances, the government has no alternative but to act. (Martin O'Hanlon, "Saskatchewan Nurses Vow to Defy NDP's Back-to-Work Order," *Globe and Mail*, 9 April 1999)
>
> [Nilson:] It is our duty to ensure health care services for the people of Saskatchewan. It is a duty we take very seriously. (*Hansard*, 8 April 1999: 457)

A few days later, Romanow combined a need to protect the public safety with an unequivocal commitment to assuring patient care to further legitimate his decision to pass back-to-work legislation a mere six hours after the strike had begun:

> 7.2: And public interest in this case meant public safety. Patient care, that's number one. And we'll be judged or elected on that in due time. I have absolutely no qualms in my heart, in my soul, in my mind that we did the best that we could to protect Medicare, to protect patient safety. (David Roberts, "Saskatchewan Nurses Back on Job," *Globe and Mail*, 19 April 1999)

The New Brunswick government speakers also emphasized the importance of providing uninterrupted health-care services to guarantee the public's well-being. According to Premier Lord:

> 7.3: The health-care system cannot cope with a strike of this magnitude for very long. (Kelly Toughill, "N.B. Hospitals Hit by Massive Strike," *Toronto Star*, 3 March 2001)

In his budget address, Minister of Finance Norman Betts stressed:

> 7.4: We know that for New Brunswickers there are some things that matter above all: ensuring quality health care ... helping those who cannot help

themselves; protecting the health and safety of New Brunswickers. (Betts, 2000)

Later, Betts explained:

> 7.5: The decision [to pass Bill 30, which would allow the government to end the legal strike] was not taken lightly. We tipped the scales toward our responsibility to the patients. ("N.B. Premier Defends Actions in Hospital Strike," *Examiner*, 6 March 2001)

Interestingly, when justifying their decision to end the hospital workers' legal strike, none of the New Brunswick government speakers mentioned, even in passing, that more than half of the workforce had been designated essential, and therefore stayed on the job, likely ensuring an acceptable level of service. The semantic move of staying quiet on important aspects of a dispute is an important component of legitimation efforts. We elaborate on it in the last chapter.

In Nova Scotia, speakers justified the introduction of Bill 68, which was designed to prevent a strike in health care by suspending the workers' right to strike for three years, by stating:

> 7.6: [Health Minister Muir:] We are acting responsibly and decisively to protect the health and safety of Nova Scotian. (*Daily News*, "N.S. Government Will Nix Nurses' Right to Strike," 15 June 2001)

> [Public Service Commission Minister and House Leader Ronald Russell:] I think it's unfortunate but necessary. I think under the circumstances we have to protect the welfare of the people of Nova Scotia, who expect to receive a standard of health care that unfortunately cannot be continued under a strike situation. (Ibid.)

In Newfoundland and Labrador, the speakers went to great lengths to convince the citizens that the government was acting on their behalf. Premier Williams highlighted two reasons for the government's decision to end the public-sector strike and impose the government's final offer on the workers – the need to bring the fiscal situation under control, and the need to avoid chaos in the health-care system. Thus, he argued:

> 7.7: There are 500,000 people in this Province besides the public sector workers. We have to look out for them as well. (*House of Assembly Proceedings*, 26 April 2004, vol. 45, no. 22)

> The Government of Newfoundland and Labrador has to have stability in its public sector services. We cannot proceed without a collective agreement. We are now into twenty-nine days of trying to negotiate a collective agreement. We worked until very, very late last night in an attempt to advance this ... It has never been this government's intention to strip contracts ... We have made every effort to try and reach solutions. (Ibid., no. 24)

In a nutshell, the need to protect the collective good of the province surpassed the vested interest of the strikers. Importantly, Bill 18 was an option of last resort, taken by a conscientious government that tried hard to avoid abrogating collective contracts.

In Alberta, Learning Minister Oberg made a sweeping argument to justify his stern warning to teachers. They should not expect the government to pull its punches if they decided to walk off the job and shut down the education system for six months. As we know, his government terminated the strike before it was even half a month old.

> 7.8: There is absolutely no way the public, the government or anybody else would tolerate kids missing six months of the year, half a year of schooling, because someone is on strike. (Kerry Williamson, "Oberg Fears Strike Can't Be Averted," *Calgary Herald*, 12 January 2002)

> Over the coming days our priorities will be to examine whether this action is causing unreasonable hardship to students, families and other third parties. ("No End in Sight for Strike," *Edmonton Journal*, 20 February 2002)

The public that the government wanted to protect was defined as students, their families, and "other third parties." Presumably, the definition did not include the striking teachers and their families. When he defended the government decision to order the teachers back to work, Oberg chose to stress the government's obligation to the students:

> 7.9: We feel it's absolutely hideous [that] students are in the middle of this. What we have done today is take students out of the equation. ("Manipulation 101," *Calgary Herald*, 22 February 2002)

The Quebec government used the value of public interest to moralize its actions in two ways. First, according to Treasury Board President

Monique Jérôme-Forget, the government's austerity plan should result in more and better public services:

> 7.10: It's clear that we want savings, but that's not the main goal. The objective is, more importantly, to give better services to people. (Mike De Souza, "16,000 Quebec Government Jobs to Disappear by 2013 under Plan," *Gazette*, 6 May 2004)

Thus, public-sector restructuring was aimed not at creating a leaner government by privatizing services and laying off workers, but rather at providing more and better services to the public. Savings were likely a welcome, yet secondary, goal; downsizing was probably collateral damage. The ensuing labour conflict was a result of the government's unwavering commitment to the public interest in the face of labour pigheadedness, as the next argument suggests. Second, the government was not willing to give in to union demands and finance them by raising taxes. Jérôme-Forget emphatically declared:

> 7.11: I don't print money. I have to take it from taxpayers' pockets. ("Quebec Government, Public Sector Unions at Impasse," *Expositor*, 20 June 2005)

The premier sent a similar yet sharper message by referring to two additional values – protecting future generations and equity. Charest would not

> 7.12: buy peace by sending the bill to future generations of Quebec ... [His] first duty is towards equity between all Quebecers and all generations. (Mike De Souza, "Public Sector Unions Warned to Keep Demands Reasonable," *Gazette*, 8 August 2005)

Taken together, probably, the above arguments were relevant to every citizen and easily understood, presented the unions in a negative light, and placed a significant pressure on them to justify their harmful actions. In a nutshell, the government argued that it worked very hard to protect and promote the interests of the whole province, including its future generations, and would not succumb to the will of an interest group. By claiming to be acting on behalf of the public in general, and weaker groups in particular, the government might have achieved two goals. First, it conducted itself as a "class act" during a very difficult time. Governments took the high road by demonstrating honesty, fairness, and selflessness while sticking to its game plan of eliminating budget deficits and provincial debts. Second, mostly implicitly, the government speakers painted the unions as a greedy self-centred interest group which was willing to play hardball with little regard for the public welfare. If we are correct, then this was a shrewd strategic move. Often, without using any explicitly derogatory language, the speakers might have managed to undermine the union's value system in the court of public opinion.

Value of Leadership

Given how we define leadership below, one would expect the value of leadership to permeate our speakers' remarks in a profound manner. We consider leadership a process of influence in which one person can enlist the aid and support of others in the accomplishment of a common task. In other words, leadership is organizing a group of people to achieve a common goal. In itself, leadership is a value. It is something people expect high-ranking personnel to have and demonstrate. In most organizations, people who are positioned high in the organizational hierarchy are expected to have a grand vision, chart a plan to accomplish it, and convince others to embrace it. In short, they are leaders and are expected to lead. However, leaders can show their mettle in a variety of ways and styles. They can be more or less rational, impartial, benevolent, brutal, and so on. Across the cases studied here, the evidence suggests that government speakers chose to emphasize several highly consistent leadership traits in their efforts to convince the public of the morality of their behaviour. Below, we discuss these elements. Each case involved at least one of the following values – integrity, fairness, responsibility, and prudence. Again, because of space considerations, we offer only a few brief examples to illustrate our arguments.

INTEGRITY

Several speakers chose to moralize their actions by reference to their personal veracity. They were elected to enact an election platform, or a vision. Although their agenda might require individual and collective sacrifices, they were still standing by their campaign promises. They would not stray from the road charted during the election campaign, even if it cost them the next election. Saskatchewan, where the NDP government (the only one in this study) had maintained a long and close relationship with the labour movement, epitomized this scenario. Premier Romanow made it clear that he had no regrets about how his government had handled the nurses' strike (ending it only six hours after it had started), even if it might have undercut his relationship with the unions and the prospects of getting re-elected. The vision he was pursuing made that cost worthwhile:

> 7.13: People of Saskatchewan said [that the] 22 percent [wage increase the union is demanding] is just not on. If [my] handling of the nurses' strike has chilled relations between the NDP and organized labour, then so be it. I took an oath of office to do the best that I could to define the public interest ... And we'll be judged or elected on that in due time ... What the voters decide, of course, is the prerogative of the voters. (David Roberts, "Saskatchewan Nurses Back on Job," *Globe and Mail*, 19 April 1999)

Romanow was fully aware of the possible consequences of his action. He chose to prevent workers, his party's closest ideological and political ally, from exercising a right their union had won after a long and bitter fight. Yet the premier was ready to pay a heavy price for being a principled politician. In itself, that stance might have increased his social capital in the eyes of the public.

In New Brunswick, Premier Lord was even more belligerent:

> 7.14: We have responsibilities as the government that I take very seriously. (*Calgary Herald*, "New Brunswick Hospital Strikers Forced to Return," 6 March 2001)
>
> I will not be taken hostage by a union. If ... union leaders ... want to work against me in the next election, so be it, I will deal with that. ("Strike Ends, Union Vows Revenge," *Observer*, 7 March 2001)

The premier's moral compass was well calibrated. He was facing an opponent who might like to take him hostage. However, this was not going to happen, at least not without a fight. He was ready to do whatever it took to protect the public interest, even if that might exact the highest political toll. The use of the word "hostage" is interesting. It is associated with terrorism, and was likely to evoke strong emotions among at least some of the audience. It implied that Premier Lord was facing a group of potential terrorists, the workers and their union, yet at least in the short term he would prevail. The demonstration of fortitude might have elicited sympathy and support from the public.

In Nova Scotia, Premier Hamm made it clear that, regardless of the union pressures:

> 7.15: I am not going to back away from the right thing to do and I think the right thing to do is to get the finances of this province under control. Just think back on how many years you've seen governments that in the end knuckle under and do things that you know didn't make sense in the long run. (Kevin Cox, "Bill; Banning Strikes Will Exact Toll, Hamm Say," *Globe and Mail*, 16 June 2001)

Our last example of this theme is from Newfoundland and Labrador, where Premier Danny Williams explained his decision to pass a bill that ended a massive public-sector strike:

> 7.16: We were given a mandate from the people to run this province on their behalf. That is exactly what we are trying to do ... This is not about 20,000 people. This is about 520,000 people and the future generations. We cannot allow anarchy to prevail in our province. (Deana Stokes Sullivan and Barb Sweet, "Tough New Bill Aimed at Ending Ugly Strike," *Leader-Post*, 27 April 2004)

The message in texts 7.13–7.16 is clear – the voters gave government a mandate to implement a recovery plan. Government would not let itself become captive to union pressure tactics and unreasonable demands. The government zeroed in on specific goals, and it had every intention of achieving them, regardless of the cost it might have to pay in the next elections.

FAIRNESS

Fairness refers to the speakers' efforts to convince the public that the government's last offer was fair and generous, and that the government was not unduly heavy-handed when ordering workers back to work and imposing its last offer on them. The logical extension of such utterances, which often remained unsaid, was likely that the unions were a greedy lot that did not appreciate how fortunate they were to be dealing with such a considerate government. In Saskatchewan, Premier Romanow could not understand why the nurses had refused

> 7.17: the best contract proposals SUN has ever received. (Martin O'Hanlon, "Saskatchewan Nurses Vow to Defy Any Court Injunction," *Calgary Herald*, 10 April 1999)

And, after SUN rejected a government offer, Health Minister Patricia Atkinson emphasized:

> 7.18: I believe that we share a strong commitment to getting our health care system working again ... and to moving forward to conclude a fair collective agreement. I want to assure you again that we have listened and heard registered nurses loudly and clearly. (Martin O'Hanlon, "Nurses Reject Offer," *Calgary Herald*, 17 April 1999)

In the Legislative Assembly, Atkinson stressed the government's strong affinity with the nurses, adding a layer of melodramatic empathy to previous arguments:

> 7.19: Registered nurses, Mr. Speaker, are our sisters, our cousins, our aunts, our mothers, our grandmothers. We know registered nurses and we have heard very clearly that there are issues that need to be addressed. (*Hansard*, 8 April 1999: 455)

Thus, the speakers portrayed the government as fair, generous, and compassionate. In addition, the public was given to believe that ordering the nurses back to work only six hours after they walked off the job was a very tough decision. This discourse left the public to infer the role the union occupied in this narrative, yet the options might have been fairly limited.

In Quebec, in late 2005, support staff in twenty junior colleges planned to walk off the job for twenty-four hours, disrupting classes for some 65,000 students and sending a warning to a government that was refusing the union's demands. Premier Charest was convinced that the government offer was fair and did not hide his disgust with the union's actions:

> 7.20: I don't agree with the unions holding parents and children and students hostage to the negotiations when in fact we should all be at the table talking. We have tabled a very reasonable offer of 12.6 percent over six years, including pay equity. The unions want four percent a year over three years. It is $6.7 billion, plus pay equity. I am convinced of the fairness of what we have put on the table and I invite the union leaders to stay at the table and negotiate. (Kevin Dougherty, "Let's Sit Down, Charest Tells Unions," *Gazette*, 23 August 2005)

In Alberta, Learning Minister Oberg made a similar plea:

> 7.21: There is enough money to make Alberta teachers the best-paid on average in the country. With the six percent increase, Alberta teachers' salary ranges will be the highest in the country. (Colette Derworiz, "Teachers among Best-Paid," *Edmonton Journal*, 2 February 2002)

In New Brunswick, the government terminated a legal strike three days after it had begun. It is not a trivial matter to order workers back to work after such a short period on the picket lines, let alone that half of the bargaining unit had been designated essential and therefore was forced to stay on the job. Perhaps this is why the New Brunswick government felt compelled to convince the public that it was not being mean or unduly harsh. Probably, the public was expected to embrace messages describing the government as compassionate and considerate, as well as a victim of circumstances beyond its control. The values of being compassionate and considerate had been first introduced in the budget address (Betts, 2000: 12):

> 7.22: The government will treat its employees fairly and compassionately and will offer those affected by Program/Service Review a range of options such as reassignments, transfer, redeployment, and temporary placement. (Kelly Toughill, "N.B. Hospitals Hit by Massive Strike," *Toronto Star*, 3 March 2001)

Later, Premier Lord indicated that his government was a victim of a situation created by others. His government had to clean up after its predecessors:

> 7.23: I sympathize with the poorly paid workers, but the cash-strapped government can't make up for 10 years of neglect in one contract [Lord's Progressive Party won the 1999 elections after a twelve-year Liberal administration]. (Ibid.)

In texts 7.19, 7.22, and 7.23, the speakers added a layer of compassion and sympathy to the value of fairness, thus stressing that the government was neither heavy-handed nor cold. It acknowledged and empathized with the workers' anguish, but its hands were tied. Along the way, the blame for the labour conflict and its consequences was attributed to the other party.

In the Newfoundland/Labrador House of Assembly, Premier Williams exonerated his hard-working government of any wrongdoing, insinuating that the other side was responsible for the deadlocked bargaining:

> 7.24: The Government of Newfoundland and Labrador has to have stability in its public sector services. We cannot proceed without a collective agreement. We have made every effort possible. We are now into twenty-nine days of trying to negotiate a collective agreement. We worked until very, very late last night in an attempt to advance this ... It has never been this government's intention to strip contracts ... We have made every effort to try and reach solutions. (*House of Assembly Proceedings*, 28 April 2004, vol. 45, no. 24)

In Nova Scotia, government speakers also stressed their fairness in dealing with the other side, their respect for workers, and unions' improper behaviour. Public Service Commission Minister and House Leader Ronald Russell stated:

> 7.25: The stance of this government is to attempt to reach an agreement with the nurses' unions in a fair and equitable fashion and at the same time, protect the health care of the people of this province. (*Hansard*, 14 June 2001: 4567)

Similarly, Health Minister Jamie Muir declared:

> 7.26: Again, I repeat how much our government appreciates the nurses and the rest of the health care workers we have in the system. There is nothing in that legislation that would prevent the collective bargaining process [sic] continuing. I would hope that what this group would do, instead of showboating, is to encourage the groups to get back to the table and to work it out at the table. (Ibid.: 4571)

The above discourse presents an unequivocal image of sympathetic and generous governments doing whatever they could to reach agreements under very trying fiscal conditions. They were not dismissive of the plight of hard-working union members. The offers they made to the unions were fair and reasonable. However, their noble behaviour got them nowhere. Mostly implicitly but sometimes explicitly (by using words such as "showboating" and "hostage"), the government speakers suggested that how the conflict had evolved was the other side's fault. Thus, by moralizing their own actions with such terms as "compassionate," "reasonable," "fair," and "making every effort possible," they distinguished fairly clearly between the good and the bad players.

RESPONSIBILITY AND PRUDENCE

In our context, the values of responsibility and prudence are interchangeable. They mean that, first, a cautious government did not want to sink the province deeper into debt and deficit by giving in to union demands. Second, balancing the budget and eliminating, or reducing, the provincial debt were moralized activities. The relevant rhetoric assigned a moral quality, or a positive normative evaluation, to this behaviour. Deficit and debt reduction were important provincial interests, which government had to protect.

During the debate preceding the vote on Bill 23, Saskatchewan Premier Romanow sent a succinct message:

> 7.27: The province simply can't afford to meet the nurses' wage demands. [I cannot understand why] they passed up the best contract proposals SUN has ever received. (Martin O'Hanlon, "Saskatchewan Nurses Vow to Defy Any Court Injunction," *Calgary Herald*, 10 April 1999)

Not only was the government fiscally prudent, it was also fair and generous to the nurses. Why did SUN reject the government offer? Was SUN ungrateful, irresponsible, or perhaps greedy? The textual strategy that juxtaposed the government's generosity at such a difficult time with the union's behaviour cast in stark relief this last possibility. Likewise, in New Brunswick, government had to reject the union demands, since it should not spend more than it could afford. Premier Lord explained that situation and stressed the need to be fair to all taxpayers:

> 7.28: The unions are asking for more money than we think is reasonable and fair to the taxpayers of New Brunswick. (Kelly Toughill, "N.B. Hospitals Hit by Massive Strike," *Toronto Star*, 3 March 2001)

Minister of Finance Norman Betts offered a similar view:

> 7.29: We want to avert a strike, but a settlement at any cost is not something we want to do. ("Mediator Looks to Stop the Bleeding," *Examiner*, 2 March 2001)

In his 1999 budget address, Betts had elaborated on the seriousness of the situation and stressed the virtue of a balanced budget:

> 7.30: The price of admission to a new century is a balanced budget. It is the foundation for a more competitive, more compassionate New Brunswick. (Betts, 2000: 8)

A year later he repeated that message, adding how

> 7.31: Deficits today are simply taxes tomorrow. Maintaining a competitive position in the "new century" requires continued fiscal prudence leading to balanced budgets with balanced results. (Betts, 2001: 7)

Similarly, in Newfoundland and Labrador, deficit and debt-elimination plans were hailed as the necessary right steps to achieving a healthy province. According to Premier Williams, a healthy fiscal situation is something the government owed to "our children and grandchildren":

> 7.32: Our government may have inherited this serious fiscal situation but we have absolutely no intention of letting our children and grandchildren inherit it from us. (Williams, 2004)

Finance Minister Loyola Sullivan added:

> 7.33: We must bring the deficit progressively and strategically lower each year in order to protect the province's credit rating ... The consequences of a rating decline would be higher interest rates, reduced access to capital markets and increased exposure to foreign exchange fluctuations. (Sullivan, 2004: 13)

In British Columbia, Health Minister Colin Hanson emphasized several elements when explaining the roots of the conflict and the government's plan to redress the situation:

> 7.34: We saw the Hospital Employees' Union getting huge increases during that period of time [i.e., when the NDP was in office, 1991–2001]. How did the province pay for those increases? It was by diverting money away from patient care in order to fund those very expensive contracts ... [Bill 37] will allow for a fair wage and a generous benefit package that will ensure that those workers are among the highest paid in Canada. (*Hansard*, 28 April 2004: 10638)

> I think when members [of the opposition] want to see the root cause of the challenges that we're facing, they should actually go look in the mirror. During the 1990s when the NDP were in office, we saw the sweetheart deals that were signed between the Premier's office and the Hospital Employees' Union, which took money out of patient care and diverted it instead into

making the support staff in this province so much higher paid – 20 to 40 percent higher than any other province. What we are doing is bringing those costs into line, because we have to put patients first. We have to make sure that we get costs in line with what other jurisdictions are facing, and that is exactly what we are accomplishing through this legislation. (*Hansard*, 29 April 2004: 10686)

Taken together, texts 7.27–7.34 show speakers articulating a sense of a fiscal crisis created by events beyond their control, an ominous future, and a pressing need for bold action to redress the situation. A tough stance in regard to public-sector working conditions in general and union demands in particular was one of the policy tools governments advocated. However, the speakers were prudent enough to moralize controversial steps such as back-to-work legislation, wage freezes or cuts, and downsizing. They related them to a discourse of competitiveness and fiscal prudence, which emphasized the imperatives of a province's competitive position, balanced budget, and zero debt. These concepts became coveted goals, a "must" that every advanced society should strive to achieve if it was to earn a ticket into "a new century," thereby guaranteeing the future of its children and grandchildren. They became the yardstick of a responsible, savvy government which was ready to lead its citizens to the "promised land" of fiscal health and economic prosperity. In short, they became moralized utilities.

Remarks such as those quoted above painted a picture of a firm but fair, resolved yet benevolent government that worked tirelessly to guarantee the future of succeeding generations by fighting the perils of fiscal mismanagement (e.g., raising taxes, yielding to union demands). This discourse, in turn, created a challenge for the unions, which had to counteract it without appearing as a greedy group in pursuit of its own narrow self-interest.

VALUE OF COLLECTIVE BARGAINING

For various reasons, each of the seven governments included in this study also moralized its stance and behaviour by affirming its commitment to collective bargaining. This institution is not a straightforward value. For those who revere it, collective bargaining is the foremost vehicle to level the industrial-relations playing field. For years, the process has given otherwise powerless workers a reasonable chance to improve their lot. Others may loathe collective bargaining with passion. They may consider it an unwelcome interference with circumstances that should be governed by the invisible hand of the market. Still others might be indifferent to it altogether; for them, collective bargaining is not a value but rather an irrelevant concept. In our case studies, government speakers took time to express their appreciation of collective bargaining. Though it was an institution that in almost each instance they did not hesitate to trample on, all of them, without exception, described it as the most appropriate mechanism for deciding on working conditions.

In Saskatchewan, the haste of the NDP government to terminate the legal nurses' strike required a justification. It was one thing to drive a hard bargain in times of fiscal constraint but quite another to deny the union a fundamental right by terminating a legal strike six hours after it had started, and then impose a collective agreement. That this was done by an allegedly union-friendly government might have deepened the union's sense of betrayal. This was not lost on the government speakers, who, at least in public, appeared to agonize over their own decision. They made an effort to demonstrate their pro-labour colours and prove that their actions were not a show of bravado by a thoughtless government. For example, Justice Minister Nilson lamented:

> 7.35: It is with considerable regret and disappointment that today this government finds itself in the position it must take the step of introducing back-to-work legislation. Our commitment to collective bargaining makes this a difficult step but one that is essential to safeguard the lives and health of Saskatchewan citizens. (Martin O'Hanlon, "Saskatchewan Nurses Vow to Defy NDP's Back-to-Work Order," *Globe and Mail*, 9 April 1999)

Health Minister Atkinson added:

> 7.36: I believe that we share a strong commitment to getting our health care system working again ... and to moving forward to conclude a fair collective agreement. I want to assure you again that we have listened and heard registered nurses loudly and clearly. (Martin O'Hanlon, "Nurses Reject Offer," *Calgary Herald*, 17 April 1999)

Thus, the speakers sugarcoated their assault on the union's right to strike and bargain by stressing that fiscal exigencies had not dulled their sense of right and wrong and, more important, had not shaken their commitment to collective bargaining. It was still a valued institution, the preferred way of "doing business" with organized labour. However, at the moment, its value was outstripped by the value of public safety.

In New Brunswick, beginning with Finance Minister Bett's 2000 budget address, government speakers emphasized that they preferred negotiated agreements to any other settlement option:

> 7.37: This year we will be at the bargaining table with a number of public sector unions representing more than 25,000 public service employees. I look forward to signing agreements with them at the conclusion of the collective bargaining process. (Betts, 2000: 12)

During the conflict, Betts reiterated this message:

> 7.38: I'll remind you that we didn't walk away from the table, CUPE walked away from the table. We still believe a negotiated settlement is the best settlement and if Mr. Kuttner [the mediator appointed by the New Brunswick Labour Relations Board] can make that happen, that'll be great. ("Mediator Looks to Stop the Bleeding," *Examiner*, 2 March 2001)

The message was loud and clear. Bill 30, the whip the government wielded to force the union members into ratifying its last offer, should not be interpreted as a show of disrespect towards organized labour and the institution of collective bargaining. Rather, "a negotiated agreement is the best settlement." But what could a willing government do if its negotiation partner walked away from the table?

More than two weeks before his government passed Bill 18, Newfoundland and Labrador Premier Danny Williams had stated unequivocally that legislation to end the strike and impose an agreement was an option of last resort. Apparently, a negotiated settlement was his first choice. But he was also quick to point out that, unfortunately, a joint agreement was not imminent because the parties were deadlocked:

> 7.39: They want to put us in a position, I think, where they're going to force us to legislate them back. Legislating an end to the nine-day-old strike remains a last resort, but will take place if I feel the public's safety is being put at risk. No such legislation has been prepared yet ... I don't see a negotiated settlement possible. I really honestly think we're too far apart. ("Newfoundland and Unions Hit Stalemate," *Nanaimo Daily News*, 10 April 2004)

After legislating the striking workers back to work, he repeated the last point:

> 7.40: If talks were very close and we were hours away, we would hold off for that period of time. (Deana Stokes Sullivan, "Back-to-Work Bill Remains on the Table," *Leader-Post*, 28 April 2004)

In short, the premier explicitly stated his support for collective bargaining over legislation yet blamed the unions for bringing the government, against its will, to consider the latter option. Seemingly, for him, legislation was inferior to a jointly negotiated agreement. However, when pushed to choose between the two values, the government had opted for the certainty and immediacy of uninterrupted services over the less than probable negotiated agreement. According to Williams, the unions, CUPE and NAPE, preferred the government to legislate the workers back to work. Although he never explained why, he put the blame for the conflict squarely on organized labour.

In Nova Scotia, government speakers highlighted the extent to which they valued collective bargaining and negotiated settlements. The Public Service Commission minister captured the essence of the arguments when he succinctly stated that Bill 68, which ended a legal strike mere hours after it had begun, was "unfortunate but necessary" ("N.S. Government Will Nix Nurses' Right to Strike," *Daily News*, 15 June 2001). The health minister added:

> 7.41: Clearly we hope the collective bargaining process will continue and will be successful. What we are concerned about is that if the collective bargaining process is not able to reach a satisfactory conclusion that is accepted by both parties, then there would be a health and safety risk to Nova Scotia and we are not prepared to accept that. (*Hansard*, 14 June 2001: 4569)

Less than two weeks later, a dejected Premier Hamm admitted that negotiation over wages was not the way to resolve the conflict. The problem was more serious. It was created by the previous administration and was structural in nature:

> 7.42: Much of the anger that has been developed in the health care delivery system will not be solved by a wage contract no matter how much money is in the envelope because it will not serve the fundamental problem in the working conditions of health sector workers in this province. (Nova Scotia, *Hansard*, 26 June 2001: 5785)

> Part of the problem that we find ourselves in here is the result of the flawed policy of the previous government. For example, we are now facing a shortage of nurses, much of that is the result of the ill-advised early retirement program five years ago which provided an exit for many, many experienced nurses. (Ibid.: 5786)

The speakers thus portrayed a government that was forced to resort to legislation. Yet Bill 68 was in no way a show of disrespect to unions and the institution of collective bargaining. Rather, it was a way to protect the health and safety of the citizens.

Likewise, in British Columbia, the speakers tried hard to show their respect for collective bargaining and negotiated settlements, thereby avoiding the appearance of being anti-labour. In other words, this was not a case of government and employers taking advantage of the situation to launch an assault on organized labour. On several occasions the speakers stated their commitment to collective bargaining and their preference for a negotiated settlement. For example, Health Employers Association of British Columbia President and CEO Louise Simard stressed:

> 7.43: We've been at the table for three months, the unions are simply refusing to negotiate. It's like bargaining with ourselves ... The union has made no attempt to negotiate with us. (James Vassallo, "Health Unions, Employers Deadlocked," *Daily News*, 5 April 2004)

The minister of skills development and labour, Graham Bruce, similarly lamented:

> 7.44: It is unfortunate that this intervention is necessary. I would much prefer that a settlement be reached through effective collective bargaining. Regrettably, this is not possible. (*Hansard*, 28 April 2004: 10607)

Once again, the speakers employed a discourse that emphasized a preference for collective bargaining together with the inevitability of legislation to end the dispute as a result of the irresponsibility of unions. The latter were "simply refusing to negotiate," thus forcing the government to pass Bill 37.

Government preference for collective bargaining and negotiated settlements figured prominently in the Quebec speakers' attempts to moralize Bill 142, which imposed a new collective agreement on some five hundred thousand public-sector workers. In the summer of

2005, a hopeful Premier Charest showed confidence in the bargaining process:

> 7.45: I am convinced of the fairness of what we have put on the table and I invite the union leaders to stay at the table and negotiate. We're going to sit down. We're going to negotiate. We'll do our best to come to an agreement. (Kevin Dougherty, "Let's Sit Down, Charest Tells Unions," *Gazette*, 23 August 2005)

Later, shortly before passing Bill 142, an exasperated and disillusioned premier admitted:

> 7.46: We've negotiated everything we could. We are now left with one conclusion: We will not be able to have an agreement on salaries and therefore the National Assembly will be called back tomorrow so that we legislate on this issue. (Rhéal Séguin, "Quebec Set to Impose Public-Sector Contract," *Globe and Mail*, 15 December 2005)

Having exhausted the option of collective bargaining, the government was down to its very last resort; hence Bill 142. Implicitly, the Quebec government blamed the unions for the crisis. If the government had "negotiated everything [they] could" and got nowhere, then logically the responsibility for the stalemate must rest with the other side.

In summary, compared with values such as fairness, responsibility, and prudence, collective bargaining is far more complex. This is because the term often carries different moral connotations depending on how speakers use it. Government speakers' utterances indicated that they all longed for jointly negotiated agreements yet opted for legislation. They tried hard to moralize their choice. The speakers crafted a reality in which a fair and diligent government had done whatever it could to reach a negotiated settlement. Alas, that government was forced by a difficult bargaining process and obstinate union to pass back-to-work legislation to restore order. In making this case, the speakers used a three-pronged moralization strategy which was based on such statements as, "We are committed to collective bargaining," "we didn't walk away from the table, the union walked away from the table," "we still believe in a negotiated agreement," "we've negotiate everything we could," and "we've been at the table for three months yet the unions are simply refusing to negotiate."

First, the speakers demonstrated their deep respect for and unwavering commitment to collective bargaining, and readily admitted the superiority of negotiated settlements. Second, they described the legislation in question, which terminated legal strikes and imposed the government's last offer, as a means of last resort that was unequivocally inferior to a negotiated agreement. Third, that unwanted legislation was a result of the union's behaviour, not the government's. In moralizing their own behaviour, the speakers thus shifted the blame for the stalemate to the intractable unions. Sometimes they did so explicitly by, for example, declaring that the unions had acted recklessly by "asking for the moon and planet Mars" (Monique Jérôme-Forget, Quebec's Treasury Board president: Kevin Dougherty, "Province Can Pay") and "taking the public hostage" (Jean-Marc Fournier, Quebec's education minister: Ingrid Peritz, "Labour Strife Disrupts Classes of 65,000 Quebec College Students," *Globe and Mail*, 22 August 2005). Sometimes, it was done more subtly, as in text 7.40. But the moral of the narrative was fairly consistent – the union had left the government no choice but to end the labour conflict through legislation. The speakers wove a discourse of integrity and dishonesty which exonerated their government of any wrongdoing and blamed the union for the confrontation and the unravelling of the bargaining process.

Union Moralization Strategy

Like their government counterparts, the union speakers used moralization- legitimation strategy to legitimate their actions and positions. In the main, they relied on two value domains – labour rights (in six cases) and public interest (in four cases). In addition, individual cases highlight ad hoc uses of the moralization strategy, with values taken from the domains of respect for working people (New Brunswick and British Columbia), living wage (New Brunswick), democracy (Nova Scotia), and representation (Quebec).

Value of Labour Rights

In all the cases except Quebec, speakers used the discourse of labour rights to moralize strikes as an expression of the union's fight for justice. In addition, this strategy was an attempt to de-moralize the government's assault on the fundamental union rights to negotiate and strike. Reacting to the government's back-to-work legislation, the Saskatchewan Union of Nurses president, Rosalee Longmoore, declared:

> 7.47: This [the nurses' defiance of the government back-to-work order] is about our rights to freely collective bargain. (Martin O'Hanlon, "Saskatchewan Nurses Vow to Defy NDP's Back-to-Work Order," *Globe and Mail*, 9 April 1999)

140   Bad Time Stories

In New Brunswick, a series of statements described the government's behaviour as an attack on labour relations and the union's democratic, legal right to strike and bargain:

> 7.48: [Marlene Ryan, president of CUPE Local 908:] [The premier] has declared war on the labour movement in New Brunswick. (Kelly Toughill, "N.B. Hospitals Hit by Massive Strike," *Toronto Star*, 3 March 2001)
>
> [CUPE negotiator Daniel Bernatchez:] [The premier's] message is that there are no more negotiations in this province. Do you believe this? I'm still in a dream. Is this real? I keep pinching myself. (Ibid.)

At one point, Ken Georgetti, President of the Canadian Labour Congress, intervened in a similar vein:

> 7.49: These workers have the democratic right to belong to a union and have the right to strike. A democratically elected government should not behave that way. ("N.B. Premier Defends Actions in Hospital Strike," *Examiner*, 6 March 2001)

The case of Newfoundland and Labrador was no different:

> 7.50: [Wayne Lucas, provincial president of CUPE:] This [the idea to introduce legislation to end the job action and impose an agreement] is about breaking the backs of unions. I'm really angry. I'm really mad. This is not the way to do things. ("Newfoundland and Unions Hit Stalemate," *Nanaimo Daily News*, 10 April 2004)
>
> [NAPE president Leo Puddister reacting to Williams's announcement that he was contemplating back-to-work legislation:] If you're not going to play by the rules, why put people through this torture? We will go gladly to any bargaining table, but we've stated our position quite clearly for 20 days: we will not talk concessions. (National Union of Public and General Employees, 21 April 2004)
>
> [Wayne Lucas, CUPE:] With a stroke of a pen [the premier] is going to make a legitimate, legal structure illegal and try to turn hard-working Newfoundlanders and Labradorians into criminals. ("Bill Expected to End Nfld. Strike," *Pembroke Observer*, 26 April 2004

In Alberta, on several occasions the ATA president, Larry Booi, protested that the government had behaved in a non-democratic manner:

> 7.51: We believe that they are taking away our right to strike, not for an emergency but for inconvenience, and now we'll hear what the courts say.

(Jeff Holubitsky, "Gov't Orders Teachers Back," *Edmonton Journal*, 22 February 2002)

[Learning Minister] Oberg is acting like a medieval monarch, not a democratic cabinet minister. (Jeff Holubitsky and Graham Thomson, "'Get Back to Negotiating,'" *Edmonton Journal*, 2 February 2002)

This [government behaviour] is an arrogant abuse of power. It's also a black day for public education and democracy in Alberta. (Tom Olsen, "Teachers Urged to Pull Voluntary Services," *Calgary Herald*, 12 March 2002)

The thrust of this legitimation strategy emphasized how government had denied unions their legal right to bargain collectively and strike. Highly aggressive and disrespectful governments were trying to resolve their fiscal problems by heaping them on the backs of their own workers and their unions. Thus, a strike that had begun as a campaign for a better health-care or education system assumed a completely different character. Using utterances such as "dream," "is it real," "do you believe it," and "war," speakers conveyed the gravity of the situation. By showing an "arrogant abuse of power," governments had resolved to "break the back of the union," leaving it little choice but to defend itself as best it could. The gist of this moralizing effort contrasted the heavy-handedness and bullying tactics of government with the unions' struggle to protect their democratic and legal right to bargain and strike. Using hyperbole such as the above, union speakers presented their unions as the victims of careless, oppressive governments that were running roughshod over union members by denying them their legal right to negotiate collective agreements and call strikes. It is possible that, by highlighting the non-democratic spirit of government behaviour, the unions added a layer of public good to their own actions. The fight for union democratic rights may have resonated with a wider public audience.

It is hard to assess the extent to which this moralization approach appealed to the public. Yet, by shifting the focus away from "pure and simple" industrial-relations matters to fundamental labour rights, speakers may have hoped to blunt the edge of the union's actions, which sometimes were illegal and/or perceived to be self-centred. In addition, perhaps unions felt compelled to justify their actions to their own membership. As stated at the outset of this study, "the right to strike was achieved in the first place by a combination of political lobbying and technically illegal activity. Governments that use the law to break the rules should have no right to expect us to obey the law" (National Union of Public and General Employees, 2006: 4). Some union actions were congruent with, perhaps even an expression of, this sentiment.

142   Bad Time Stories

Value of Public Interest

For several years prior to striking, the Saskatchewan nurses had warned the government and employers about their deteriorating working conditions and the erosion of service quality, but to no avail. They felt that it was their professional duty to champion change because the government was dragging its feet. Since the government had refused to listen, a more aggressive approach was warranted. And so the nurses and their union were fighting on behalf of the public. One nurse bluntly stated:

> 7.52: We are striking for the safety of our patients because they're not being ensured safe care right now. There's not enough nurses and it's a dire, dire situation right now. (Martin O'Hanlon, "Nurses Defy Back-to-Work Order," *Calgary Herald*, 9 April 1999)

In the same vein, another nurse added:

> 7.53: We haven't made any mistake. We have to take a stand and now it's not only for ourselves but it's for our patients' safety and for all of Saskatchewan. (Martin O'Hanlon, "Saskatchewan Nurses Vow to Defy Any Court Injunction," *Calgary Herald*, 10 April 1999)

In British Columbia, union speakers explained that the province-wide job action should restore order to a chaotic health-care system. Since the early 2000s, the Campbell government had dictated contracts in health care, laid off workers, and closed down hospitals. The unions maintained that the current job action would force the government to reconsider the merit of such heavy-handed practices:

> 7.54: [Pail Moist, CUPE national president:] This [upcoming province-wide strike] is not to create chaos. It's to bring order to the chaos created by [Premier] Gordon Campbell. (Don Harrison, "Health-Care Workers to Strike on Sunday," *Province*, 23 April 2004)

> [Chris Allnutt, HEU secretary-business manager and chief spokesperson for the multi-union bargaining association:] Public health care is on the line. Government [2002] legislation shredding our last contract resulted in closed hospitals, service cuts, and mass layoffs of more than 6,000 skilled and dedicated workers – mostly women. And if government and health employers have their way in this round of bargaining, the chaos and privatization that's infected our health care system for the past two years will

expand. (HEU, News Release, "Health Care Workers on Strike to Protect Health Care and Decent Jobs," 25 April 2004)

The strike was not only about specific union matters. It also aimed to force the government to address system-wide issues related to the poor, and deteriorating, state of the health-care system.

In Alberta, Larry Booi, the ATA president, stressed that the Alberta teachers were not a "trigger-happy" lot who took delight in walking off the job. They felt a strong professional obligation to fight for better public education. Booi was convinced that teachers were the only group capable of forcing the government to invest properly in the system. He argued that the strike action was a weapon that teachers used responsibly and reluctantly, out of a strong sense of moral duty:

> 7.55: [A strike] is a weapon of last resort and we're down to last resorts. (Susan Hagan, "Strike Position Draws Near," *Edmonton Journal*, 11 September 2001)

> Not only have we not abused the strike weapon, we haven't used it for 10 years. (Don Braid, "ATA Boss Carries a Big Stick," *Calgary Herald*, 15 January 2002)

> Teachers are the only ones who are standing up for proper funding for education. (Jeff Holubitsky, "Huge Gap between Teacher Demands, Board Budgets," *Edmonton Journal*, 3 January 2002)

In other words, teachers and their leaders were acting conscientiously, on behalf of all Albertans. They did not take their action lightly; in fact, they felt guilty. But they had no other choice – they had to protect a system that was central to the well-being of society, a system that the government was failing. In many other utterances, the ATA president painstakingly portrayed the teachers as conscientious professionals who were mindful of the consequences of their actions, yet were obligated to take a stand on behalf of all Albertans against a government that did not value public education. They were not a reckless, greedy lot chasing more money. Rather, they were in the vanguard of a quest for a better education system that would benefit students, their parents, and society at large. The strike was an act of desperation:

> 7.56: Teachers go home at the end of the day feeling guilty because they know with all those kids with high needs, they didn't get to a lot of the kids

who need their help the most. (Lynne Koziey, "Alberta Releases Class Size Figures," *Calgary Herald*, 20 January 2002)

But the strike is not about higher wages. It is about three things: classroom conditions, wages, and recruitment and retention of teachers. (Colette Derworiz, "Teachers Strikes Divide Albertans," *Calgary Herald*, 23 January 2002)

We exhausted every possible option before going on strike. We didn't interfere with diploma exams, we gave plenty of notice before striking, we didn't defy the back-to-work order, when we won back our right to strike we didn't go back out. (Maria Canton, "Teachers Poised to Begin Job Action," *Calgary Herald*, 11 March 2002)

Interestingly, the last statement contrasts with several of our case studies where striking unions defied back-to-work orders and stayed on the picket lines. The ATA elected to return to work even though the court approved the continuation of the province-wide strikes. The teachers continued their struggle by withdrawing from several extra-curricular activities, but their strikes were over. Perhaps this was their way of showing their deep sense of responsibility and commitment to the students, their parents, and the profession. Implicitly, perhaps the above statement was an "otherization" move, whereby Booi contrasted the admirable stance of the ATA with the despicable behaviour of the government.

Similarly, in Quebec, the union speakers emphasized that they were fighting on behalf of all Quebecers to preserve high-quality public services. The government plan to modernize the public sector would result in fewer, and inferior, services, a plan the unions were trying to thwart:

7.57: [Claudette Carbonneau, CSN president:] We won't let the government transform public-sector jobs into cheap labor and weaken the quality of services to the Quebec population. (Mike King, "Charest 'Swimming' in Troubled Water," *National Post*, 30 December 2004)

[Jean Lacharite, CSN central council president:] The government has to reinvest in the public sector. These services improve the quality of life for people living in the province. (Brion Robinson, "Unions Ready to Turn the Heat on Liberals," *Sherbrooke Record*, 27 April 2005)

A unique instance of using public interest to moralize a union's behaviour occurred in Nova Scotia. Joan Jessome, president of the NSGEU, suggested that Bill 68 was an attack on democracy. From that it followed that the union was fighting to protect democracy in Nova Scotia:

> 7.58: This is about the survival of democracy in this province. That is what we are fighting for. (Kevin Cox, "Union Sets June 27 for Nova Scotia Health-Care Strike," *Globe and Mail*, 23 June 2001)

Similar to their government counterparts, in texts 7.52–7.58 the union speakers legitimated their opposition to the government's policies and actions using a discourse emphasizing the value of public interest. Most likely, the purpose of this rhetoric was twofold: to convince the audience that the unions were pursuing broad interests on behalf of the public as a whole; and, in so doing, to counter the claim of some government speakers that organized labour was nothing more than a greedy interest group. In addition, and again like government speakers, union speakers used this strategy to undercut government actions. Overall, they did not mince words when blaming the government for the poor state of public services, for not being more forthcoming at the bargaining table, and, overall, for the existing dispute.

Ad Hoc Value Domains

Union speakers sometimes cited values that were not mentioned in other cases. In New Brunswick, for example, speakers used the value of a living wage to moralize their actions. They emphasized the poor economic situation of the union members as a key to understanding the strike. Some were so poor that they needed to hold two jobs to eke out a living.

> 7.59: [Marlene Ryan, CUPE Local 908 president:] We don't even make above the poverty line. Many hospital workers are forced to take two jobs to make ends meet. (Kelly Toughill, "N.B. Hospitals Hit by Massive Strike," *Toronto Star*, 3 March 2001)

Apparently, a moral basis for the strike was the long-held belief that workers deserved to earn a living wage. Relative to the other six cases, this type of rationalization was unusual. Generally, union leaders avoided using the financial plight of their members, and the desire to improve it, as a legitimation strategy. As stated above, in other health-care conflicts, strikers (especially nurses) argued that job actions were a means to forcing governments to improve service quality. Thus, they appeared as advocates on behalf of weaker groups. In this case, perhaps because the workers (maintenance and janitorial staff, food and laboratory workers, clerical staff and registered nursing assistants) might have had less direct contact with patients than registered nurses, and perhaps because their economic situation justified an immediate adjustment, the speakers advocated on their behalf, emphasizing the need to improve wages.

Some union speakers used the value of respect for working people to moralize their union's behaviour and delegitimate the government's actions. In Nova Scotia, Joan Jessome, NSGEU president, used the value of respect to moralize the union's actions:

> 7.60: This is going to drive nurses out of the province. I can't believe that they can say they value health-care providers and then turn around and take away every single right they have negotiated away from them. ("Nurses Protest 'Draconian' Bill," *Trail Times*, 15 June 2001)

Two weeks later, she repeated this message:

> 7.61: This government sat in the house for the past 13 days, laughed in our faces, showed us no respect and then passed a bill that took away our rights. ("N.S. Tories Pass Anti-Strike Bill; Workers Vow to Defy It," *Leader-Post*, 28 June 2001)

In British Columbia, speakers tried to convince the public that the unions fought, at least in part, to restore government's respect for workers. Chris Allnut of the HEU did not pull any punches when talking to reporters on the issue:

> 7.62: The Campbell Liberals continue to demonstrate nothing but disdain for the women and men working on health care's front line. Once again, this premier and his government have callously rewritten the law to suit their privatization agenda in health care and violated the legal rights of tens of thousands of workers in the process. (HEU News Release, "Bill 37 a Shocking Betrayal of Health Care Workers," 28 April 2004)

> We must stand up to unjust laws that deprive working people of their fundamental rights. The legislation is unjust and must be challenged. (Oliver Moore, "B.C. Strikers Switch to 'Protest Lines,'" *Globe and Mail*, 29 April 2004)

Taken together, texts 7.60–7.62 suggest that the unions fought for fairness at the bargaining table, respect for all working people, and a better health-care system for the public as a whole. Although they almost never stated it explicitly, they implied that unions were likely among the few groups that were willing and able to stand up to the government. Probably, they hoped that the public would embrace the message and support the union's stance in these disputes.

At the outset of this chapter, we argued that moralization differs from the other three legitimation strategies. Authorization, rationalization, and, as we will show in the next chapter, mythopoesis provide the audience with a relatively clear and practical yardstick to answer the "why" questions that are the core of legitimacy – Why should we do this? Why should we do this in this way? Why should we believe you? Authorization relies on the speaker's status. We are expected to believe a speaker because of her status in a given hierarchy. Instrumental rationalization focuses on tangible utilities and the means to their improvement or preservation. Frequently, speakers can, and do, provide concrete data to ground their arguments and win public support for their positions. Mythopoesis crafts stories that explain why and how protagonists are rewarded or punished for their actions. Theoretically, this should make it easier for an audience to accept some kinds of behaviour and reject others. In contrast, moralization asks the public to choose between sets of values, or between different interpretations of similar values. At least in the context of labour conflicts, unambiguous measures may not be readily available for one to make an educated choice. For example, it may be difficult to establish that keeping students in school is less, or more, ethical than striking to promote teachers' working conditions and the quality of the education system. In this chapter we demonstrated how each party tried to convince stakeholders that its values were superior to those of the opponent.

Being political organizations, both unions and governments did not take the public for granted and worked hard to win its support by using a strategy that stressed the value of public interest. Both government and union speakers tried to demonstrate how, despite the hardship caused by their actions, they were humane and used legislation, or job action, as a means of last resort, and they were doing that with the public interest in mind. In other words, they were not pursuing a narrow self-interest (unions) or practising union bashing (governments), but truly cared about the public's collective good. For both government and union, this discourse seems intended to demonstrate their compassion and high morals when being engaged in controversial actions. While emphasizing that it was acting with the public interest in mind, each side deflected blame for the conflict onto its opponent. Government could attribute back-to-work legislation to a union's greed and inflexibility at the bargaining table. For unions, a strike action had been taken because of the government's lack of consideration for the public in general and workers in particular. Thus, overall, this strategy not only aimed at cleansing the speaker and his/her organization of any moral wrongdoing but also sought to tarnish the opponent.

To convince the public of the moral imperatives of its actions, each side presented the public with a sense of a looming catastrophe with disastrous long-term implications requiring bold and immediate action. In this way, tough and utilitarian decisions were also rendered ethical. Government speakers invoked the image of "our children and grandchildren" as the helpless group who would bear the brunt of the current generation's misdeeds. For example, increased deficits or growing debts were not simply a drag on today's finances, but rather were presented as a financial hardship that would cripple future generations – borrowing today was simply reaching into the bank accounts of our children. By grounding an event in a well-understood popular narrative, the government rendered a complex situation and an unnerving experience comprehensible and accessible. Using simple images such as the above, or that of a sinking ship which must be rescued, might have helped shape "a consensus of expectations and choice of responses" (Hirsch, 1986: 824). To illustrate, in Newfoundland and Labrador, Premier Danny Williams declared:

> 7.63: Our government may have inherited this serious fiscal situation but we have absolutely no intention of letting our children and grandchildren inherit it from us. (Williams, 2004)

Later, in the House of Assembly, Williams stated:

> 7.64: We have to look out for our children and grandchildren in this Province. (*House of Assembly Proceedings*, 26 April 2004, vol. 45, no. 22)

In Prince Edward Island, a case we discuss in chapter 9, the provincial treasurer, Wayne D. Cheverie, echoed the above message:

> 7.65: This structural deficit if left unchecked will mortgage the future of our children, leaving them with mountains of debt and few, if any, services at all. (Cheverie, 1994: 2)

In this way, an appeal for fiscal restraint was presented as a solution to a problem that might plague our children, not just us. Probably, most people could identify with the responsibility associated with paying mortgages, raising children, and guaranteeing their future. In texts 7.63–7.65, the speakers crafted a simple, accessible message that was likely to resonate with most people's everyday life experiences. It was designed to reduce the abstract and arcane concepts of deficits and debts to the more familiar and vexing matters of paying loans on time and rearing children. A complex financial reality was thus made more comprehensible to the public, rendering those who did not embrace this script morally suspect.

Union speakers, too, crafted a grim if accessible picture that, they hoped, would strike a chord with the public and evoke a favourable response to their arguments and actions. The images they used evoked two calamities – deteriorating services and poor working conditions, which intuitively should result in poor services. The "doomsday" images were used to send a simple, clear message about the gravity of a situation. In addition, the speakers employed images of stubborn, brutal, and thoughtless government to justify and popularize solutions painted as inevitable. The likely intended result was a strong endorsement from the public, which should thank the union for making a bold move to right a catastrophic situation.

Interestingly, though perhaps odd at first glance, both parties' moralization strategies stressed their concern for labour rights. Unions fought to defend their ability to negotiate collective agreements and call strikes. Governments had deep respect for labour rights but were saddled with irrevocable constraints forcing them to undermine them, only temporarily of course. The question is which argument gained moral superiority in the public mind, the one advocating defending labour rights or the one promoting their suspension.

Apparently, the speakers were not satisfied with merely establishing the utility of their actions. They felt compelled to demonstrate that their actions were the right thing to do, something that "had you been in our shoes you would most likely have done yourself." Not surprisingly, however, both sides considered some linguistic strategies inappropriate. Governments were careful not to disparage collective bargaining and strikes. As we have shown, they were diligent in underlining their solid commitment to institutions and practices that were sacrosanct for unions. In addition, they carefully separated the union leadership from the union members. Government speakers showed respect for the members and their plight, but did not hesitate to attack the leaders for being irresponsible, stubborn, and greedy. The union speakers, for their part, were generally careful to outline a broad agenda as the pretext for their positions. They were reluctant to use money as the main reason for their disagreement with government; it was a collective good they were fighting to protect, or promote. Thus, using the strategy of moralization, speakers amplified certain aspects of the situation while muting others. This linguistic oscillation played an additional important role in the overall use of moralization, since it enabled speakers to de-moralize their opponents. It was through moralization that speakers drew the lines separating villains from heroes, bullies from Robin Hoods, and dictators from benign leaders. The greater the amplitude, the clearer were those lines, and the greater the likelihood that stakeholders would embrace the dichotomy. The roles the protagonists assigned to themselves and their opponents were used to craft legitimating stories, as the next chapter demonstrates.

Chapter Eight

Mythopoesis-Legitimation Strategy

According to van Leeuwen (2008), legitimation may be achieved through storytelling or mythopoesis. Stories may valorize or idealize the actions of a particular actor or course of action (moral tales), or may depict the menacing consequences of embarking on an ill-advised course of action (cautionary tales). In moral tales, "protagonists are rewarded for engaging in legitimate social practices or restoring the legitimate order … Cautionary tales, on the other hand, convey what will happen if you do not conform to the norms of social practices" (van Leeuwen, 2008: 117–18). In moral tales, the audience is shown exemplary behaviour that enforces social norms vis-à-vis an experience to which they can relate. Cautionary tales vividly demonstrate the perils of going against the wisdom of legitimate social practices.

To illustrate, van Leeuwen (2008: 118–19) draws on children's experiences of "going to school for the first time." As they enter a new reality, children must adapt to prevailing social practices, such as waiting for permission to speak, being on time, interacting with other children, and following instructions. In children's books, moral tales feature children who are forced to leave the security of their home and negotiate various obstacles yet finally overcome the "trauma" of this separation so that they can experience a "happy ending." Cautionary tales, by contrast, underline the negative consequences of either not following this pattern or failing to respond to new challenges in a socially acceptable manner. These tales present children (and their parents) with often graphic accounts of the joys of conducting themselves in a manner deemed appropriate by society, as well as the risks of not adhering to the established moral code.

In his analysis, van Leeuwen has found that often a cautionary tale is embedded within a moral one, setting out an example to follow and a warning to heed. In these instances, the details of the story might be less important than the message conveyed. Research on the value of storytelling in organizations confirms that "the utility of storytelling ... lies less in its accurate rendition of events and more in its ability to create meaning in an organization" (Suddaby, Foster, and Trank, 2010: 158). "Meaning" in this context is the accepted social and economic order, or accepted reality, of the organization or the accepted need to change it. In short, storytelling is more than a way to pass time. It serves the important function of educating an audience by portraying what constitutes a legitimate and/or an illegitimate practice. To be effective, the storyteller should exercise a degree of "poetic license" (Gabriel, 2000). Such license serves to highlight certain aspects of an event while neglecting or diminishing others so that the moral can be readily apprehended. As well, it is instrumental in making sense of events that may otherwise be difficult to understand, or may not be connected to a larger narrative. In our analysis of public-sector labour conflict, mythopoesis provides a lens through which we can better understand how union and government speakers rendered meaningful a single event or a variety of events spanning months, years, and even decades.

Below, we discuss how each of our parties attempted to legitimate its own behaviour and undercut its opponent's by using the strategy of mythopoesis. Tables 4 and 5 provide summaries of the stories speakers from each side crafted in each of the seven cases. We do not wish to repeat these case-based stories. Instead, we try to intertwine each side's seven stories into a single coherent plot or theme. As we explain in chapter 2, there are many available analytical frameworks for dealing with this strategy. We opted for two that enabled us to organize the data in a manageable, practical, and meaningful manner – Campbell's (1949) "The Hero's Journey," and our variation on Booker's (2004) "Overcoming the Monster." These frameworks are specific instances of the more general van Leeuwen model. Their explanatory power is a result of their ability to reduce complex, and sometimes chaotic, events to a comprehensible plot by imposing artificial boundaries on how complex information is presented and used. This allowed us to begin charting new ground in industrial-relations research.

In the case of government, we argue that van Leeuwen's notion of moral and cautionary tales squared with Campbell's "The Hero's Journey," which is the basic pattern found in many narratives from around the world. Campbell describes seventeen phases in the journey, which can be roughly divided into three main stages – departure (separation), initiation, and return. Our discussion of the government use of mythopoesis follows these three stages. In *The Hero with a Thousand Faces* (1949), Campbell holds that numerous myths from various times and regions share a fundamental structure marked by several stages. These myths all present variations of a theme common to the depiction of an ideal: "A hero ventures forth from the world of common day into a region of supernatural wonder: fabulous forces are there encountered and a decisive victory is won: the hero comes back from this mysterious adventure with the power to bestow boons on his fellow man" (Campbell, 1949: 23). Whereas Campbell is not especially worried about whether stories are moral or cautionary, the hero's journey comprises elements of both, and in more than one way. A hero to some may be a villain to others; a hero at one period may morph into a scoundrel years later; the hero's road to redemption may be paved by both moral and corrupt experiences; and the hero's journey is likely to confront her with anti-heroes. In the story of the three little pigs, for example, the audience witnesses both the exemplary actions of the industrious third pig who chooses the more difficult path of building with bricks, and the hasty actions of his two lazy friends who pay with their lives for taking a shortcut in constructing their houses out of sticks and straw. We will demonstrate that speakers presented their governments as heroes going against formidable evil forces to secure a better future for society. Society, it was hoped, would embrace this story and support the government's valiant effort.

Elements of the hero's journey are also included in Booker's (2004) "Quest" and "Voyage and Return" plots, which are two of the seven basic plots that he discusses. As Booker explains: "Far away, we learn, there is some priceless goal, worth any effort to achieve: a treasure; a promised land; something of infinite value ... the story remains unresolved until the objective has been finally, triumphantly secured" (ibid.: 69). This is the gist of the quest plot. The essence of the voyage and return plot is "that its hero or heroine (or the central group of characters) travel out of their familiar, everyday 'normal' surroundings into another world completely cut off from the first, where everything seems disconcertingly abnormal ... [eventually] they can be released from the abnormal world, and can return to the safety of the familiar world where they began" (ibid.: 87). In Booker's analysis, the two plots end with a "thrilling escape" and the winning of "the life-transforming treasure" (ibid.: 83, 106). Unlike Booker, however, Campbell stresses the importance of the relationship between the hero and his community. In his version, the hero returns to the community with treasures to be distributed among the public. This account renders the Campbell theme a better fit with our data.

In the case of the unions, we use the theme of "The Princess in the Castle." The theme is similar to and yet different from Booker's (2004) "Overcoming the Monster" storyline. "The essence of [this plot] is simple. Both we and the hero are made aware of the existence of some superhuman embodiment of evil power ... It is always deadly, threatening destruction to those who cross its path or fall into its clutches. Often it is threatening an entire community or kingdom, even mankind and the world in general. But the monster often also has in its clutches some great prize, a priceless treasure or a beautiful 'Princess.' [Eventually, the hero] wins the treasure, or the hand of the 'Princess.' He has liberated the world ... from the shadow of this threat to its survival" (ibid.: 23).

According to Booker, the story is likely to run through five stages, from anticipation and call through the thrilling escape from death and the death of the monster. The reality of our cases is less dramatic. Whereas union speakers identified government as the villain, they were careful not to cross a line; they never depicted a premier or any of a premier's ministers as "some superhuman embodiment of evil power." In addition, the union stories lacked a cathartic ending, or an opportunity for stakeholders to emit a sigh of relief, such as the final stage in Booker's plot. If government defeat in the next elections might be tantamount to the crushing of the monster, then this did not happen in six of the seven cases. However, one of Booker's five stages, the frustration stage, likely exists here. At this stage, "the hero seems tiny and very much alone against such a supernaturally strong opponent." What we will try to show below is that the essence of the plot outlined by Booker exists in our case studies. Our hero (unions) faced up to a monster (the government) that held the princess (a public service) prisoner in a castle (government policies and legislation).

The princess-in-the-castle plot combines moral and cautionary tales in a very straightforward way, differentiating unequivocally between the good and the bad. Given that research on the value of storytelling in organizations corroborates that the utility of storytelling lies in its ability to create meaning, both government and union speakers tried to educate the public by stressing what constituted legitimate and/or illegitimate practices.

Government Uses of Mythopoesis

The first stage in Campbell's "The Hero's Journey" paradigm is departure. It may be likened to van Leeuwen's notion of children leaving home to attend their first day of school. In the context of government rhetoric, we define this stage as the "blindside," which refers to those times when government speakers describe the present government as suddenly encountering a calamitous situation (usually financial) which they had not anticipated and which indeed no one saw coming. In the "blindside" stage, government speakers argue that the expected surplus projected earlier suddenly became a looming deficit, or that the provincial debts were far worse than they could possibly have imagined. In this stage, government speakers portrayed themselves as having been thrust by forces beyond their control into a menacing world that threatened to destroy the province unless tough action was immediately taken (stage two).

In stage two, Campbell argues that the hero overcomes obstacles and wins a decisive victory. Such battles, however, are never easy. In government rhetoric, this stage was marked by a speaker's description of the difficult and painful path that lay ahead. In order to avoid the dark future of crippling debt and deficit, government and citizens must pull together and face the adversity head-on. Campbell defines this stage as "initiation." For van Leeuwen, it represents the lessons that the child must learn in navigating the difficulties of the first days of school. We refer to this stage as "painful but necessary," since government speakers openly admitted that the measures they proposed – and that were the only way out of the crisis – required painful sacrifices. The pain, however, brought with it the promise of future blessings, of ushering in a golden age of prosperity and well-being.

Concurrently with envisioning the painful but curative measures that lay ahead, government speakers promised the third and final stage, "return." This is when the hero (according to Campbell) or child (according to van Leeuwen) returns to the community/home ready to dispense the treasures acquired on the journey. Importantly, the hero returns home a different person – the man who left is now a hero; the child is now a student. As well, the hero fully realizes his new status by sharing the treasure with members of his community or family. In our analysis, "return" is characterized by the *promise* of *future* prosperity, which was always envisioned as possible and probable. The promise refers to the outcome of completing the difficult path laid out in stage two. Promises in government rhetoric were typically projected into a far-off future – a time that when, or if, it came might render the current government but a distant memory. The promise of fiscal prosperity was often related in terms of the happy endings (blissful future) for one's children and/or grandchildren. While the pain of remedy was immediate, the joy that it brought would be a long time coming, which, in the context of government rhetoric, spoke not to the deficiency of the medicine but rather to the gravity of the disease.

Stage 1: Departure, or the Blindside

Though our dividing of government rhetoric into three stages follows a logical trajectory and implies a certain sequence and duration, actual instances often lumped all three stages within a single utterance. Typically, a premier or provincial treasurer would announce that a number of events had led to a large budgetary deficit, that these events were unanticipated by the government, and that they now must be dealt with. This deficit if left unchecked would mortgage the future of our children, leaving them with mountains of debt and few, if any, public services. The theme demonstrates the intermingling of moral and cautionary tales as well as the conflating of Campbell's three stages. First, the government had been blindsided by events that were unanticipated; second, the events must be dealt with; third, while failure to do so would leave our children with mountains of debt, confronting those events might be painful but would result in future prosperity.

At the outset of "the hero's journey," Campbell asserts that the protagonist first receives a call to enter an unusual world of remarkable powers and events. He terms this "a call to adventure." Though our data are taken from the actual world, government speakers nonetheless spoke of a persistent element of "unusually overwhelming events" that called for unorthodox measures. While the monsters and demons that government encountered were not fantastic in a spiritual or otherworldly sense, they were nonetheless presented as powerful entities, sometimes with apocalyptic powers that threatened to destroy entire provinces. In addition, Campbell observes that heroes rarely set forth of their own accord; more often they are compelled to act. In a similar fashion, van Leeuwen's analysis demonstrates that children begin school not of their own volition. Rather, their age demands formal schooling, the laws of the land demand schooling, and they are taken by their parents to school. Whether or not they are in accord, the youngsters find themselves at school. Government rhetoric presented the elements of force majeure that compel one to apply unorthodox, and perhaps unpopular, means of coping. In the case of Newfoundland and Labrador, Premier Danny Williams spoke on TV about the danger of "drowning in our own debt." Yet then he stated that his

> 8.1: government may have inherited this serious fiscal situation but we have absolutely no intention of letting our children and grandchildren inherit it from us. (Williams, 2004)

Later, Williams reiterated how he

> 8.2: had no way of knowing what kind of a fiscal mess we were going to be left in this Province. There was no possible way of seeing that that [the previous Liberal] government could do the eternal, perpetual damage that they have done to the people of our Province. (*House of Assembly Proceedings*, 26 April 2004, vol. 45, no. 22)

Similar instances are found in other cases. In Nova Scotia, Premier John Hamm described the present difficulties as having been inherited:

> 8.3: Part of the problem that we find ourselves in here is the result of the flawed policy of the previous government. (*Hansard*, 26 June 2001: 5786)

British Columbia's health minister, Colin Hansen, was more pointed in his criticism of the previous government:

> 8.4: You have to go back to a time when the NDP [the labour-oriented New Democratic Party] government was in power in this province [1991–2001]. This was a time when the HEU executive had a key to the back door of the Premier's office. (*Hansard*, 28 April 2004: 10638)

In these instances, not only was the current government blindsided by a sudden fiscal crisis, but also the problem could be traced to a previous government that had been reckless with the province's money.

But what happened when there was no previous government to blame? In the case of Alberta, the governing Progressive Conservatives had been in power since 1971. Therefore, in her 2002 budget address, Finance Minister Patricia Nelson stated the following:

> 8.5: As I stand here today ... March 19 ... it's a year ago today that my colleagues and I were sworn in to Cabinet. Little did I know what this year would bring ... The worst drought in Alberta's recorded history, forest fires raging through the summer, a dropping Canadian dollar and collapsing stock market, mounting expectations and increasing costs, dramatic drops in the price of oil and gas, and Canada joining the war on terrorism. For the first time in many, many years we watched as a group of fine Alberta men and women went off to war thousands of miles from home. The world is a very different place than a year ago today. (Nelson, 2002: 1)

In their totality, the above data demonstrate how government presented itself as having been thrust into a vortex of crippling events and forces. But, even though the government could neither have anticipated nor forestalled the present calamities ("the world has changed"), it would nonetheless embark on the difficult but virtuous path it proposed, so that the obstacles could be overcome and a boon returned to the community. These were the cards that the current government had been dealt and now it must choose the right path and overcome the obstacles ahead. In the case of Alberta, this meant saying no to the ATA demands and ordering the striking teachers back to work. In addition, following the arbitrator's decision to award the teachers higher wage increases than what the government had offered, the government accepted the award yet refused to finance it. This, in turn, resulted in teacher layoffs across the province (Reshef, 2007: 687–8).

Excluding the case of Alberta, our cases point to the possible interconnectedness of moral and cautionary tales. While governments portrayed themselves as behaving in a moral manner, they tended to depict their predecessors in terms of a cautionary tale stressing how an ethical government should *not* conduct itself. The previous government did not take the straight and narrow path. Rather, it chose an easy route with disastrous consequences that the current government was now forced to address.

Stage 2: Initiation, Painful but Necessary

In discussing the second stage of the hero's journey, Campbell draws attention to the many difficulties and/or obstacles that our hero must overcome, especially the continual temptation to simply run away or refuse the quest, to take the easy way out. In the current context, our analysis suggests that the second stage contains similar elements – recognizing the challenge ahead and then embracing without any equivocation the difficulties that it offers. The hero's journey is not so much that as it is the transformative process of a person *becoming* a hero. The struggles not only define the heroic actions of the individual but also serve to transform the individual into a hero. Such a process is not easy, requiring one to endure a great deal of blood, sweat, and tears. The greater the challenge the more heroic are the actions of the protagonist, who is both defined and transformed by her performance in this second stage.

We are not arguing that governments are heroic actors, or that they are necessarily transformed by seminal events into heroic beings. Rather, in the second stage, adversity was encountered and its challenge embraced by ethical governments that had the courage and audacity to act responsibly rather than opportunistically. This stage involved governments that had to implement difficult and unpopular measures, which were necessary for achieving a happy ending. Frequently, speakers made it amply clear that embarking on this journey might cost their government the next election, yet it was the right thing to do. They were ready to sacrifice their political future for the collective good of securing a better life for future generations.

To complete the heroic journey one must successfully pass through the second stage. To simply walk out of the classroom, for instance, would define the student as a "dropout" or failure. Similarly, in using mythopoesis, government speakers depicted the option of backing away from making the tough but correct decision as one that was as socially inappropriate as the choice to drop out. And so we find Quebec Premier Jean Charest stating that the financial challenges

> 8.6: are what they are and that reality is inescapable and we all have to deal with it. (Philip Authier, "Premier Vows to Stand His Ground: Poll Shows Quebecers Back Unions' Agenda," *Gazette*, 7 September 2005)

Echoing this outlook, New Brunswick Premier John Hamm stated emphatically:

> 8.7: I am not going to back away from the right thing to do. (Kevin Cox, "Bill Banning Strikes Will Exact Toll, Hamm Says," *Globe and Mail*, 16 June 2001)

In this case, Hamm contended that he knew what the right thing to do was, and that he was committed to pursuing that course of action regardless of popular opinion.

If Hamm were to "back away from the right thing to do," then he would face the serious charge of being a "quitter." And to be a hero requires that one press on, even in the face of overwhelming adversity that may require the hero to sacrifice herself. New Brunswick's Finance Minister Norman Betts stated this sentiment in stark terms:

> 8.8: Very simply, the message is this – New Brunswick is at a crossroads and there is a choice of directions we can take. We can choose as a province to continue down a well-worn path of deficits and debt, or we can choose a new path that will lead New Brunswick to fiscal, economic, and social success. (Betts, 2001: 30)

The "well-worn path" is an allusion to the following admonition from the Gospel of St Mathew: "Enter ye in at the strait gate: for wide is the gate, and broad is the way, that leadeth to destruction, and many there be which go in thereat: because strait is the gate, and narrow is the way, which leadeth unto life, and few there be that find it" (Mt 7: 13–14). The more difficult path via the narrow gate is both difficult to find and hard to enter, but it alone holds the promise of future blessings. Though such a path may be found by few, it "leadeth unto life."

Because the popular well-worn path had led to deficits and debt, Betts opened his 2000 budget address steadfast in his resolve to chart a new course vis-à-vis the narrow gate:

> 8.9: We are setting a course for change – a course to make New Brunswick more economically competitive and socially compassionate. (Betts, 2000: 1)

This is not an isolated incident, spanning as it does the range of data available to us. In 1992, when Saskatchewan Finance Minister Ed Tchorzewski tabled his first budget, he declared:

> 8.10: Saskatchewan faces a finance crisis of immense proportion ... And it's going to take all of us to be part of the solution for Saskatchewan, because if all of us come together now to tackle this unprecedented financial crisis, we will make the 1990s Saskatchewan's decade ... Now, Mr. Speaker, difficult decisions were demanded, and difficult decisions were made. But our children did not create this financial crisis, and we have no right to burden them with it ... Let us look forward to the day when we can tell our children

that, though we entered the 1990s plagued by financial crisis, we made the difficult decisions. We turned a new page in our history and put this Province firmly on the path to prosperity. (Tchorzewski, 1992: 1, 6, 11)

In this instance, the difficult path was presented as the one necessary for reaching the promised land of prosperity.

The perils of not addressing a difficult situation, or of shirking one's responsibility to do the right thing, were often vividly couched in cautionary, sometimes momentous, discourse. For instance, besides encountering the possibility of "mountains of debt," we find speakers telling us how

> 8.11: expenses are growing ... borrowing has increased ... federal transfers have been reduced ... gross debt and debt service costs are climbing ... (Betts, 2000: 8)

All of this led to a grim future. Newfoundland and Labrador Premier Danny Williams warned:

> 8.12: the numbers are staggering ... we are in the very real danger of drowning in our own debt. (Williams, 2004)

Similarly, Quebec Treasury Board President Monique Jérôme-Forget declared:

> 8.13: There is no more money in the chest than there was in the spring, and summer hasn't made the financial picture any less precarious. (Peggy Curran, "Contract Talks," *Gazette*, 15 August 2005)

It follows that not doing the right thing would be ethically wrong and practically more costly than the current problem.

The precariousness of the financial picture threatened the health and welfare of the community. Like passing through the narrow gate, the path to prosperity was depicted as requiring sacrifice, toil, and pain. In outlining his government's plan to put Newfoundland and Labrador on the road to prosperity, Premier Danny Williams openly admitted that it would

> 8.14: require hard work and sacrifice by everyone. We cannot expect to improve our lives without first enduring some short-term pain in return for long-term and meaningful benefits. We have a plan that focuses on achieving a balance. It's about making decisions for the right reasons – not for political reasons. (Williams, 2004)

As in the hero's journey, the pain is necessary for transforming the protagonist into a hero and for serving as the canvas on which the hero's deeds are painted. Tough situations provide the opportunity for heroes to prove themselves, which is to say that tough ethical people are capable of making tough decisions. In this context, the collective sacrifice was a barometer of the government's capacity to lead.

The ability to make idiosyncratic decisions and endure the consequences is a core attribute of a hero. In leaving one's community, the hero is often depicted as having answered a higher call, or having responded to a vision that was revealed to him alone. The hero is presented as the one pure soul who has bravely gone against the tide of popular opinion, and has found and entered in through the narrow gate. Our data reveal several such instances. In British Columbia, Graham Bruce, minister of skills development and labour, declared that his government had

> 8.15: made a commitment ... when we took over, that we would do things that were right, not popular ... a right decision, not a popular decision. (*Hansard*, 28 April 2004: 10645)

Newfoundland and Labrador Premier Danny Williams expressed a similar sentiment when he stated that his government's plan was "about making decisions for the right reasons – not for political reasons" (Williams, 2004). New Brunswick Premier John Hamm boldly pledged that he was

> 8.16: not going to back away from the right thing to do ... Just think back on how many years you've seen governments that in the end knuckle under and do things that you know didn't make sense in the long run. (Kevin Cox, "Bill Banning Strikes Will Exact Toll, Hamm Says," *Globe and Mail*, 16 June 2001)

In a similar vein, Saskatchewan's premier, Roy Romanow, emphatically declared:

> 8.17: I took an oath of office to do the best that I could to define the public interest. And public interest in this case meant public safety. Patient care, that's number one. And we'll be judged or elected on that in due time. I have absolutely no qualms in my heart, in my soul, in my mind that we did the best that we could to protect Medicare, to protect patient safety ... What the voters decide, of course, is the prerogative of the voters. (David Roberts, "Saskatchewan Nurses Back on Job," *Globe and Mail*, 19 April 1999)

Speakers' talk of blazing a trail on the straight and narrow provide an image of a government that has accepted "the call to adventure." While this call may bring with it a high price, the cost of not embarking on the journey is presented as far more dire, and as morally wrong.

Ostensibly, there is an important distinction between Campbell's paradigm and our study of government uses of mythopoesis. For Campbell, the hero's journey is the trajectory of a single protagonist, replete with self-actualization, transformation, and growth. As such, the narrative follows an individual actor as he completes a solitary quest before returning to the community with a trove of treasure. Government speakers, however, rarely if ever spoke in such solitary terms. Rather, the quest for redemption was framed in terms of a collective effort. It rested on a group that had to join forces to overcome significant obstacles in order to enter a new era marked by prosperity, growth, and stability. The heroic journey of the government consisted of calling a spade a spade, identifying long-term goals, charting a frequently unpopular path out of the crisis, rallying the public to embrace the new vision, and implementing the plan. Strictly speaking, however, the original final "returning-to-the-community-with-a-boon-to-distribute" stage was missing.

This emphasis on all members joining together to accomplish a great feat distinguishes government discourse from Campbell's analysis of the hero's journey, which focuses on the individual. The case of Saskatchewan, for instance, is representative of government speakers' propensity to contextualize the journey in terms of the community. Finance Minister Ed Tchorzewski opened his 1992 budget address by declaring his government's intention to restore the province to its former glory:

> 8.18: Today we begin rebuilding Saskatchewan together ... This financial difficulty cannot be wished away, but it can and it will be resolved by working together. And it's going to take all of us to be part of the solution for Saskatchewan, because if all of us come together now to tackle this unprecedented financial crisis, we will make the 1990s Saskatchewan's decade. (Tchorzewski, 1992: 1)

While the financial crisis was seen as "unprecedented," it nonetheless could be overcome if all agreed to be "part of the solution." Saskatchewan was not alone in this sentiment.

The need for "everyone" to commit themselves to hard work and sacrifice distinguishes our government speakers' discourse from Campbell's paradigm of the hero's journey. But if, as Campbell argues, the hero's journey is archetypal, then it should be regarded as having universal significance and being universally understood. Government speakers' propensity to frame the hero's journey in terms of the community reflects an implicit understanding that, if the journey is to be successful, then the community itself must embrace it and the hardships it presents. Such a message would presumably resonate with audience members because of the fundamental understanding that no one can accomplish the present journey on his own. Perhaps at one time each participant in the collective effort to combat deficits and debts resembled Campbell's original and individual hero, but he came to understand that a group effort was the appropriate means of securing the coveted reward.

Stage 3: Return, A Golden Age

Return is the final stage of the hero's journey. The hero returns to his community with knowledge, power, and wealth to be shared among all. In sharing in the rewards, members of the community can be regarded as participating, or at least validating, the journey completed by the hero. As noted in van Leeuwen's (2008: 119) analysis, the child does not simply remain at school. She is expected to be educated and become a productive member of society. If the hero never returned, then the community would be left to suffer the loss. Unlike the previous stages, this stage serves an especially important social function in that the rewards shared with the community make it a better place, not only materialistically but morally as well. Of course, applying such a stage to government discourse is problematic because here the notion of return is mostly used to rally support for the journey. The anticipated boon may never come during the tenure of the current government. Or, as in the case of Alberta, it may come but not be distributed fairly among the community.

In delivering his 1999 budget, Finance Minister Eric Cline began by reiterating how the people of Saskatchewan had chosen the right but difficult path before serving notice that a better future would soon ensue:

> 8.19: Mr. Speaker, ladies and gentlemen, Saskatchewan people *have* made the difficult decisions. We *have* turned a new page. We *are* on the path to prosperity – moving forward, working together to build the economy we want and the society we dream of. (Cline, 1999: 2; emphasis in original)

In this instance, Cline reassured his audience that they were in fact already on the path to prosperity, that it had taken its first tentative steps forward. That is not to say, however, that the destination had been reached. Rather, the course must be stayed since the progress made merely marked the beginning of a lengthy journey. In fact, according to Cline, this was exactly what the people of Saskatchewan wanted:

> 8.20: Saskatchewan people want a balanced, responsible approach to lower taxes, as finances permit. (Ibid.: 17)

The promised land of fiscal health and prosperity was within reach.

The sense of a closer-than-ever brighter future surfaced again in Newfoundland and Labrador Premier Danny Williams's *State of the Province Address*. Though Williams warned of the danger of "drowning in our own debt," he promised that the measures adopted by his government would restore "the seaworthiness of the vessel so we can launch out into the deep with confidence and success." Curiously, no port was mentioned. Rather, the ship of state would be returned to seaworthiness so that it could sail with "confidence and success." Importantly, in line with the notion of the community that must pull together, Williams's metaphor depicted a vessel wherein all crewmembers must share in the responsibility of readying it so that it could sail forward. The actions taken by the government and embraced by the people

> 8.21: hold promise for a brighter future. There is reason for optimism. There is reason for hope. (Williams, 2004)

With all hands on deck, so to speak, the ship of state would sail into waters that were more peaceful and that held the promise of a more prosperous future. Such a future was one that would surely benefit all the people of the province.

Similar promises can be found across the data. In the case of Quebec, the Treasury Board President, Monique Jérôme-Forget, held that while all Quebecers should expect to share in short-term sacrifice, all would similarly benefit:

> 8.22: I promise that, four years from now, there will be a hell of a lot more [services] than there are today ... It's clear that we want savings, but that's not the main goal. The objective is, more importantly, to give better services to people. (Mike De Souza, "16,000 Quebec Government Jobs to Disappear by 2013 under Plan," *Gazette*, 6 May 2004)

Though "services" may be less inspiring than the image of sailing into a golden sunset, the sentiment would seem to be similar in that the public stood to benefit if it supported the government's austerity plan. It should be noted that such a specific timeline is unique. It is more customary to find speakers, like Danny Williams, pointing towards some vague point in the future when the benefits would be realized. This is in fact the only instance in our data where a government speaker assigned such a specific time frame to the receipt of benefits. In the very same case, Quebec Premier Jean Charest presented the timeline in more general terms:

> 8.23: My first duty is towards equity between all Quebecers and all generations. (Mike De Souza, "Public Sector Unions Warned to Keep Demands Reasonable," *Gazette*, 8 August 2005)

Similarly, Saskatchewan Finance Minister Ed Tchorzewski asked constituents to look forward not four years but rather

> 8.24: to the day when we can tell our children that, though we entered the 1990s plagued by financial crisis, we made the difficult decisions. We turned a new page in our history and put this Province firmly on the path to prosperity. (Tchorzewski, 1992: 11)

In a similar vein, Premier Danny Williams reminded Newfoundlanders:

> 8.25: We have to look out for our children and grandchildren in this Province. (*House of Assembly Proceedings*, 26 April 2004, vol. 45, no. 22)

In this context, the hero's journey may take quite some time and the reward returned to the community may only occur much later. The future may thus be presented as a golden age that seems to recede before us continually. And yet government speakers were quick to point out that right decisions had been made even if their fruits had yet to be realized. To extend the metaphor provided by Danny Williams, we could say that though it takes much time and effort to turn the ship of state around, it takes still longer for it to reach the safety of calm waters. The rewards, then, may not be reaped by the current generation. Yet members of this generation were able to "change [the] future together," to quote New Brunswick Finance Minister Norman Betts (2000: 12). The future may have been altered and yet, like all of our futures, it remains continually beyond our grasp, with only the promise that one day our ship may arrive.

Overall, we have applied the theme of the hero's journey to government use of mythopoesis. As with probably any other discourse, its effectiveness relied on "institutional vocabularies," which means the "structures of words, expressions, and meanings used to articulate a particular logic or means of interpreting reality. Institutional vocabularies are the primary means by which institutional logics are articulated and manipulated" (Suddaby and Greenwood, 2005: 43). The hero's journey discourse highlighted the current government's leadership and ethical behaviour, absolved it from guilt, justified its austerity measures, prepared the public for sacrifice, and promised a better future. It is the first two elements in this list that prompted us to apply the hero's journey theme to governments. In the cases we used, government speakers often made it amply clear that they had opted for austerity measures even though doing so might have cost them the next election. This was the right thing to do. In other words, they had a choice and decided to shun the "easy way out." In the current context, this was a version of the hero's journey.

We have mentioned that our version of the hero's story differs from the original by its emphasis on the importance of the collective to the success of the hero's mission. In addition, unlike the original version, here there was someone to blame for the calamity that the hero was forced to redress. The previous government, or force majeure in the case of Alberta, was the obvious culprit. Since in most cases the incumbent government party won the next election, the current account of the hero's journey story might have appealed to a large segment of the voting population.

Union Uses of Mythopoesis: The Princess in the Castle

While we have argued that government discourse could be fruitfully thought of as the hero's journey, union discourse required a different archetype that we have termed "the princess in the castle." As we have said earlier, this plot is similar in its essence to Booker's (2004) "overcoming the monster." In this storyline, the hero is "drawn into the struggle not just on his own behalf but to save others; to save all those who are suffering in the monster's shadow; to free the community or the kingdom the monster is threatening; to liberate the 'Princess' it has imprisoned" (ibid.: 33). The princess in the castle represents a public treasure that is as fragile and vulnerable as it is precious and sacred.

The responsibility of defending this treasure falls upon its guardian(s), who must now act to stave off the looming danger. In real life, a community has found itself besieged by a malevolent force, the government, that threatens to destroy something that is valuable and essential to its well-being. The princess, that is, a service and a group of stakeholders (e.g., teachers, students), requires succor. The prince, here the unions, is expected to take up arms and assume his natural position as the princess's saviour.

While the government discourse presented a journey out into the wilderness where the dragon of debt and deficit had to be slain, the union discourse presented the government itself as the threatening dragon. Thus, while the government discourse largely identified threats as external entities, the union discourse identified the threat as originating with the rulers of the kingdom. The threat was not a dragon from a misty mountaintop, but rather the king himself who had turned against the very thing which was most treasured by his subjects. The union discourse appeared to be less comprehensive than the government's, less sweeping in its narrative arc, and more direct and pointed. While government might vaguely describe how we all had to pull together to fight debt and deficit, union speakers frequently drew a line between the good and the bad, between government and the workers and other stakeholders whom the union was protecting. From union speakers we heard much less about the future of our children and grandchildren. Such concerns were overshadowed by the immediacy and enormity of the current danger. In contrast to government speakers, who often spoke in generalized terms of an abstract future lingering beyond the horizon, union speakers were very specific, invoking explicit pieces of legislation or government policies that dominated the mind of present-day workers and recipients of affected services.

The "princess in the castle" connotes a straightforward narrative about a gallant knight fighting an evil force who is threatening a helpless princess locked up in a castle. However, in real life our fearless, chivalrous knight is a union hampered by organizational imperatives and political concerns. To be successful, its actions have to appeal to members, service recipients and their families, and the public at large. Sometimes, a "lean discourse" about a mean government that is undercutting an essential service through austerity policies may not be enough to gain the support of every "significant other." The story should be more nuanced and dramatic than that. Below we outline rhetorical dimensions that speakers used to make their narrative more compelling and attractive to various audiences.

Power Inequality

Government speakers drew an ominous picture of the external forces that were gathering to destroy the well-being of their provinces. To fight them successfully, government had to apply extraordinary measures. Likewise, union speakers demonstrated their own storytelling virtuosity by painting a dramatic image of the evil power, namely the government, that had assaulted them and their constituencies, thereby forcing them to retaliate. An element the speakers emphasized was the inherent imbalance of union-government power. The saviour of the princess must fight against a formidable opponent. Naturally, defeating an adversary that holds a considerable power advantage is not a trivial matter. If the knight in shining armour is to have any chance of success, she will have to use unorthodox methods that may cause short-term pain. Larry Booi, the ATA president, made this very point:

> 8.26: We have to do this [province-wide teachers strike] if we want to see things changed. It is a weapon of last resort and we're down to last resorts. (Susan Hagan, "Strike Position Draws Near," *Edmonton Journal*, 11 September 2001)

> If they order us back, the fight isn't over. If you think you can wave a legislative wand and make all the problems go away, it's not going to be that way and we will find other ways to fight it ... The only guarantee is if we don't take strong action, nothing is going to change. (Jeff Holubitsky, "Alberta Teachers Ready to Work to Rule," *Edmonton Journal*, 22 January 2002)

> We will do whatever is necessary to carry this struggle on. If the government slams one door shut, we will find another to open. If the government clamps the lid down, there is going to be more heat and more pressure. (Colette Derworiz, "CBE Teachers Reject Contract Offer," *Calgary Herald*, 28 January 2002)

> Nobody's minimizing the loss of extracurricular activities for kids. But tell me what other choices teachers have that aren't simply a meek acceptance of a really vile [arbitration] process. (Tom Olsen, "Teachers Outline Next Step in Fight," *Calgary Herald*, 19 March 2002)

In some cases, union leaders had to escalate their fight and even adopt illegal measures in order to have a chance of having their demands accepted. They told a vivid story of desperation, of a union that was fighting a ruthless opponent and therefore had to go the distance to protect its members and the general public. They were careful to stress that their illegal action must not be construed as a show of disrespect to the legal system, but was something that they had been forced to do. This is how Saskatchewan Union of Nurses President Rosalee Longmoore explained the situation:

> 8.27: I would like to say to the judge and this court that the action we took was not done easily or taken lightly and was meant as no show of disrespect of this court. I could not ask nurses to go back to work because their issues had not been dealt with and until this was done I could not ask my members to go back to work. While [I] took the court order very seriously, [I] was prepared to disobey it and face going to jail because [I] couldn't ask nurses to return to work in intolerable conditions without any hope of improvement. The members had to make individual choices whether to stay off the job or go back to work. [I] felt that SAHO and the provincial government were using the court to circumvent the collective bargaining process. (Anne Kyle, "Nurses' Union Faces 1-Million Fine for Defying Legislation," *Star-Phoenix*, 26 June 1999)

> The government and employers are using the fine to punish us for proving them wrong, I guess, because their rationale for [the back-to-work legislation] was that the system couldn't withstand a strike for more than six hours. But in fact the system withstood the strike for 10 to 11 days. (David Roberts, "Saskatchewan Nurses Pay for Illegal Strike," *Globe and Mail*, 9 July 1999)

Taken together, texts 8.26 and 8.27 suggest a "David versus Goliath" theme that was diligently cultivated by union speakers. To accentuate this image, some union speakers added a layer of "shock and awe" to their discourse, highlighting the enormity of their adversaries' callousness and bullying tactics. In the case of Nova Scotia, for instance, Joan Jessome, president of the NSGEU, reacted to the government's introduction of Bill 68 with disbelief:

> 8.28: I just can't believe they can say they value health-care providers and then turn around and take away every single right they have negotiated away from them. (*Trail Times*, "Nurses Protest 'Draconian' Bill," 15 June 2001)

On the one hand, the government had assured nurses that they were essential to the province's future. Yet, on the other hand, Bill 68 was designed to prevent a strike in health care by suspending the employees' right to strike for three years while giving the government the right to determine any collective agreement, or provision thereof. In this way, Jessome implied that the government was saying one thing but doing another.

Like Jessome, Daniel Bernatchez, CUPE negotiator in New Brunswick, was shocked by Premier Bernard Lord's support of Bill 30:

> 8.29: His message is that there are no more negotiations in this province. Do you believe this? I'm still in a dream. Is this real? I keep pinching myself. ("Service Reductions Planned as Hospitals Gird for N.B. Strike," *Standard*, 28 February 2001)

In British Columbia, Chris Allnutt of the HEU expressed outrage with the government's abuse of power to get its way:

> 8.30: This premier and his government have callously rewritten the law to suit their privatization agenda in health care and violated the legal rights of tens of thousands of workers in the process. (HEU News Release, "Bill 37 a Shocking Betrayal of Health Care Workers," 28 April 2004)

In the case of Newfoundland and Labrador, Wayne Lucas, provincial president of CUPE, portrayed Premier Danny Williams as having but to reach for a pen to render a great wrong:

> 8.31: With a stroke of a pen [the premier] is going to make a legitimate, legal structure illegal and try to turn hard-working Newfoundlanders and Labradorians into criminals. ("Bill Expected to End Nfld. Strike," *Pembroke Observer*, 26 April 2004)

Not only did Lucas's statement implicitly acknowledge the tremendous power wielded by the premier, but it also depicted the perversion of that power – the king would transform the legal strike into an illegal one so that he could punish severely his hard-working subjects.

In a democracy one would expect those with power to use it in a responsible manner, and to treat others with respect and consideration. Yet union speakers often depicted government as not only irresponsible but as gleefully, or unabashedly, abusing their power. In the case of Alberta, ATA president Larry Booi characterized Klein's introduction of Bill 12, the Education Services Settlement Act, as

8.32: an arrogant abuse of power. It's also a black day for public education and democracy in Alberta. What was tabled is not arbitration. It is legislative smashing of fair collective bargaining and teachers' rights. (Tom Olsen, "Teachers Urged to Pull Voluntary Services," *Calgary Herald,* 12 March 2002)

Compared with Jessome's depiction of the Nova Scotia government, however, Booi's comments appear tame:

8.33: This government sat in the house for the past 13 days, laughed in our faces, showed us no respect and then passed a bill that took away our rights. ("N.S. Tories Pass Anti-Strike Bill; Workers Vow to Defy It," *Leader-Post,* 28 June 2001)

Union speakers crafted a discourse of victimization that portrayed government as insensitive bullies who had chosen to operate beyond the pale of social norms. It was a cautionary tale of governments that had ceased to conduct themselves in a responsible, humane manner and were now behaving like omnipotent dictators who felt a sense of Schadenfreude in the suffering of labour. Yet the unions did not shirk their responsibilities to their respective constituencies, and they did not pull their punches. They were ready to defend the weak and less fortunate. Yes, sometimes they had to resort to illegal measures, and occasionally their actions were painful – but what other choices did they have? This sense of duty and anxiety was further emphasized when the unions presented themselves as the only ones capable of holding the government accountable and taking it to task for its wrongdoing. They were the only ones who were ready to face up to the redoubtable opponent and spare no effort in saving the besieged princess.

The "Princess's" Sole Protectors

Compared with government, union uses of mythopoesis were more concrete, tangible, and focused. In the hero's journey, it was noted how government spoke of a nebulous danger lurking ahead and how certain actions, judiciously chosen, would lead to the coming of a golden age. In the union discourse, the lines were more clearly drawn, the danger more immediate, tactile, and visible – patient care was suffering, students were drowning in a sea of overcrowded classrooms, union members were being bullied by an insensitive government, and democracy was at risk from specific legislation or policy. In the case of Saskatchewan, for example, a nurse at a Regina hospital was reported to have said that she and her colleagues were

> 8.34: striking for the safety of [their] patients because they're not being ensured safe care right now. There's not enough nurses and it's a dire, dire situation right now. (Martin O'Hanlon, "Nurses Defy Back-to-Work Order," *Calgary Herald*, 9 April 1999)

In Quebec, chief CSQ negotiator Brent Tweddell said:

> 8.35: What [was] on the table [was] basically going to impoverish people. (Kevin Dougherty, "Thorny Negotiations Ahead as Quebec Proposes Six-Year Contract to Unions," *Gazette*, 19 June 2004)

Following the "clarification phase" where the speakers pinpointed the problem, they continued to portray their union as the only group willing, and able, to stand up for an important cause, the "saving of the princess." In the case of Alberta, for example, what was in peril was the institution of education, according to the ATA's Larry Booi:

> 8.36: Teachers are the only ones who are standing up for proper funding for education. (Jeff Holubitsky, "Huge Gap between Teacher Demands, Board Budgets," *Edmonton Journal*, 3 January 2002)

This might have been due to three factors. First, the government apparently did not care about education. Second, there was a lack of knowledge among the general population regarding proper funding levels for the education system. Third, unions might have been the only organization that possessed the wherewithal needed to defend the besieged institution of education.

To guarantee popular support for their sometimes controversial actions, union speakers were careful to relate their discourse to a broad spectrum of stakeholders. In the case of Saskatchewan, the union presented itself as standing up for a health-care system that existed to benefit everyone. In the words of that Regina hospital nurse again:

> 8.37: We have to take a stand and now it's not only for ourselves but it's for our patients' safety and for all of Saskatchewan. (Martin O'Hanlon, "Nurses Defy Back-to-Work Order," *Calgary Herald*, 9 April 1999)

For Nova Scotian NSGEU President Joan Jessome, the union's actions signalled a commitment to the fundamental rights of all Nova Scotians. The strike was not simply about health care. Rather:

> 8.38: This is about the survival of democracy in this province. That is what we are fighting for. (Kevin Cox, "Union Sets June 27 for Nova Scotia Health-Care Strike," *Globe and Mail*, 23 June 2001)

Similarly, in British Columbia, chief union spokesperson Chris Allnutt declared that the union

> 8.39: must stand up to unjust laws that deprive working people of their fundamental rights. The legislation is unjust and must be challenged. (Oliver Moore, "B.C. Strikers Switch to 'Protest Lines,'" *Globe and Mail*, 29 April 2004)

In these instances, the union was presented as having acted, or having planned to act, on behalf of and in the best interests of the larger community. This is the stage in the storyline where the audience may feel constricted and threatened yet at the same time relieved that there is a hero who is ready to face up to the monster. The union, it would seem, was uniquely well suited to identify the threat and to stand up on behalf of the larger community when others could not, or would not, do so. It follows that the coveted trophy of public opinion and support should go to the union.

A CLEAR TARGET

As with government discourse, we find that moral and cautionary tales often appear simultaneously in union uses of mythopoesis. Yet this is where the similarity ends. The union speakers focused on a concrete, and often personal, target – the government, that is, the premier and particular politicians. The battle lines were clearly drawn, the targets were brought into focus and were highly visible. In government discourse, by contrast, the citizens were told how they must all "pull together" in order to ward off the somewhat arcane and impersonal (unless it was the previous government) threat of financial turmoil. Unions were almost never specifically mentioned in any of the government speeches pertaining to the future financial vitality of a province. We never heard, for example, how readying the province for a future of economic and social bliss would entail a hard-line approach towards unions. Consistent with the theme of the hero's journey, we were told of a menacing threat and how government action would tackle it and lead the province to a brighter future. Seemingly, unions became embroiled in conflicts with governments because they happened to be in the line of fire of public-sector restructuring and austerity measures.

Union speakers, however, identified governments, premiers, and other specific politicians as villains who were threatening the fragile princess. Debts and deficits did not imperil classroom and/or hospital conditions – high-ranking politicians did. Democracy was not being besieged by an emerging financial shortfall. Rather, government was conducting itself in a way that undermined public services and fundamental human rights. The problem was not ancillary to the labour conflict, or the result of the flawed policies of a previous government. Instead, the problem was the other party; it had a face and a name, it was concrete and personal. It was a self-centred government that had little to no regard for unions, working people, and public-service clients. The unions' use of mythopoesis gave their troubles visual and tactile qualities that were absent in the government texts. For example, in Quebec, CSQ President Claudette Carbonneau declared:

> 8.40: We won't let the government transform public-sector jobs into cheap labor and weaken the quality of services offered to the Quebec population. The CSN will also never tolerate public-sector employees going two years without a raise. The government did everything to stall public-sector negotiations [this year]. 2005 will again be a hot year because of the numerous union allegiances forced by fusions imposed by Bill 30. (Mike King, "Charest 'Swimming' in Troubled Water," *National Post*, 30 December 2004)

Others made more pointed accusations. For example, Michael Murray, reacting to the government's decision to award performance bonuses to school board directors who earned between $83,000 and $147,000 a year, stated:

> 8.41: These types of Mickey Mouse demands have been on the table for two years. It was like telling people, "don't get sick, don't get injured or else you'll be replaced and reassigned to another job in the school board." ... We had never seen demands like this before. It is somewhat scandalous ... it's awful that the government offers bonuses to those making $147,000 a year. (Rhéal Séguin, "Unions Delay Walking out at Schools in Quebec," *Globe and Mail*, 13 September 2005)

176   Bad Time Stories

Similarly, Carole Roberge, president of the SPGQ, responding to the news that some union leaders had calculated that in fact the government had a margin of manoeuvre of $6 billion, declared:

> 8.42 The figures do not lie. But they [the government] are lying with the figures. (Kevin Dougherty, "Province Can Pay," *Gazette*, 28 September 2005)

And Réjean Parent, CSQ president, responded this way to Treasury Board President Jérôme-Forget's statement that "with their reduced demands, the unions are only asking for the moon and planet Mars. I'm inviting them to come back down to Earth":

> 8.43: She should get out of the basement and come back to Earth. (Kevin Dougherty, "Province Can Pay," *Gazette*, 28 September 2005)

Likewise, in Alberta, ATA President Booi blamed Learning Minister Oberg for the brewing conflict:

> 8.44: The question among teachers is, what is going on with Dr. Oberg? In that statement [that the Alberta teachers are being used as pawns by the Canada Teachers Federation, which is trying to win high settlements that can be applied across Canada], he has gone from being unreasonable to being hysterical. He is either in denial of obvious troubles, or he is putting an unreasonable spin on things so he is losing credibility." (Tom Olsen and Scott McKeen, "Teachers 'Pawns' in Wage Fight," *Edmonton Journal*, 17 December 2001)

> Oberg is acting like a medieval monarch, not a democratic cabinet minister with thinking like this [considering using days allocated to the Easter break and March break to help the students catch up after the strike]. He can't rule by executive decision, especially if he's not willing to put up the money that will be needed to pay teachers for giving up that time. (Jeff Holubitsky and Graham Thomson, "'Get Back to Negotiating,'" *Edmonton Journal*, 2 February 2002)

> When the lights go out in our classrooms, across the province, Dr. Oberg is partly responsible for throwing the switch. (Rick Pedersen, "Strike Clearly Going Forward," *Edmonton Journal*, 3 February 2002)

By putting a name and a face on their adversary, union speakers provided themselves and their audience with a crystal-clear rallying point – the problem was not as nebulous as "the economy" or "world affairs," but a concrete, uncaring, and belligerent premier (or a specific minister) who was intent on targeting the union and who did not understand that one could not simply pile more patients or students into already full spaces. It was much more difficult for the government, by comparison, to protest against the forces that were undermining the fiscal situation and the well-being of its province. Droughts, floods, a rollercoaster economy, even public coffers plundered by their predecessors, these were all abstractions that could not be so easily protested against. Certainly, they could be complained about, but it would be silly indeed to hear of the agriculture minister protesting the latest drought, or the minister of finance spearheading a demonstration against the economic downturn in the United States.

Summing Up

We have argued that, while government discourse fits well with Campbell's archetype of the hero's journey, union discourse is more suited to the theme of the princess in the castle, a version of Booker's overcoming-the-monster plot. We have highlighted the importance of time as an interpretive resource. For government, because the future was uncertain, legitimating an effective action strategy required speakers to engage in "temporal work" to negotiate tensions among possible different conceptions of what had happened in the past, what was at stake in the present, and what might hopefully emerge in the future. Government speakers were inclined to construct a narrative that looked back to an earlier time to explain how we had arrived at this moment, before proclaiming the actions that must now be taken to realize a blissful future. In general, the past was the source of the current troubles; the present provided an opportunity for redemption; and the future promised a boon for those embarking on this journey and their offspring. The government was committed to the journey and the hardship it entailed, even if it led to political defeat.

The temporal range invoked by unions was more limited. Speakers' uses of mythopoesis were more straightforward since they did not conceive of their struggles in terms of a long-range journey, but rather presented a head-to-head conflict occurring at this moment and in this place between guardians of key public institutions and those who would not hesitate to harm them. Typically, they relayed the simple message that an institution important to us all was facing government attack, or neglect, and that they were standing up in its defence. In the main, these were stories of alarm and protest, of pluck in the face of a grave danger. Their time frame was usually short, limited to the here and now, and so the arc of a possible eventful journey was partial. Yet, within these shorter-range journeys, there were acts of heroism since those who dared to free the princess sacrificed portions of their incomes, risked their own freedom, public denunciation, and even jail terms. Taken together, for governments, the princess in the castle might be conceived as a chapter, or an episode, in their journey to a better future. For unions, metaphorically, the princess in the castle was a matter of life and death, a hill to die on.

Perhaps most revealing about both government and union uses of mythopoesis is that mythopoesis appears at all. If government deemed it necessary to make cuts to education and union would fight those cuts, then why was it necessary for either side to bother with crafting stories? Perhaps it was because stories provide speakers with a powerful way to simplify complex situations and actions, rendering them more accessible and meaningful to an audience. Statements about sinking ships and future generations likely resonate better with audiences than lectures about growing deficits, shaky financial markets, volatile exchange rates, and accumulated debts. These latter issues may be beyond the comprehension of many, but most people are likely to grasp the tales told by the people dealing with such weighty matters and their implications. Thus, the telling of stories becomes a way not only to justify certain actions but also to enable us to understand and talk in a meaningful manner about the complex problems confronting our society. This is simply to say that the speakers presented here conceived of their situations and resolutions in terms of narrative. But, while narratives may weave together and contain many instances, how government and union speakers used those narratives and for what ends differed markedly.

Chapter Nine

It Is Not All the Same (Stories from Another Book?)

The previous chapters may have left some readers with the impression that the behaviour of unions and governments during labour conflicts is largely scripted. The rhetoric of their legitimation strategies follows a predictable pattern, with plots that adhere to a similar storyline. Unions react in pretty much the same way to government intervention in industrial relations, and governments respond similarly to union behaviour that they deem inappropriate. The pattern that emerges follows one of two basic forms. First, organized labour beats the war drums once it suspects that government is assaulting its right to collective bargaining and strike and/or the well-being of union members. Or, second, government retaliates against union behaviour (e.g., refusal to negotiate wage rollbacks, threats of a strike, a strike, forging an alliance with other unions in response to government policy) by unilaterally intervening in an existing dispute. As a result, broadly speaking, the union discourse would justify strikes or other service withdrawal tactics, whereas the government's narrative would likely defend its austerity measures and retaliation against the union's proposed or actual job actions. However, public-sector labour disputes can evolve in a variety of ways, and occasionally produce discourses that differ markedly from the ones we have discussed. Not all government-union conflicts are the same. Some defy assimilation. The following four cases illustrate this point.

The first case is that of Prince Edward Island (P.E.I.). On 25 January 1993 Catherine Callbeck became the first elected female premier of P.E.I., the smallest province in Canada. Her Liberal Party won thirty-one seats in a thirty-two-seat legislature. In June of that year, the P.E.I. government predicted a deficit of $25.4 million for the 1993–4 fiscal year. In early 1994 the figure was revised to $69.4 million, an increase of $44 million. An austerity plan to fight the deficit was looming. The subsequent government rhetoric should now be familiar to readers. It included a self-absolving statement – the government had no way of anticipating a set of events that were beyond its control but had now culminated in a fiscal emergency – followed by a typical pattern: a clarion call for a collective sacrifice that was vital for the future of "our children"; a declaration of war on the deficit yet, as per the Islanders' wish, not through the raising of taxes – hence, the need for government to cut "our hard-working" public-sector employees' wages and benefits; and a reminder that leadership meant taking tough, if unpopular, decisions such as those proposed by this responsible government.

In March 1994 Lieutenant Governor Marion L. Reid delivered the Speech from the Throne. In a section entitled "Balancing the Budget," she set the stage for the austerity plan that would be detailed in the upcoming budget address:

> 9.1: With federal transfer payments to the province reduced by more than $100 million over the past three years, with interest payments on our debt now amounting to nearly seventeen percent of our total spending, and with a resistance amongst all Canadians to further tax increases, Prince Edward Island must act decisively to get its financial house in order ... My government has been successful in controlling expenditures, and yet the first-year deficit reduction is proving to be elusive ... our plan to balance the budget by the end of 1996 is still firmly in place, and our resolve is strong. We are now convinced, however, that reaching this goal can be accomplished only if all segments of the Island community share in the sacrifice. (Reid, 1994: 9)

A month later, the provincial treasurer, Wayne D. Cheverie, delivered the budget address. He echoed the above message, substantiated the gravity of the situation, and outlined policy tools his government would apply to put "our financial house in order":

> 9.2: In June of 1993, we were predicting a deficit for that fiscal year of $25.4 million. The final deficit figure, however, will be $69.4 million, an increase of $44 million ... Reductions in [the federal government's] equalization [payments] combined with the cap on established programs financing transfers have led to a large structural budgetary deficit. These events were unanticipated by the Government, but now must be dealt with ... this structural deficit if left unchecked will mortgage the future of our children, leaving them with mountains of debt and few, if any, services at all.

Last autumn, I decided to open the budget making process ... I wanted to hear more from Islanders. I held a series of four Roundtable Meetings across Prince Edward Island. These meetings were attended by representatives of a broad range of groups and organizations ... The consensus from the Roundtable sessions was that a long term plan was needed to reduce the deficit, and that Government should place more emphasis on economic growth and reducing costs instead of increasing taxes ... The majority of people told me that taxes in Prince Edward Island are already high enough, and should not be looked at as a way to generate more money for the government.

... The single largest area of Government spending is in wages and benefits ... almost 47 cents out of every dollar brought into Government, go back out in the form of wages and benefits to our employees ... our Government consistently has resisted such actions [i.e., wage cuts and layoffs], in hope that the economy would improve, and with careful management we could achieve our deficit reduction objective through other means. However, it is now clear that we cannot deal effectively with our deficit problem without addressing this "half" of Government spending. This is ... a regrettable but an inescapable conclusion. Our public sector employees work hard for their living, and deserve the wages and benefits they earn, and yet if adjustments are not made at this time, we will put at risk the ability of the Province to provide all citizens with essential programs and services ... We will do everything possible to avoid layoffs, and see this approach [i.e., wage rollbacks] as being a reasonable alternative ... leadership means doing the right thing, at the right time, and while these measures are tough, they are a necessary remedy. (Cheverie, 1994: 2, 3, 6, 9–10, 14–16)

The government asked the unions to negotiate the wage rollbacks, but they refused. Consequently, on 19 May, the government passed Bill 70, the Public Sector Pay Reduction Act. The bill suspended collective bargaining for all monetary terms in the public sector for one year, and rolled back the wages of all public-sector employees. The wages of those earning $28,000 per year or less were cut by 3.75 per cent, and of those making more than $28,000 per year by 7.5 per cent. Interestingly, this heavy-handed intervention did not trigger a major clash with the public-sector unions. Media coverage of the matter was scant, and we could not find any union texts in response to the government's retrenchment policy and Bill 70. Notably, this is the only case in our study where the government party lost the election following its intervention in industrial relations. Unfortunately, as we have stated several times, given the nature of the data, a causal relationship between the two events cannot be established.

This case shows that a government's assault on labour's right to strike and negotiate agreements, a theme that runs throughout all of the case studies, does not always result in open conflict with unions. In P.E.I., the unions refused to negotiate the government-imposed wage rollbacks. However, beyond that, they did not escalate the conflict. We could not find any written indication that they protested Bill 70 in any way. Perhaps, forbidden to strike, the unions were reluctant to break the law by spearheading a job action. Or perhaps, given the popularity of the government and its strength in the legislature, the unions assumed that they would not be able to garner much public support if they organized a collective resistance. Regardless, this was a situation that one would have thought would escalate and blossom into "open war." But it did not.

In stark contrast to the cases we have discussed so far are those situations where unions, or stakeholder groups (e.g., students' parents), implored a government to intervene in a conflict but it refused. In New Brunswick, on 25 September 2000, the court stenographers' bargaining unit went on strike. The unit included all of the sixty-three court stenographers in the province. However, only a third were allowed to stay off the job, since the employer (the government) had declared forty-two stenographers as essential. This might have been the main reason why the strike, which ended on 30 January 2001, lasted ninety-eight days. With two-thirds of the bargaining unit at work, the courts could handle close to a full caseload. Thus, the government was under no real pressure to end the strike. The workers asked for a wage increase of 19.0 per cent over three years. The employer offered 1.5 per cent per year over three years. Throughout the long dispute, the workers, all of them women, implored the government to intervene, but to no avail. According to the union spokesman, Ed Grenier of CUPE:

> 9.3: There's no doubt in our minds that had this been a predominantly male group, we would have been at the table negotiating an end to this strike. (Brad Green, "Stenographers Say Government Sexist," *Cambridge Reporter*, 4 November 2000; see also "Court Stenos Vow to Stay on Strike for Years in Dispute with New Brunswick Government," *Cobourg Daily Star*, 12 January 2001)

The government's response was that it had

> 9.4: established a standard settlement offer of 1.5 percent as a pattern for public sector negotiations. If [it] breaks the pattern for stenos, [it] would

have to do the same for other groups lining up to negotiate new contracts. (*Cobourg Daily Star*, 12 January 2001)

This narrative resurfaced throughout the conflict. The government's reluctance to intervene was aided by the fact that the political and economic effects of the strike were minimal, since most members of the bargaining unit were forced to stay on the job. The strike ended with an arbitrator awarding the stenographers a 15.0 per cent wage increase over four years.

The next case took place in Alberta on 16 February 2007, when about six hundred teachers in the Parkland School Division went on strike. The strike ended on 19 March after twenty-two working days. The teachers had been without a contract since their three-year agreement expired in August 2006. The length of the new contract was a key obstacle in the negotiations. The teachers wanted a one-year deal whereas the school board insisted on a multi-year contract. Ultimately, the two sides agreed to refer the dispute to arbitration. Throughout the strike, various groups pressured the government to intervene. The government consistently refused. Premier Ed Stelmach explained:

> 9.5: As a former school trustee myself, I firmly believe in the authority of the local school board. That's one of their responsibilities and we're going to leave it with them. (David Howell, "School's Out in Parkland," *Edmonton Journal*, 16 February 2007)

A month later, the education minister, Ron Liepert, stressed:

> 9.6: The [school] board and the ATA each have a responsibility to resolve this issue. ("For Students' Sake, End Parkland Strike School Impasse," *Edmonton Journal*, 9 March 2007))

Employment Minister Iris Evans added:

> 9.7: We fought hard [as trustees] to have local collective bargaining, and I think now they have to follow through with their commitment to that. (Jim MacDonald, "Province Not Ready to Intervene in Parkland Teachers Strike," Canadian Press, 12 March 2007)

Though this situation was different, it is possible that Stelmach's Progressive Conservative government was reluctant to recreate the drama its predecessor had gone through nearly five years earlier (see chapter 4). Thus, the 2001–2 government mantra that "teachers and students belong in the classroom" was now dimmed by a discourse stressing the sanctity of free local collective bargaining.

Our fourth and last example, already mentioned briefly in chapter 3, is from Ontario. Between 6 November 2008 and 28 January 2009, about 3,350 contract faculty, teaching assistants, and graduate assistants went on strike at York University. Close to 50,000 students were forced to miss classes. The university offered the workers 9.25 per cent wage increase over three years. CUPE, the union representing the striking workers, demanded an 11.0 per cent wage hike over two years, enhanced benefits, and more job security. According to the university:

> 9.8: The union's overall demands add up to a "totally unrealistic" 41 per cent hike. ("York Students Hit Again," *Toronto Star*, 7 November 2008)

Two other campus groups, maintenance workers and clerical staff, had ratified contracts similar to those offered to the striking workers. Throughout the strike, the Liberal government of Dalton McGuinty was pressured to intervene. But it took the government eighty-five days before it succumbed to public pressure and legislated the workers back to work. Two weeks before ending the dispute, John Milloy, the minister of training, colleges and universities, said:

> 9.9: I appreciate the frustration of the parents and the students. [I] urge and encourage both sides to resolve [the dispute] as quickly as possible. (Keith Leslie, "Province Won't Force York Settlement," *Globe and Mail*, 14 January 2009)

A day later he acknowledged that he did not want to intervene in a dispute at an autonomous institution and added:

> 9.10: There is a process which is unfolding and we're going to see what happens. (Murray Campbell, "Angry over Strike," *Globe and Mail*, 13 January 2009)

Respect for collective bargaining thus figured prominently in this part of the government narrative.

There was at least one other reason for the government's procrastination. Senior officials admitted that the government was reluctant to intervene in the dispute because of the precedent-setting 2007 Supreme Court ruling in a dispute between the British Columbia government and unionized health-care support workers (Benzie, Rushowy, and Loriggio, 2009; Coyle, 2009). In chapter 3 we noted that, in its landmark decision, the Supreme Court declared that collective bargaining was protected by the Charter of Rights of Freedoms (Supreme Court of Canada, 2007). Therefore, governments should not rush to abrogate duly negotiated collective agreements. The Court accepted the "Principles Concerning Collective Bargaining" issued by the International Labour Organization (ILO), including the following:

> (§77. J) It is acceptable for conciliation and mediation to be imposed by law in the framework of the process of collective bargaining, provided that reasonable time limits are established. However, the imposition of compulsory arbitration in cases where the parties do not reach agreement is generally contrary to the principle of voluntary collective bargaining and is only admissible [in cases of essential services, administration of the state, clear deadlock, and national crisis].

In this narrative, then, the constitutional right to collective bargaining figured as a prominent reason for not passing a back-to-work bill earlier. The premier initially decided to allow the parties "reasonable time" to settle their differences; eventually, however, he came to the conclusion that they were "clearly deadlocked" and that the dispute could no longer be waged on the backs of the students:

> 9.11: I am now convinced that the two sides are in deadlock, that there is no reasonable prospect of resolution through the traditional bargaining process, so time's up. (Karen Howlett and Elizabeth Church, "York Union Vows to Fight Back-to-Work Legislation," *Globe and Mail*, 27 January 2009)

On 29 January the government passed Bill 145, an Act to Resolve Labour Disputes between York University and Canadian Union of Public Employees, Local 3903. The bill ordered the workers back to work and referred the dispute to a mediator-arbitrator, who eventually awarded the workers a yearly 3.0 per cent wage increase over three years. It should be noted that Bill 145 outlined five principles that restricted the mediator-arbitrator's terms of reference. These principles are presented in chapter 3.

The four cases discussed above demonstrate that unions may not always respond aggressively to austerity measures, and that governments may sometimes prefer to remain on the sidelines during public-sector labour disputes. We have offered various anecdotal explanations for these phenomena. A more systematic analysis of the determinants of conflict behaviour is beyond the scope of this book. Perhaps more important in the context of our study is the recognition that a discourse is socially constructed to fit particular circumstances and mindsets. Put differently, discourse is likely delimited by context. At the same time, discourse can shape context. In the case of Alberta, for example, the government discourse formed a context where the protection of free collective bargaining was paramount, clearly exceeding the need for government intervention. Researchers may wish to explore the following questions: To what extent are discourses tailored to fit shifting agendas? To what extent are they cast in the mould of a prevailing ideology and how do they change over time and across events? What makes social actors more or less opportunistic/dogmatic in the way they respond to similar circumstances at different times? Can one find systematic patterns in the conflict behaviour of the parties? Are discourses crafted to suit current interests simply for pragmatic reasons?

Chapter Ten

Findings and Conclusions

Our study has endeavoured to address how public-sector unions and governments mobilized language to legitimate their actions during conflicts. Our approach does not focus on collective bargaining and strikes, which usually figure prominently in research on labour conflict. Rather, we have explored how, when in conflict, government and union seek support for their actions through the use of discourse. To that end, we have used language for data and critical discourse analysis as our analytical tool.

In this book, language is the medium not merely for relating a course of action but also for explaining why that course is necessary and preferable to others. In this way, language itself has served as the focus of our study. We have tried to show that the language used was seldom neutral. Instead, it constituted a "contested terrain," or "discursive struggle," that was no less important than labour conflicts' more obvious economic, political, and behavioural manifestations. After all, as Nelson (2003: 449) states in the epigraph to our book, "human conflict begins and ends via talk and text. We generate, shape, implement, remember and forget violent behavior between individuals, communities or states through specific discourse. It is discourse that prepares for sacrifice, justifies inhumanity, absolves from guilt, and demonizes the enemy." Within this general context, following van Leeuwen (2008) and van Leeuwen and Wodak (1999), we have demarcated and explored actors' rhetoric of legitimation across four textual strategies – authorization, rationalization, moralization, and mythopoesis.

Our findings suggest that the authorization-legitimation strategy was used in each one of the seven case studies. The most prevalent type was personal-authorization legitimation. Speakers likely expected the audience to accept what they said because of who they were, high-ranking union or government personnel. We identified a further authorization-legitimation strategy that we termed "public authorization." Here, speakers called upon the general public, specific groups (e.g., teachers, nurses), or broadly defined groups (e.g., workers, taxpayers, students, and their parents) to endorse position statements and actions "because this is what the people want."

Naturally, speakers also provided concrete reasons why the public should embrace their agenda and behaviour. This rationalization-legitimation strategy comprised two types – instrumental and theoretical. While these strategies were fairly easy to spot, they depended heavily on the less recognizable features of context to achieve their discursive power. (Context is the collection of circumstances that form the setting for an event or utterance and in terms of which it is understood and assessed.) Rationalization strategies may appear logical and persuasive within their context, yet, once the context itself is deconstructed, the strategies may become deflated. The reason is that, frequently, context is constructed to amplify contingencies which should promote an agenda and downplay others which may undercut it. Once this is exposed, arguments may lose their original "bite" and veracity.

Moralization, the third legitimation strategy in our framework, is closely linked with rationalization. We often found a single passage intertwining both strategies. Government speakers, for instance, may tell us that they have passed back-to-work legislation because of public safety. Union speakers may argue passionately that they launched a job action to improve a much-neglected public service. Such arguments combine a utility (protecting the public; improving a public service) with a moralized action (it is the right step to take). Frequently, controversial actions were pitched as the "right decisions" in a hope that the audience would find them more palatable.

The last legitimation strategy we have discussed is mythopoesis or storytelling. It comprises two basic genres – moral and cautionary tales. We have observed these two genres but have also found that government and union discourse followed two archetypal plots – "the hero's journey" and "the princess in the castle" respectively. Borrowed from Campbell (1949), the hero's journey is essentially a tale of a protagonist who sets out to overcome the tests that lie ahead before returning home to share the boon with the community. It is a story that endows the main character with a great deal of fortitude and capacity for action. In reading the government texts, one quickly realizes that future happiness requires immediate bold action and a great deal of resolve and resilience. The union discourse followed a theme we call "the princess in the castle," an instance of Booker's (2004) "overcoming the monster" plot. Unlike the hero's journey, here the community does not face the enemy without. Now, it is those who should be protecting the kingdom's greatest treasure who are endangering it. The resulting struggle, therefore, is within the community itself. Within this context, the unions are those who are ready to stand up to the government in an effort to salvage a deteriorating service.

We will now elaborate briefly on the above findings. First, authorization is legitimation by reference to authority. Our data revealed that the parties relied heavily on personal authorization, in which the audience was expected to accept what was being said because of the authority vested in the speakers' positions. Speakers on both sides of a conflict were, by and large, officers who occupied positions of great authority and status in the organization's hierarchy. For instance, a premier or other high-ranking government official might ask the public to accept at face value that there was no more money for wage increases, or that a 3.0 per cent wage increase was generous and fair, simply because of who they were. Similarly, union leaders would rely on their status when asking the public to endorse a strike in an essential service to prevent further government neglect of this service.

In addition, in a few cases, government speakers used impersonal authorization, in which they justified their actions by invoking and reifying key economic indicators like deficits, debts, and inflation rates, or entities such as the market, financial community, and budget. Speakers would commonly argue that certain steps "had" to be taken because these entities "demanded" or "expected" them. For example, a budget, though a product of human activity, may be reified and presented as an independent entity that restricted the actions of all the stakeholders, including those responsible for its creation.

An appeal to an impersonal authority often carried ominous overtones. We were told how the financial markets would not tolerate debts and deficits, how our credit rating was in danger of being downgraded, and how a hike in interest payments threatened to cripple future generations. By devaluing the agency of human beings, speakers using impersonal authorization created a sense of inevitability in the face of force majeure. Government must act decisively and summarily if we are to control our own destiny.

Less common was impersonal authorization by reference to an expert (used only once by the Newfoundland government). Here, a particular course of action had to be pursued because of expert advice. In this scenario, speakers may point to a consultant's report or a financial expert's advice in justifying austerity measures. As we all know from reading the news, however, experts do not always agree, and reference to an expert may open the door for the other side to point to their own expert, leaving the audience with a possible stalemate or unnerving confusion.

We identified a further authorization-legitimation strategy that we termed "public authorization." Here, speakers again called upon the general public, specific groups (e.g., teachers, nurses), or broadly defined groups (e.g., workers, taxpayers, the sick and their families) to endorse their agenda, their arguments, and their behaviour. Legitimation is the answer to "the spoken or unspoken 'why' question – 'Why should we do this?' or 'Why should we do this in this way?'" (van Leeuwen, 2008: 106). Within public authorization, this form of legitimation frequently took the form of, "because this is what the people want," or "this is what the people have asked us to do." In other words, public authorization is a case of "direct democracy" where the constituents supposedly tell the leaders what they want them to do without going through any intermediary bodies. Government speakers explained that they had embarked on a particular course of action because they had communicated with the people, or taxpayers, and the people had told them what they wanted. The speakers might then tell us that the public would not tolerate a tax hike or a teachers' strike. Therefore, back-to-work legislation simply expressed the public sentiment.

For the union's part, we found that speakers often legitimated their actions by telling us that the public could no longer tolerate massive cuts to education or health care, and that it wanted someone to take a stand against the cuts being made to public services. The union was the only group who could meet the challenge. In this way, the speakers answered the "why" question by saying that the public was not willing to tolerate overcrowded classrooms or excessive hospital wait-times. The union was the only group willing, and powerful enough, to stand up on behalf of the people and take on the government. In addition, naturally, the union speakers often stressed that they had received a mandate to act from their members, a private case of public authorization.

This legitimation strategy is a departure from and an extension of personal authorization. In personal authorization, the audience should pay heed because of who the speaker is vis-à-vis the organization (e.g., premier, union president). In public authorization, the audience should listen because the speaker is telling them what they themselves have expressed. For both government and union speakers, public authorization implied that they were expressing the will of the public, or a significant part thereof. They were not pursuing their own narrow self-interests but rather society's collective good. Yet, as before, the people were expected to believe the speaker because of who she was. Therefore, public authorization derives its potency from the speaker's authority.

We have noted, however, that occasionally this presented a paradox vis-à-vis the concept of leadership that speakers, especially from the government, often used to justify unpopular decisions. Users of public authorization claimed that they were simply giving the people what they wanted. On its own, such a statement might have implied that the speakers were not leading but simply following popular opinion. But on other occasions speakers shunned public authorization and ruminated on the burden of leadership, which meant making "tough, unpopular choices" regardless of public opinion and potential cost. Therefore, we are left with some basic and troubling questions. First, why would some speakers refer to public authorization? Does such a strategy imply that the speaker is reluctant to demonstrate leadership? Is it a show of leadership or populism? Is such a move simply a manoeuvre to manipulate the audience and put pressure on the other side? Was an appeal to public authorization a rhetorical strategy to build consensus, or at least to portray one's own party as a unified front? Was public authorization invoked when speakers felt it would help their cause, since they were likely to use whatever legitimation strategy was best able to succeed at a given moment?

Our findings reveal that public authorization was almost never challenged. Even when it was challenged (Nova Scotia), the challenge itself took the form of public authorization ("the people want ..." versus "the people have not been heard"). Though it may present a strong stance, public authorization can be thwarted. For instance, speakers' claims of public authorization can be met with certain basic questions: How many people approached you? How many of them supported you? How many opposed your position? How did these people tell you what they wanted? In cases of public consultation, how were the public representatives chosen? Who facilitated the consultation process? Given the sweeping and general tone of public authorization, it is puzzling why such questions were rarely if ever posed, to government and union speakers alike.

Naturally, speakers did not rely only on their status when they tried to justify their actions and swing public opinion in their favour. They also provided theoretical and concrete reasons why the public should embrace their position. This rationalization-legitimation strategy comprised two types – theoretical and instrumental. Theoretical- rationalization arguments are essentially self-explanatory. They are based on short axiomatic expressions that justify actions on the basis of some kind of truth, such as "this is life" or "this is the way things are." Thus, unions can explain a controversial collective action by saying that "governments only understand power." A government can defend its behaviour by saying that "unions always want more." These arguments rest on conventional wisdom, or that which speakers consider as such. They require little elaboration and should be immune to any counter-arguments. The weakness of theoretical rationalization surfaces when another party refuses to accept it or produces its own version of the truth, an alternative natural order.

Instrumental-rationalization statements stressed the utility an action was supposed to protect or advance. While these efforts were fairly easy to detect, they depended heavily on the less recognizable features of context to achieve traction. Like water to fish, context is essential even though it may escape notice. Rationalization strategies may appear logical and pervasive within their context, yet once the context itself is scrutinized the strategies may lose some of their rhetorical power. This is because, frequently, context is socially constructed to support specific actions that are geared towards securing specific utilities. We have likened the role of context to the rails on which trains run, since it provides rationalization with the means to operate while demonstrating how various points are connected. Context provides rationalization with a coherent and meaningful medium for expression, but it also prescribes its scope and may effectively conceal the often-arbitrary track of the fictional rails on which it runs.

Our study has largely examined how the parties rationalized their own actions. But we noticed a further and more dynamic phenomenon at work – both theoretical and instrumental rationalizations were often used simultaneously to delegitimate the opposition. In other words, rationalization was used both to paint a negative picture of the opposition and to legitimate the position of the speaker's organization. In this way, rationalization may serve a double-faced or Janus-like function, looking both ways at once. For example, we were often told that a government's use of back-to-work legislation was expressive of its duty, since the legislation had been passed to protect citizens and keep society running. But such legitimation seldom stopped there. Instead, it was marshalled to further delegitimate, sometimes implicitly, the action of a union that had denied the public an essential service. Conversely, union speakers would often explain that their strike action was necessary to demonstrate the gravity of their concerns and to force the government to listen. This stance portrayed government as carelessly sloughing off the impending crisis, as all too willing to simply kick the can farther down the road.

Such usages demonstrate the utility of this rhetorical strategy, which can be employed as a weapon of defence and offence, of justification and accusation, both to legitimate one's own actions and to cast a long shadow on one's adversary. On the one hand, a strategy like rationalization may go far in legitimating the actions of a group, since its stark depiction provides a high degree of explanatory power that helps us appreciate the difficulties faced by the group. Yet, on the other hand, the very explanation would seem to create a potentially unbridgeable chasm that locates the entities on different sides of the rhetorical fence. While such elasticity is a strength, the strategy may leave little room for concession and compromise. Used as a discourse of conflict, it remains a strategy of separation or bifurcation, for it drives the sides apart by driving a rhetorical wedge between them. Perhaps this is one of the reasons that the cases we studied appeared to be mired in endless debate and acrimony, and why there seemed to be very little compromise and concession between the parties. Possibly this is why all the cases were ended following heavy-handed unilateral legislation, or the intervention of a third party.

If, as indicated by the epigraph at the beginning of our book, conflict begins with words, then perhaps we should not be surprised to find that the words used depict an escalation of conflict. Like an arms race in which both sides race to a continually receding finish line, the rhetorical strategies that we have explored seem far more capable of producing conflict than resolving it. Rationalization, furthermore, can be particularly "dangerous" in that it often attributes the present conflict to a basic function or even to the core identity of the other group, which may well poison the water in which the actors swim. Clearly, however, just as the parties can immerse themselves in a discourse of conflict, they can also embark upon a discourse of conciliation that can facilitate an end to the conflict. A discourse that separates the parties from each other and highlights the reasons for conflict is not an act of God. However, at least in our cases, a discourse of conciliation and appeasement seems harder to come by. This may be a result of our non-random sample of cases, or of the fact that peaceful bargaining processes might not be as newsworthy as conflicts and so are not "discursive events."

Rationalization is closely linked with moralization, the third legitimation strategy. We often found a single passage evidencing both moralization and rationalization. What is salient about the close proximity of rationalization to moralization is that the "tough utilitarian decisions" also came to be presented as the "right decisions," and vice versa. Government speakers, for instance, might tell us that they have passed back-to-work legislation because of public safety. Passing legislation to end a strike and protect the public is an instance of instrumental legitimation. It is also an instance of moralization, since the government likely had weighed the value of free collective bargaining and the union's right-to-strike against the value of public safety and decided that public safety was morally superior. For their part, union speakers seemed at a disadvantage, since they often had to justify strikes in public services for which there were no alternatives. Nonetheless, they might tell their audience that, while they understood concerns regarding patient safety, their decision to strike was in fact guided by their desire to save health care – a moralized utility – from the hands of government. In some ways, the situation often comes to resemble conventional wisdom in that the "right" path is presented as more difficult than the broader and easier path leading down the "wrong" way.

In conducting our study of moralization, we were struck by the way in which moralization made itself known to an audience. Often, moral values were implied or intimated. In his discussion of moralization, van Leeuwen (2008) notes how discourses relating to moral values are rarely explicit. These intimations are "the tip of a submerged iceberg of moral values. They trigger a moral concept, but are detached from the system of interpretation from which they derive, at least on a conscious level" (ibid.: 110). In a particular passage examined in this book, for instance, it would be obvious that moralization was the dominant discursive strategy, and yet it was not always clear how we knew that. It might be likened to hearing a joke and then laughing. The response is immediate and one rarely pauses to consider why the joke is funny.

Why was moralization often presented without explicit explanation or attributes (e.g., good/bad, right/wrong)? Perhaps it was because elaboration was unnecessary and might have blunted the effect. For Habermas (1976: 36), the triggering of a moral concept enables moral discourse to be transformed into "generalized motives" that are "widely used to ensure mass loyalty." In our analysis, this may be considered similar to those instances when, for example, government speakers described how austerity now must be embraced, even if reluctantly, for the sake of our children and grandchildren. No elaboration on why the future of our progeny should be a concern to us was provided. In addition, nowhere in the data was their any qualification of this statement, let alone any response to or rebuttal of it. Perhaps that was because it struck a deep cultural chord to which most, if not all, citizens would assent; as parents, after all, we willingly, and routinely, make sacrifices so that our children can enjoy a better life. Such a conundrum leads us far beyond the scope of our current investigation. But it does cast in relief van Leeuwen's (2008) observation about the difficulty of concretizing methods for identifying moral evaluations. We can but humbly agree with his conclusion that "as discourse analysts, we can only 'recognize' them [moral evaluations], on the basis of our commonsense cultural knowledge. The usefulness of linguistic discourse analysis stops at this point" (ibid.: 110).

Perhaps the idea of moral conduct carries weight because it assumes a close bond with the audience. In saying that unions were attempting to "hold the public hostage" (see text 7.14), for instance, government speakers implied not only that they were above such an action but also that everyone would grasp its significance and universally condemn it. Describing the holding of hostages as immoral is redundant, and, possibly more important, it also suggests that one is not intimately connected with the values of one's audience. When union speakers blamed the government for making "Mickey Mouse demands" (see text 8.41), they did not go on to explain that such demands were comically silly and therefore they would not accept them. Like having to explain a joke to someone, an explanation might emphasize the degree of separation between the speaker and audience while deflating its power.

Possibly that is one of the strengths of moralization – it presumes a close cultural intimacy between the speaker and the audience. To invoke moralization implies that one is well attuned to the listeners' value system. You do not have to say explicitly that hostage taking is wrong or that Mickey Mouse demands are ridiculous and therefore unacceptable; it is a well-known and widely accepted truism. Because the speaker knows the audience, an explanation likely is not required. Such knowledge is inside knowledge, presumably available to those who are intimately connected with the wider interests of the community to which one belongs. We "recognize" moralization on the basis of our "commonsense cultural knowledge." Perhaps this is the profound strength of moralization. If you "get it," then you are an active participant in the cultural knowledge being referenced. You are an insider who does not need to have an action's moral significance explained to you. Moralization is expressive of the deep bonds that hold us together.

Van Leeuwen (2008: 117) notes how legitimation "can also be achieved through storytelling." As mentioned above, two basic genres of storytelling – the moral and the cautionary – are identified in his analysis, and both are evident in our case studies. Yet we have also observed two different archetypes, with government discourse following "the hero's journey" and union discourse "the princess in the castle." Government texts, following the "hero's journey" template, repeatedly made the point that today's financial woes are a mortgage on our children's and grandchildren's future, and that addressing this challenge requires immediate action and a great deal of fortitude. Such far-sightedness was inevitably presented as a powerful impetus to act without delay, and, as part of that characterization, time was often visibly manipulated in the following ways.

First, the financial problems of today were painstakingly attributed to the past, especially to previous government mismanagement. Government speakers were almost unanimous in condemning the misguided decisions of earlier government leaders who had created the current predicament. Previous governments were not prudent; they did not make the tough but "right" decisions. Instead, they preferred the disastrous but easy choice to pass the buck. All of this had conspired to land the present government in an immensely difficult situation, which, if not immediately confronted, would surely result in catastrophe. Second, these problems were projected into the future by speakers who evoked grim images of children labouring under a mountain of debt, or sinking beneath the waves of staggering deficits. If the dragon living in the mountain is not slain now, then it might be too big for succeeding generations to vanquish.

Third, such a future was then superimposed onto the present so that it became a pivotal moment brimming with hope, potential, and significance. These depictions of past and future created a situation in which immediate actions became critical and therefore inevitable. The present contained the antidote for counteracting a poisonous past. If applied quickly and resolutely, it would lead to a much-improved future for our descendants. Renowned scholars Porter and Rivkin (2012: 60) have observed that, in the United States, government budgets "have shifted from investing in the future toward paying for the past." This comment also fits our narrative. Whether, and when, governments hobbled by deficits and debts will be able to rebalance their portfolio of paying for past mismanagement with expenditures towards the future remains to be seen.

Within the context of union discourse, we followed elements of Booker's (2004) "overcoming the monster" plot. We have called the theme "the princess in the castle." As pointed out above, this discourse, unlike the hero's journey, depicted the crisis as existing *within* the castle walls. The threat to the community was not some external monster seeking to raze the castle; the menace was internal – coming from the very people who should be protecting the kingdom's greatest treasure. The resulting struggle, therefore, is not between a united kingdom and a nebulous force beyond, but is rather being waged between two different groups inside the community itself. Within this context, union speakers became trusted confidants who were privileged holders of key information that was not available to the wider community. Because union speakers held this crucial knowledge, it was incumbent upon them to warn others of the dire consequences of their rulers' actions.

While constructions of the past and future figured prominently in government uses of mythopoesis, union speakers conferred less significance on them. They did on occasion describe how pressure had been building and services were eroding, but they tended in general to stress the immediacy of the problem and its solution. Union discourse was also far less preoccupied with visions of the future; or at least, the dire future consequences of which government speakers warned were usually painted instead on the canvas of the present. Though we did occasionally hear of how a current action was important for preserving the institution of democracy or collective bargaining, we did not find the action presented in terms of children slaving under a future totalitarian regime without any rights at all. Rather, in the main, the consequences were contained in the present time. It was most common to hear that there were already too few nurses, that line-ups were too long, and that too many classrooms were overcrowded. It was a crisis crying out for an immediate solution. Whether union narratives would have achieved a different impact by portraying their present struggles within the context of future generations remains an interesting question.

The competing mythopoetic archetypes underscore an important point – relatively, unions were reactive and government proactive. In the cases we examined, government speakers frequently declared that "now is the time for action," but this action was portrayed as pre-emptively heading off a burgeoning threat. The sweeping arc of government discourse looked consistently back and deep into the future to explain and animate the present conflict. Union speakers, in contrast, depicted the threat as one now engulfing them. Such a threat was sometimes the product of a misguided past and less often one looming beyond the horizon of tomorrow; most frequently, it was seen as current and pressing. Equally, however, both parties used blame and fear to justify immediate and bold action. By according blame to the previous, or current, government, both government and union speakers argued that the harsh actions they were now taking were a direct consequence of others' blunders and neglect. To avoid the catastrophic consequences of others' recklessness, the current responsible government/union leadership "must" take "tough" steps, and it must do that now or else.

It is worth pointing out that the union and government archetypes were not necessarily presented in their entirety in every instance. Put differently, the entire trajectory of the hero's journey or the princess in the castle was not contained in every passage. We did find, however, that individual statements contributed to the total structure. Like shards of pottery, each of the various discursive pieces in our data possessed a certain place and, when glimpsed in their totality, presented a distinctive pattern.

What is perhaps most intriguing in our research is the prevalence of mythopoesis. Both government and union speakers seemed predisposed to present their arguments in the form of a story. Whether speakers were warning of impending financial doom or the catastrophic erosion of services, workers being impoverished, or a government becoming bankrupt, they most often reached for the dramatic, creative, and perhaps more memorable strategy of mythopoesis to explain themselves. Noted media theorist and cultural critic Neil Postman (2000) has argued that what most distinguishes humanity is its penchant for storytelling. Perhaps we conceive of our actions within the larger trajectory of narrative, or perhaps stories are simply the mechanism for enabling us to express and understand ourselves. Or, possibly communication via stories renders the message more coherent and memorable. Precisely why stories are so pervasive remains beyond the scope of our investigation. Nonetheless, our research demonstrates both the prevalence of storytelling and the need to pay close attention to those stories.

In this book we offer a novel and insightful way of examining labour conflict. The phenomenon has been studied extensively, but so far as we know it has not yet been approached from the perspective offered here. The focus of our study has been language, and how union and government personnel mobilized it to advance their interests vis-à-vis one another. Our data set has allowed us to engage in critical discourse analysis from the points of view of two adversaries, government and union, across seven cases of labour conflict. Thus, we have been able to observe how two parties engaged in a series of discursive struggles concurrently. We have attempted to demonstrate how governments and unions dealt with one another when their relationship was strained; how they attacked and counterattacked, appealed to significant others for support, and strategically highlighted and dimmed various elements of the conflict.

Critical discourse analysis is used to demonstrate how a group uses discourse to assert itself against opponents, gain followers, and persuade others to adopt its agenda. A typical CDA exposes how influential actors manipulate language to propagate, more or less subtly, social maladies such as misogyny, anti-Semitism, racism, xenophobia, and war mongering. One result is a clear-cut separation between the powerful and the vulnerable, the demonizing and the demonized, society's pillars and rabble. In contrast, our data set has enabled us to explore what happens when two adversaries use language to show how the opponent abuses its power and turns established institutions into structures of domination. We should note that, compared with the above-mentioned discourses, the discourse of labour conflict is less inflammatory and shows a greater degree of decorum. Still, according to government, unions used strikes "to take the public hostage." And government, in the union discourse, took advantage of its sovereignty to inflict misery upon thousands of workers with a stroke of a pen, or the wave of a magic wand. Ours is thus an original application of CDA in that we did not discern a single authoritative narrative that clearly distinguished between the oppressors and oppressed.

Our data did not permit us to conduct any causal analysis to examine the effects of the discourses the parties developed. We cannot confirm the extent to which behaviour and attitudes were inspired, animated, intensified, and moderated by words. This is a shortcoming that, we hope, future research will remedy. It is customary to indicate that "actions speak louder than words." Still, this study suggests that the importance of words, at least to the actors, should not be underestimated. Earlier, we quoted Max Weber, who argued that "every system of authority attempts to establish and cultivate the belief in its legitimacy" (1977: 325), and the German philosopher Dolf Sternberger, who asserted that "the desire for legitimacy is ... deeply rooted in human communities" (1968: 244). Perhaps this is why, here, the parties were compelled to supplement their actions with words. In fact, our impression is that words and actions went hand in hand. The parties craved popular support and sought to achieve that through legitimation efforts. Actions such as budget cuts, back-to-work legislation, and strikes in essential services were promoted, justified, and defended using elaborate and imaginative statements. Semantic creativity made it possible for governments to abrogate existing collective agreements while declaring respect for collective bargaining, and roll back wages and downsize the public-sector workforce yet proclaim their admiration of working people. Linguistic dexterity enabled union leaders to make passionate arguments about their unshaken commitment to groups such as students and patients, while simultaneously inspiring their members to complicate the lives of these groups by walking off the job. In short, language enacted the protagonists' practices. Yet, at the same time, practices gave meaning and purpose to language. Perhaps "language and practices 'boot strap' each other into existence in a reciprocal process through time. We cannot have one without the other" (Gee, 2011: 18).

This book is about language, and as such it stresses the words and discourses the actors articulated. Yet there were some propitious linguistic possibilities the parties left untouched. It is impossible to establish whether or not they did that consciously, for strategic reasons. However, those occasions have given us pause. We have already noted above the generally non-inflammatory nature of most of the statements in our database. Excluding a few instances (e.g., texts 8.43, 8.44), the union speakers avoided personal, derogatory accusations. In addition, we rarely heard how nasty politicians tried to bust unions. When a union speaker made such an allegation, it was uttered in a fairly mild manner (e.g., texts 5.28, 7.48). Government speakers, for their part, were respectful (at least verbally) of the institutions of collective bargaining and collective representation of workers. They did not hesitate to accuse unions of being greedy and stubborn, but they never suggested that unions should cease to exist, or that they were the cause of the government's fiscal woes. Furthermore, like their union counterparts, government speakers did not blame particular union leaders for any of the conflicts.

As we have mentioned on a number of occasions, both parties rarely used concrete data to ground their claims and debunk their opponent's. Governments did not provide data to support assertions about the fairness of their last offer, or about the effects of a wage raise on the economy, or about how many people told them that they loathed tax increases. Unions were not concrete about the state of public services, or how strikes were related to service improvement, or how a new policy would impoverish workers. This is puzzling, for there was no shortage of data that speakers could use for these purposes. We speculate that they preferred sweeping, axiomatic, accessible arguments to more complex propositions that were difficult to develop and grasp. It is also possible that the mass media we used as the main source of data are by nature less suitable for such grounded argumentation. In any event, we would like to point out that sometimes what the parties did not say might be as instructive as what they did. In summary, the evidence suggests that discourse played an important role in labour conflict. The parties spent time and effort crafting elaborate arguments to justify their behaviour. But they did not always need to do that. Some of the governments in our sample had been elected to carry out restructuring plans involving austerity measures. Several unions did nothing wrong in executing legal job actions. Still, in each case the parties felt compelled to engage in the discourse of legitimation. Second, the actors did not remain indifferent to each other's statements. They felt that the "war of words" was important enough to merit engagement.

None of this corroborates the proposition that discourse shapes attitudes and behaviour. Until such causality is substantiated, we may have to be satisfied with the notion that "ours is a discourse-based global society," and that discursive interventions are a key aspect of life and are necessary in many local fields (Graham, Keenan, and Dowd, 2004: 217). If this is true, then discourse matters, and analysis of it is a worthy endeavour.

References

Adams, Roy J. 2001. "Public Employment Relations: Canadian Developments in Perspective." In *Public-Sector Labour Relations in an Era of Restraint and Restructuring*, ed. Gene Swimmer. 212–27. New York: Oxford University.

Adams, Roy J. 2006. *Labour Left Out: Canada's Failure to Protect and Promote Collective Bargaining as a Human Right*. Ottawa, ON: Canadian Centre for Policy Alternatives.

Adell, Bernard, Michel Grant, and Allen Ponak. 2001. *Strikes in Essential Services*. Kingston, ON: Industrial Relations Centre, Queen's University.

Alberta, Health. 1994 and 1995. *Health Workforce in Alberta*. Edmonton, AB.

Alberta, Health Planning Secretariat. 1993. *Starting Points: Recommendations for Creating a More Accountable and Affordable Health System*. Edmonton, AB.

Alberta, Personnel Administration Office. 1995, 1996, and 1997. *Public Service Commissioner's Annual Report: Profile of the Alberta Public Service*. Edmonton, AB.

Alberta Teachers' Assn. v. Alberta. 2002a. ABQB 240.

Alberta Teachers' Association. 2002b. *Memorandum*. 22 February.

Alyward, Joan Marie. 2003. *Budget Speech 2003: Building Our Future Together*. Government of Newfoundland and Labrador. 27 March.

Amer, Mosheer M. 2009. "'Telling-It-Like-It-Is': The Delegitimation of the Second Palestinian Intifada in Thomas Friedman's Discourse." *Discourse & Society* 20 (1): 5–31.

Andresani, Gianluca, and Ewan Ferlie. 2006. "Studying Governance within the British Public Sector and Without: Theoretical and Methodological Issues." *Public Management Review* 8: 415–31.

Armstrong, Jane. 2004. "B.C. Health-Care Workers Walk Out." *Globe and Mail*. 26 April.

Aucoin, Peter. 1995. *The New Public Management – Canada in Comparative Perspective*. Montreal, QC: Institute for Research on Public Policy.

Bennett, Dean. 2012. "Alberta Budget Update Projects $2 to $3B Deficit as Resource Revenue Slumps." *Canadian Press*. 30 August.
Benzie, Robert, Kristin Rushowy, and Paola Loriggio. 2009. "Why McGuinty Lets York U. Strike Drag on." *Toronto Star*. 22 January.
Betts, Norman. 2000. *Changing Our Future Together: Budget 2000–2001. March.* Fredericton, NB: Department of Finance.
Betts, Norman. 2001. *Changing Our Future Together: Budget 2001–2002.* Department of Finance, Fredericton, NB. March.
Billing, Michael. 2003. "Preface: Language as Forms of Dearth." In *At War with Words*, ed. Mirjana N. Dedaić and Daniel N. Nelson. vii–xxii. Berlin: Mouton de Gruyter. http://dx.doi.org/10.1515/9783110897715.vii.
Boivin, Jean. 1975. "Collective Bargaining in the Public Sector: Some Propositions on the Cause of Public Employee Unrest." In *Collective Bargaining in the Essential and Public Service Sectors*, ed. Morley Gunderson. 3–36. Toronto, ON: University of Toronto Press.
Boivin, Jean, and Ester Déom. 1995. "Labour-Management Relations in Quebec." In *Union-management Relations in Canada*, ed. Morley Gunderson and Allen Ponak. 455–94. Don Mills, ON: Addison-Wesley.
Booker, Christopher. 2004. *The Seven Basic Plots: Why We Tell Stories*. New York: Continuum.
Bourdieu, Pierre. 1998. The Essence of Neoliberalism. December. http://mondediplo.com/1998/12/08bourdieu.
Bradshaw, James, and Wendy Stuec. 2012. "Across Canada, Cash-Strapped Governments Target Education." *Globe and Mail*. 4 March.
British Columbia Labour Relations Board. 2004. In the Matter of an Application ... Between Health Employers Association of British Columbia and Facilities Subsector Bargaining Association and Hospital Employees' Union. 30 April.
British Columbia Teachers' Federation v. British Columbia, 2011 BCSC 469.
Camfield, David. 2007. "Renewal in Canadian Public Sector Unions: Neoliberalism and Union Praxis." *Relations Industrielles* 62 (Spring): 282–304.
Campagnolo, Iona. 2004. *Speech From the Throne*. British Columbia. 10 February.
Campbell, Joseph. 1949. *The Hero with a Thousand Faces*. Princeton, NJ: Princeton University Press.
Canadian Business. 1995. "Tory Hack and Slash: Just Who Is on Mike Harris's Get Lost List?" 68. 15 August.
Cheverie, Wayne D. 1994. *Province of Prince Edward Island: Budget Address*. Government of Saskatchewan. 12 April.
Chilton, Paul. 2004. *Analyzing Political Discourse*. London: Routledge.

Cline, Eric. 1999. *Budget Address: Moving Forward Together.* Saskatchewan Finance. March.
Courchene, Thomas J., and Colin R. Telmer. 1998. *From Heartland to North American Region State.* Toronto, ON: University of Toronto Press.
Coyle, Jim. 2009. "Parsing Stalemate Won't End It." *Toronto Star.* 28 January.
Dare, Bill. 1997. "Harris's First Year: Attacks and Resistance." In *Open for Business, Closed to People*, ed. Diana Ralph, André Régimbald, and Nérée St-Amand. 20–6. Halifax, NS: Fernwood.
Dedaić, Mirjana N. 2006. "Political Speeches and Persuasive Argumentation." In *Encyclopedia of Language and Linguistics*, ed. Keith Brown. 2nd ed. Vol 9. 700–6.
De Souza, Mike. 2004. "16,000 Quebec Government Jobs to Disappear by 2013 under Plan." *Gazette.* 6 May.
Dougherty, Kevin. 2005a. "Public-Sector Unions Tell Quebec." *Gazette.* 21 June.
Dougherty, Kevin. 2005b. "Province Can Pay: Government Denies It Has $6 Billion of Wiggle Room." *Gazette.* 28 September.
Duncan, Dwight. 2009. *2009 Ontario Budget: Confronting the Challenge; Building Our Economic Future.* Toronto, ON: Service Ontario Publications.
Dunleavy, Patrick, Helen Margetts, Simon Bastow, and Jane Tinkler. 2006. "New Public Management is Dead – Long Live Digital-Era Governance." *Journal of Public Administration: Research and Theory* 16 (3): 467–94. http://dx.doi.org/10.1093/jopart/mui057.
Dyck, Rand. 1996. *Provincial Politics in Canada: Toward the Turn of the Century.* Scarborough, ON: Prentice Hall.
Edmonton Public School Board No. 7 and the Alberta Teachers' Association. 2002. S.A. 2002, c. E-05.
Fairclough, Norman. 1989. *Language and Power.* London: Longman.
Fairclough, Norman. 2005. "Discourse Analysis in Organization Studies: The Case for Critical Realism." *Organization Studies* 26 (6): 915–39. http://dx.doi.org/10.1177/0170840605054610.
Fairclough, Norman, and Ruth Wodak. 1997. "Critical Discourse Analysis." In *Discourse as Social Interaction. Discourse Studied: A Multidisciplinary Introduction*, vol. 2. ed. Teun A. van Dijk. 258–84. Thousand Oaks, CA: Sage.
Fattore, Giovanni, Hans F.W. Dubois, and Antonion Lapenta. 2012. "Measuring New Public Management and Governance in Political Debate." *Public Administration Review* 72 (2): 218–27. http://dx.doi.org/10.1111/j.1540-6210.2011.02497.x.
Fekete, Jason. 2011. "Unions Brace for Tens of Thousands of Job Cuts in Public Service." *Vancouver Sun.* 1 December.

Fudge, Derek. 2005. *Collective Bargaining in Canada: Human Right or Canadian Illusion.* Toronto, ON: NUPGE.

Gabriel, Yiannis. 2000. *Storytelling in Organizations: Facts, Fictions, and Fantasies.* London: Oxford University. http://dx.doi.org/10.1093/acprof:oso/9780198290957.001.0001.

Gabriel, Yiannis. 2004. "Narratives, Stories and Texts." In *The Sage Handbook of Organizational Discourse,* ed. David Grant, Cynthia Hardy, Cliff Oswick, and Linda Putman. 61–77. Thousand Oaks, CA: Sage. http://dx.doi.org/10.4135/9781848608122.n3.

Gazette. 2004. "Union Labours Against Premier." 7 September.

Gazette. 2005. "Solidarity Forever! Quebec Leads Continent in Unionized Workforce." 13 July.

Gee, James Paul. 2011. *An Introduction to Discourse Analysis: Theory and Method.* 3rd ed. New York: Routledge.

George, Susan. 1999. *A Short History of Neoliberalism.* March. http://www.globalexchange.org/resources/econ101/neoliberalismhist.

Globe and Mail. 2001. "Campbell in Charge." 18 May.

Globe and Mail. 2004. "Board Orders Defiant B.C. Workers Back to Work." 30 April.

Graham, Phil, Thomas Keenan, and Anne-Maree Dowd. 2004. "A Call to Arms at the End of History: A Discourse-Historical Analysis of George W. Bush's Declaration of War on Terror." *Discourse and Society* 15 (2–3): 199–221.

Grant, David, and Cynthia Hardy. 2003. "Introduction: Struggles with Organizational Discourse." *Organization Studies* 25 (1): 5–13. http://dx.doi.org/10.1177/0170840604038173.

Grant, David, Cynthia Hardy, Cliff Oswick, and Linda Putnam. 2004. "Introduction: Organizational Discourse: Exploring the Field." In *The Sage Handbook of Organizational Discourse,* ed. David Grant, Cynthia Hardy, Cliff Oswick, and Linda Putnam. 1–36. Thousand Oaks, CA: Sage. http://dx.doi.org/10.4135/9781848608122.n1.

Grant, David, Tom Keenoy, and Cliff Oswick. 1998. "Defining Organizational Discourse: Of Diversity, Dichotomy and Multi-Disciplinarity." In *Discourse and Organization,* ed. David Grant, Tom Keenoy, and Cliff Oswick. 1–13. Thousand Oaks, CA: Sage.

Grant, Michel. 2003. "Quebec: Toward a New Social Contract – From Confrontation to Mutual Gains?" In Mark Thompson, Joseph B. Rose, and Anthony E. Smith (eds.), *Beyond the National Divide: Regional Dimensions of Industrial Relations.* 51–96. Published by McGill-Queen's University Press for the Canadian Industrial Relations Association and the School of Policy Studies, Queen's University, Kingston, ON. 51–96.

Gunderson, Morley. 2005. "Two Faces of Union Voice in the Public Sector." *Journal of Labor Research* 26 (3): 393–413. http://dx.doi.org/10.1007/s12122-005-1012-6.

Gunderson, Morley, and Douglas Hyatt. 1996. "Canadian Public Sector Employment Relations in Transition." In *Public Sector Employment in Time of Transition*, ed. Dale Belman, Morley Gunderson, and Douglas Hyatt. 243–81. Madison, WI: Industrial Relations Research Association.

Habermas, Jürgen. 1976. *Legitimation Crisis.* London: Heinemann.

Haddow, Rodney, and Thomas Klassen. 2006. *Partisanship, Globalization, and Canadian Labour Market Policy.* Toronto, ON: University of Toronto Press.

Hagan, Susan. 2001. "Strike Position Draws Near." *Edmonton Journal*, 11 September.

Haiven, Larry. 2003. "Saskatchewan: Social Experimentation, Economic Development and the Test of Tome." In Mark Thompson, Joseph B. Rose, and Anthony E. Smith (eds.), *Beyond the National Divide: Regional Dimensions of Industrial Relations*, 159–96. Published by McGill-Queen's University Press for the Canadian Industrial Relations Association and the School of Policy Studies, Queen's University, Kingston, ON.

Hansen, Colin. 2011. *Budget Speech 2011.* British Columbia. 15 February.

Hardy, Cynthia, Ian Palmer, and Nelson Phillips. 2000. "Discourse as a Strategic Resource." *Human Relations* 53 (9): 1227–48. http://dx.doi.org/10.1177/0018726700539006.

Hibbs, Douglas A., Jr. 1976. "Industrial Conflict in Advanced Industrial Societies." *American Political Science Review* 70 (4): 1033–58. http://dx.doi.org/10.2307/1959373.

Hirsch, Paul M. 1986. "From Ambushes to Golden Parachutes: Corporate Takeovers as an Instance of Cultural Framing and Institutional Integration." *American Journal of Sociology* 4 (January): 800–37. http://dx.doi.org/10.1086/228351.

Holubitski, Jeff. 2002. "Gov't Orders Teachers Back." *Edmonton Journal.* 22 February.

Hospital Employees' Union. 2003. *Impact of Contracting Out on Health Workers, Public, Reduced in Framework Agreement.* 17 April.

Hutchinson, Brian. 2012. "BC Liberals Are the Clear Winners in Tentative Deal with Teachers." *National Post.* 27 June.

Johnsrude, Larry. 1997. "Why Women Are Less In-Kleined to Vote for Ralph." *Edmonton Journal.* 2 February.

Joseph, John E. 2006. *Language and Politics.* Edinburgh: Edinburgh University Press. http://dx.doi.org/10.3366/edinburgh/9780748624522.001.0001.

Kaufman, Bruce E. 1982. "The Determinants of Strikes in the United States, 1900–1977." *Industrial & Labor Relations Review* 35 (4): 473–90. http://dx.doi.org/10.2307/2522662.

Korpi, Walter, and Michael Shalev. 1979. "Strikes, Industrial Relations and Class Conflict in Capitalist Societies." *British Journal of Sociology* 30 (2): 164–85. http://dx.doi.org/10.2307/589523.

Leblanc, Neil J. 2001. *Budget Address: Province of Nova Scotia*. Nova Scotia House of Assembly, 29 March.

Lessa, Iara. 2006. "Discursive Struggles within Social Welfare: Restaging Teen Motherhood." *British Journal of Social Work* 36 (2): 283–98. http://dx.doi.org/10.1093/bjsw/bch256.

Lewin, David, and Shirley B. Goldenberg. 1980. "Public Sector Unionism in the U.S. and Canada." *Industrial Relations* 3 (Fall): 239–56. http://dx.doi.org/10.1111/j.1468-232X.1980.tb01096.x.

Liepert, Ron. 2012. *Budget 2012: Investing in People*. Government of Alberta. February.

Lipset, Seymour Martin. 1960. *Political Man: The Social Bases of Politics*. Garden City, NJ: Doubleday and Company.

Martens, Martin L., Jennifer E. Jennings, and P. Devereaux Jennings. 2007. "Do the Stories They Tell Get Them the Money They Need? The Role of Entrepreneurial Narratives in Resource Acquisition." *Academy of Management Journal* 50 (5): 1107–32. http://dx.doi.org/10.5465/AMJ.2007.27169488.

Martinez, Elizabeth, and Arnoldo Garcia. 1996. *What is Neoliberalism?* August. http://www.corpwatch.org/article.php?id=376

McAdam, Doug. 1982. *Political Process and the Development of Black Insurgency, 1930–1970*. Chicago, IL: University of Chicago Press.

McLellan, Ray. 1997. "Alternative Service Delivery in Ontario: The New." *Public Management*. Toronto: Ontario Legislative Library.

McMillan, Melville L. 1996. *Leading the Way or Missing The Mark? The Klein Government's Fiscal Plan*. Edmonton, AB: Western Centre for Economic Research. University of Alberta.

Metcalfe, Les, and Sue Richards. 1990. *Improving Public Management*. London: Sage.

Mumby, Dennis K., and Robin P. Clair. 1997. "Organizational Discourse." In *Discourse as Social Interaction. Discourse Studied: A Multidisciplinary Introduction*, vol. 2. ed. Teun A. van Dijk. 181–205. Thousand Oaks, CA: Sage.

Nelson, Daniel. 2003. "Conclusion: Word Peace." In *At War with Words*, ed. Mirjana N. Dedaić and Daniel N. Nelson. 449–62. Berlin: Mouton de Gruyter. http://dx.doi.org/10.1515/9783110897715.449.

Nelson, Patricia L. 2002. *Budget 2002 Address: The Right Decisions for Challenging Times*. Alberta. 19 March.

NSGEU and NSNU and Province of Nova Scotia. 2001. 13 August.
NUPGE. 2004. *Newfoundland Tories Legislating End to Public Sector Strike.* 21 April.
NUPGE. 2006. *The Attack on Workers' Rights in Canada: A Public Sector Focus.* Document 5.
NUPGE. 2007. Quebec Court Rules Forced Union Mergers Unconstitutional. 4 December.
NUPGE. 2010. http://www.labourrights.ca/.
Nursall, Kim. 2012. "Majority of BC Teachers Vote in Favor of Contract Agreement." Canadian Press. 29 June.
Oake, George. 1992. "Saskatchewan Gets Tax Hikes in NDP Budget." *Toronto Star.* 8 May.
Ochs, Elinor. 1997. "Narrative." In *Discourse as Social Interaction. Discourse Studied: A Multidisciplinary Introduction. Volume 1,* ed. Teun A. van Dijk. 185–207. Thousand Oaks, CA: Sage.
O'Donnell, Sarah. 2012. "Infrastructure Deficit More Worrisome Than Budget Deficit, Premier Says." *Edmonton Journal,* 15 November.
OECD. 1993. "Public Management Developments." France.
Olsen, Tom. 2002. "Tories Shelve Strike Order: Teacher Walkouts to Continue." *Calgary Herald,* 20 February.
Ontario Ministry of Education. 1996–7. *Elementary and Secondary Education: Quick Facts.* (http://www.edu.gov.on.ca/)
Ontario Progressive Conservative Party. 1994. *Common Sense Revolution.* 3 May.
Osborne, David, and Ted Gaebler. 1992. *Reinventing Government: How the Entrepreneurial Spirit Is Transforming the Public Sector.* Reading, MA: Addison-Wesley.
Osborne, Stephen P. 2006. "The New Public Governance?" *Public Management Review* 8 (3): 377–87. http://dx.doi.org/10.1080/14719030600853022.
Panitch, Leo, and Donald Swartz. 1988. *The Assault on Trade Union Freedoms: From Consent to Coercion Revisited.* Toronto, ON: Garamond.
Peritz, Ingrid. 2005. "Labour Strife Disrupts Classes of 65,000 Quebec College Students," *Globe and Mail.* 22 August.
Perspectives on Labour and Income. 2005. "Fact Sheet on Unionization." Ottawa, ON: Statistics Canada. August.
Point, Steven L. 2011. *Speech from the Throne.* British Columbia. 3 October.
Polti, Georges. 1917. *The Thirty-Six Dramatic Situations.* Ridgewood, NJ: The Editor Company.
Poole, Michael. 1984. "Comparative Approaches to Industrial Conflict." In *International Perspectives on Organizational Democracy,* ed. Bernhard Wilpert and Arndt Sorge. 197–213. New York: John Wiley.
Porter, Michael E., and Jan W. Rivkin. 2012. "The Looming Challenge to U.S. Competitiveness." *Harvard Business Review* 90 (March): 54–62.

Postman, Neil. 2000. *Where Do We Go from Here: The Quest for Narratives in a Technological Society.* The 2000 Laing Lectures sponsored by Regent College in Vancouver, BC.

Potter, Jonathan, and Margaret Wetherell. 1987. *Discourse and Social Psychology: Beyond Attitudes and Behavior.* Beverly Hills, CA: Sage.

PricewaterhouseCoopers. 2003. *Directions, Choices, and Tough Choices.* 22 December.

Provis, Chris. 1996. "Unitarism, Pluralism, Interests and Values." *British Journal of Industrial Relations* 34 (4): 473–95. http://dx.doi.org/10.1111/j.1467-8543.1996.tb00486.x.

Rae, Bob. 1997. *From Protest to Power: Personal Reflections on a Life in Politics].* Toronto, ON: Penguin.

Rapaport, David. 1999. *No Justice, No Peace: The 1996 OPSEU Strike against the Harris Government in Ontario.* Ottawa, ON: McGill-Queen's University Press.

Rees, Albert. 1952. "Industrial Conflict and Business Fluctuations." *Journal of Political Economy* 60 (5): 371–82. http://dx.doi.org/10.1086/257272.

Reid, Marion L. 1994. *Speech From the Throne.* Saskatchewan. 9 March.

Reisigl, Martin. 2008. "Analyzing Political Rhetoric." In *Qualitative Discourse Analysis in the Social Sciences*, ed. Ruth Wodak and Michat Krzyzanowski. 96–120. New York: Palgrave MacMillan.

Reshef, Yonatan. 1986. "Political Exchange in Israel: Histadtrut-State Relations." *Industrial Relations* 3 (Fall): 303–19. http://dx.doi.org/10.1111/j.1468-232X.1986.tb00687.x.

Reshef, Yonatan. 2007. "Government Intervention in Public Sector Industrial Relations: Lessons from the Alberta Teachers' Association." *Journal of Labor Research* 28 (4): 677–96.

Reshef, Yonatan, and Sandra Rastin. 2003. *Unions in the Time of Revolution: Government Restructuring in Alberta & Ontario.* Toronto, ON: University of Toronto Press. http://dx.doi.org/10.1007/s12122-007-9019-9.

Rose, Joseph B. 1998. *Industrial Relations in Ontario.* Working paper. McMaster University, Hamilton, ON.

Rose, Joseph B. 2004. ""Public Sector Bargaining: From Retrenchment to Consolidation." *Industrial Relations.*" *Relations Industrielles* 2 (Spring): 271–92. http://dx.doi.org/10.7202/009542ar.

Scholes, Robert. 1981. "Language, Narrative, and Anti-Narrative." In *On Narrative*, ed. W.J.T. Mitchell. 200–8. Chicago, IL: University of Chicago Press.

Schwartz, Herman M. 1997. "Reinvention and Retrenchment: Lessons from the Application of the New Zealand Model to Alberta, Canada." *Journal of Policy Analysis and Management* 16 (3): 405–22. http://dx.doi.org/10.1002/(SICI)1520-6688(199722)16:3<405::AID-PAM3>3.0.CO;2-L.

Shaw, Gordon, Robert Brown, and Philip Bromiley. 1998. "Strategic Stories: How 3M Is Rewriting Business Planning." *Harvard Business Review* 76 (May-June): 41–50.

Shepherdson, David K. 2011. *Industrial Relations Outlook 2012: Going Sideways, with a Twist.* Ottawa, ON: Conference Board of Canada. November.

Shorter, Edward, and Charles Tilly. 1974. *Strikes in France, 1830–1968.* Cambridge: Cambridge University Press.

Snow, David A., E. Burke Rochford, Jr, Steven K. Worden, and Robert D. Benford. 1986. "Frame Alignment Processes, Micromobilization, and Movement Participation." *American Sociological Review* 51 (4): 464–81. http://dx.doi.org/10.2307/2095581.

Snow, David A., and Robert D. Benford. 1988. "Ideology, Frame Resonance, and Participant Mobilization." *International Social Movement Research* 1: 197–217.

Sorbara, Greg. 2007. *Ontario Budget: Investing in People; Expanding Opportunity.* Toronto, ON: Publications Ontario.

Statistics Canada. 1998. *Annual Estimates of Employment, Earnings and Hours: 1985–1997.* Ottawa, ON: Catalogue no. 72F0002XDB.

Statistics Canada. 2000. *Education in Canada.* Ottawa, ON: Catalogue no. 81-229-X1B.

Stern, Robert N. 1978. "Methodological Issues in Quantitative Strike Analysis." *Industrial Relations* 17 (1): 32–42. http://dx.doi.org/10.1111/j.1468-232X.1978.tb00109.x.

Sternberger, Dolf. 1968. "Legitimacy." In *International Encyclopedia of the Social Sciences*, ed. David S. Miller. Vol. 9, 244–48. Macmillan Company & Free Press: 244–48.

Suchman, Mark C. 1995. "Managing Legitimacy: Strategic and Institutional Approaches." *Academy of Management Review* 20 (July): 571–610.

Sudbury Star. 2004. "Newfoundland Labor Leaders Gird for Battle over Wage Freeze." 7 January.

Suddaby, Roy, and Royston Greenwood. 2005. "Rhetorical Strategies of Legitimacy." *Administrative Science Quarterly* 50 (March): 35–67.

Suddaby, Roy, William M. Foster, and Chris Quinn Trank. 2010. "Rhetorical History as a Source of Competitive Advantage." *Advances in Strategic Management* 27: 147–73. http://dx.doi.org/10.1108/S0742-3322(2010)0000027009.

Sullivan, Loyola. 2004. *Protecting Our Future: Budget Speech 2004.* Government of Newfoundland and Labrador.

Sullivan, Paul. 2002. "And in the War against Unionism." *Globe and Mail.* 29 January.

Supreme Court of Canada. 2007. *Health Services and Support – Facilities Subsector Bargaining Assn. v. British Columbia.* SCC 27.

Swimmer, Gene. 2001a. "Public-Sector Labour Relations in an Era of Restraint and Restructuring: An Overview." In *Public-Sector Labour Relations in an Era of Restraint and Restructuring*, ed. Gene Swimmer. 1–35. Don Mills, ON: Oxford University Press.

Swimmer, Gene, ed. 2001b. *Public-Sector Labour Relations in an Era of Restraint and Restructuring*. Don Mills, ON: Oxford University Press.

Swimmer, Gene, and Tim Bartkiw. 2003. "The Future of Public Sector Collective Bargaining in Canada." *Journal of Labor Research* 24 (Fall): 579–95. http://dx.doi.org/10.1007/s12122-003-1015-0.

Tchorzewski, Ed. 1992. *Budget Speech*. Saskatchewan. 7 May.

Thomas, Paul G. 2003. *A Canadian Perspective on "the New Public Service*. Toronto, ON: Commentary at the Annual Conference of the Institute of Public Administration of Canada.

Thompson, Mark. 1986. "The Future of Voluntarism in Public Sector Labour Relations." In *Essays in Labour Relations Law: Papers Presented at the Conference on Government and Labour Relations: The Death of Voluntarism*, ed. Geoffrey England. 103–29. Don Mills, ON: CCH Canadian.

Thompson, Mark, and Gene Swimmer. 1995. "The Future of Public Sector Industrial Relations." In *Public Sector Collective Bargaining in Canada: Beginning of the End or End of the Beginning?* ed. Gene Swimmer and Mark Thomson. 430–46. Kingston, ON: IRC.

Thompson, Mark, and Joseph B. Rose. 2003. "Regional Differences in Canadian Industrial Relations: Is There a 'Canadian' System?" In *Beyond the National Divide: Regional Dimensions of Industrial Relations*, ed. Mark Thompson, Joseph B. Rose, and Anthony E. Smith. 307–24. Published by McGill-Queen's University Press for the Canadian Industrial Relations Association and the School of Policy Studies, Queen's University, Kingston, ON.

Thomson, Graham. 2001. "Klein Hints at Hefty Pay Hikes for Teachers." *Edmonton Journal*, 6 April.

Vaara, Eero, and Janne Tienari. 2008. "A Discourse Perspective on Legitimation Strategies in Multinational Corporations." *Academy of Management Review* 33 (4): 985–93. http://dx.doi.org/10.5465/AMR.2008.34422019.

van Dijk Teun, A. 1997. "The Study of Discourse." In *Discourse as Structure and Process*, vol. 1. ed. Teun A. van Dijk. 1–34. Thousand Oaks, CA: Sage. http://dx.doi.org/10.4135/9781446221884.n1.

van Leeuwen, Theo. 2008. *Discourse and Practice: New Tools for Critical Discourse Analysis*. New York: Oxford University Press.

van Leeuwen, Theo, and Ruth Wodak. 1999. "Legitimizing Immigration and Control: A Discursive-Historical Analysis." *Discourse Studies* 1 (1): 83–118. http://dx.doi.org/10.1177/1461445699001001005.

Watson, Tony J. 2003. *Sociology, Work and Industry.* 4th ed. New York: Routledge.
Weber, Max. 1977. *The Theory of Social and Economic Organization.* New York: Free Press.
Weiler, Joseph M. 1986. "The Role of Law in Labour Relations." *Labour Law and Urban Law in Canada* 51: 1–65.
White, Bob. 1987. *Hard Bargains: My Life on the Line.* Toronto, ON: McClelland and Stewart.
White, Graham. 2000. "Revolutionary Change in the Ontario Public Service." In *Government Restructuring and Career Public Services*, ed. Evert Lindquist. 310–45. Toronto, ON: Institute of Public Administration of Canada.
Williams, Danny. 2004. *State of the Province Address.* 5 January. http://www.gov.nl.ca/financialsituation/premieraddress.html.

Index

Alberta, government of: on being blindsided by events, 157–8; recent economic record of, 30–1, 32–3; restructuring of civil service, 31–2
Alberta Parkland School Division strike (2007), 183–4
Alberta teachers' strike (2002): back-to-work legislation, 50–1, 64, 68, 107, 140–1, 171–2; government leadership during, 129; government moralization legitimation, 123; impersonal authorization in, 74–5; instrumental rationalization in, 101, 104, 105–6, 107, 110, 112; overview of, 50–1, 64–8; public authorization in, 80; theoretical rationalization in, 114–15, 117; union moralization legitimation, 140–1; union sees government as enemy, 176; union use of power-inequality rhetoric, 169; union working for public interest in, 143–4, 173; use of storytelling in, 88
Allnutt, Chris, 142–3, 146, 171, 174
Alyward, Joan Marie, 57
Anstey, Reg, 59
anti-union legislation, 38, 181–2. *See also* back-to-work legislation

Atkinson, Patricia, 128, 134
authorization legitimation, 13–14, 72–6, 147

back-to-work legislation: by Alberta government, 50–1, 64, 68, 107, 140–1, 171–2; by B.C. government, 48–9, 64, 132–3, 137, 146, 171; defying of, 170; government's justification of, 133–9; and instrumental rationalization, 101–2, 103, 104, 106; and moralization legitimation, 138–9, 194; by New Brunswick government, 45, 57, 121–2, 129, 135, 140, 171; by Newfoundland and Labrador government, 45, 60, 135–6, 140, 171; by Nova Scotia government, 47, 61, 89, 136–7, 146, 170–1, 172; by Ontario government, 23, 35, 184–5; pattern of use by governments in industrial relations, 20–1, 22–4; by Quebec government, 24, 52–3, 68–9, 103, 137–8; by Saskatchewan government, 44, 55, 101, 102, 106, 115–16, 128, 134–5, 139, 170; union view of, 139–41
Bauman, Robert, 49

Belikka, Jerry, 107
Bernatchez, Daniel, 82–3, 116, 140, 171
Betts, Norman: advocates a balanced budget, 74, 131–2; budget address of 2000, 56–7; justifies back-to-work legislation, 121–2; on making tough choices, 160; on preference for collective bargaining, 135; on reaching prosperity, 166
Booi, Larry: on back-to-work legislation, 171–2; on collective bargaining, 66; on government as enemy, 117, 140–1, 176; on lack of union power, 169; on union fight for education, 112, 143–4, 173
British Columbia, government of: economic situation, 37–8; fight with teachers, 38, 39–42; neoliberalism of, 37–8, 115
British Columbia health workers' strike (2004): background to, 38–9; back-to-work legislation, 48–9, 64, 132–3, 137, 146, 171; collective bargaining during, 137; government leadership during, 132–3; overview of, 48–9, 62–4; public authorization in, 79–80; theoretical rationalization in, 113, 116–17; union reaction to government use of power, 171; union use of lack-of-respect strategy, 146; union working for public interest in, 142–3, 174
Bruce, Graham, 137, 162

Callbeck, Catherine, 179
Campagnola, Iona, 40
Campbell, Gordon, 62, 114. *See also* British Columbia, government of

Carbonneau, Claudette, 111–12, 144, 175
Charest, Jean: aim of restructuring public sector, 68; on back-to-work legislation, 103; leadership of, 124, 128; on reaching prosperity, 166; speaks for Quebecers, 78; on standing up to economic challenges, 159; view of collective bargaining, 138. *See also* Quebec, government of
Cheverie, Wayne D., 148, 180–1
Chisholm, Robert, 91
Cline, Eric, 164–5
collective action, 4–5
collective bargaining: government attitude towards, 133–9, 140; Supreme Court decision on, 22–3, 185; union view of, 66, 139–41
Common Sense Revolution, 33–6
concrete evidence: in Alberta teachers' strike, 87, 88, 90; lack of, 81, 113, 200–1; in Nova Scotia strike, 89
context for instrumental rationalization, 104–8, 111–13, 188, 192
contracting out, 35–6, 38, 63–4, 69, 113–14, 124. *See also* privatization
Corbett, Frank, 91
critical discourse analysis (CDA), 10–11, 198–201

Dexter, Darrell, 91
discourse, 9
discourse analysis, 9–10, 11, 186
discursive dominance, 11
Drummond, Don, 37
Dunford, Clint, 107

emotion, 87–8
Evans, Iris, 183

evidence. *See* concrete evidence
expert advice, 75, 190. *See also* impersonal-authorization legitimation

Fairclough, Norman, 10
fairness, 127–30
Fournier, Jean-Marc, 139
framing, 10

Gaudet, Wayne, 90
Georgetti, Ken, 140
government: attitude toward collective bargaining, 133–9; blindsided stage of mythopoesis, 156–8, 196; and context of instrumental rationalization, 104–8; cost of intervention in labour conflicts, 43, 54; golden age stage of mythopoesis, 164–7; "The Hero's Journey" as framework story of, 152–4, 177, 188–9; impersonal authorization by, 189–90; initiation stage of mythopoesis, 158–64; instrumental rationalization by, 94, 99, 100–4; leadership by, 125–33; need of legitimacy, 12; overview of legitimation strategies, 95–6; pattern of intervention in industrial relations, 20–6; public authorization by, 76–81, 84–6, 89–92, 190; refusal to intervene in strikes, 182–4; theoretical rationalization by, 113–16; thoughts on use of mythopoesis, 196, 197–8; unilateral actions by, 3–4; use of narrative by, 148–9, 178; working in the public interest, 11, 76–81, 84–6, 120–5, 147–8. *See also* specific provincial governments and specific strikes
Grenier, Ed, 182

Hamm, John: on being blindsided by previous government, 157; election of, 60; and instrumental rationalization, 102; leadership of, 127; part in strike negotiations, 80, 89–90; on standing up to economic challenges, 159–60; on taking the right path, 162; view of collective bargaining, 136–7
Hansen, Colin: on being blindsided by previous government, 132–3, 157; on contracting out health jobs, 38, 63; on deficit numbers, 41; representing the public will, 79–80
"The Hero's Journey" (Campbell), 152–4, 177, 188–9
Horner, Doug, 33

impersonal-authorization legitimation, 74–5, 189–90
instrumental-rationalization legitimation: combined with theoretical rationalization, 192; context of government, 104–8; context of union, 111–13, 188; defined, 94; described, 99–100, 147; government examples of, 100–4; importance of context to, 192; and moralization, 99–100, 103–4, 193–4; thoughts about, 192–3; union examples of, 99–100, 108–10
integrity, 125–7
interest groups, unions as, 81, 83, 110, 112

Jérôme-Forget, Monique: as focus of union anger, 139; on future benefits of sacrifice, 165–6; restructuring public service, 68, 69; shows

218 Index

leadership, 103, 124; on state of finances, 161
Jessome, Joan: on government's callousness, 72–3, 146, 170, 172; on union fight to save democracy, 109, 111, 144–5, 174
Johnson, Byron, 37

Klein, Ralph: acting on behalf of people, 80, 92; and back-to-work legislation, 68; cuts to teachers, 65; election of, 64; as storyteller, 88. *See also* Alberta, government of

Lacharite, Jean, 144
Lambert, Susan, 41–2
leadership, 77, 125–133, 191
Leblanc, Neil, 60
legitimacy, 12–13, 19
legitimation strategies, 13–19, 95–8. *See also* specific legitimation strategies
Liepert, Ron, 183
Longmoore, Rosalee, 81–2, 108, 139, 170
Lord, Bernard: acting on behalf of people, 121; on being blindsided by previous government, 74; election of, 56; leadership of, 126, 129, 131. *See also* New Brunswick, government of
Lucas, Wayne, 140, 171

McCraken, John, 109
McGuinty, Dalton, 36–7, 184, 185
mediation, 23, 41–2, 61, 66–7
metaphors, 85–6, 165
Milloy, John, 184
Moist, Pail, 142
moral evaluation, 15–16

moralization legitimation: and back-to-work legislation, 138–9, 194; described, 119–20, 147, 188; government use of, 120–5, 130; and instrumental rationalization, 99–100, 103–4, 193–4; relationship to rationalization, 15–16; and theoretical rationalization, 118; thoughts on, 193–5; unions' use of, 139–41
Muir, Jamie, 89, 102, 122, 130
Murray, Michael, 175
mythopoesis: described, 16–17, 96, 151–2, 188–9; government stage of being blindsided, 156–8, 196; government stage of initiation, 158–64; government stage of reaching golden age, 164–7; government use of "The Hero's Journey" as framework, 152–4, 177, 188–9; thoughts on, 196–8; union emphasis on power inequality, 169–72; union fight to save democracy, 172–4; union use of "The Princess in the Castle" framework, 154, 167–8, 177–8, 189; unions make government focus of their fight, 174–7

narratives/stories, 16–17, 18, 88, 148–9, 178. *See also* mythopoesis
Nelson, Patricia, 158
neo-liberalism: in Alberta, 30, 105, 115; of B.C. government, 30, 37–8, 115; described, 26–9; in Saskatchewan, 115–16
New Brunswick, government of, 55–7, 159–60
New Brunswick court stenographers' strike (2000), 182–3

New Brunswick hospital workers' strike (2001): back-to-work legislation, 45, 57, 121–2, 129, 135, 140, 171; collective bargaining in, 135, 140; government leadership during, 126, 129, 131–2; impersonal authorization in, 74; instrumental rationalization of, 110; moralization legitimation, 121–2; overview of, 45, 57; public authorization in, 82–3; theoretical rationalization in, 116; union reaction to government use of power, 171; union uses living-wage argument, 145–6

Newfoundland and Labrador, government of, 57–9, 165, 166

Newfoundland and Labrador public-service strike (2004): back-to-work legislation, 45, 60, 135–6, 140, 171; collective bargaining in, 135–6, 140; government leadership during, 127, 130, 132; impersonal authorization in, 74; and instrumental rationalization, 102, 104; moralization legitimation, 122–3; overview of, 46, 57, 59, 60; personal authorization in, 73; public authorization in, 78–9, 83–4, 85–6; third-party authorization in, 75; union view of government's use of power, 171

New Public Management (NPM), 26–9, 35–6

Nilson, John, 101, 106, 114, 121, 134

Nova Scotia, government of, 60

Nova Scotia public service strike (2001): back-to-work legislation, 47, 61, 89, 136–7, 146, 170–1, 172; collective bargaining in, 136–7; government leadership during, 127, 130; and instrumental rationalization, 102, 104, 109, 111; moralization legitimation in, 122; overview of, 47, 60–1; personal authorization in, 72–3; public authorization in, 80, 89–92; union use of lack-of-respect strategy, 146; union view of government's use of power, 170–1; union working for public interest in, 144–5, 174

Oberg, Lyle: and back-to-work legislation, 68, 107; as focus of union anger, 141, 176; justification of offer to teachers, 66, 74–5, 101, 105–6; leadership of, 129; and moralization legitimation, 123; and theoretical rationalization, 114–15, 117

Ontario, government of: recent economic record of, 33–7; uses back-to-work legislation, 23, 35, 184–5; and York University strike, 184–5

organizational discourse, 8–9

"Overcoming the Monster" (Booker), 152, 153–4

Parent, Réjean, 176

personal-authorization legitimation: combined with public authorization, 81, 87, 190–1; described, 187–8; examples of, 72–3; thoughts on, 189–90

persuasion, 11

Peters, Erik, 36

petitions, 90

Point, Steven L., 41

political discourse, 11

Prince Edward Island, government of: economic situation of, 179–81; legislates wage rollbacks, 181–2

"The Princess in the Castle," 154, 167–8, 189

privatization, 26–7, 31, 32, 62, 63, 146, 171. *See also* contracting out

public-authorization legitimation: combined with personal authorization, 81, 87, 190–1; counteracting, 88–92; described, 188; effectiveness of, 87–8; by government, 76–81; and public interest, 76–7; speaker is one of the group, 83–7; thoughts on, 190–1; by union, 76–7, 81–4, 92, 190; weaknesses of, 92–3, 191

public interest: government speaking for, 11, 76–81, 84–6, 120–5, 147–8; and public- authorization legitimation, 191; unions speaking for, 76–7, 142–5, 147–8, 172–4

public opinion, 73

Puddister, Leo, 84, 140

Quebec, government of: on reaching prosperity, 165–6; restructuring of civil service, 68–9; scope of economic difficulty, 161

Quebec public-service strike (2005): back-to-work legislation, 24, 52–3, 68–9, 103, 137–8; collective bargaining during, 137–8; government leadership during, 128; instrumental rationalization in, 103, 109–10, 111–12; moralization legitimation in, 123–4; overview of, 52–3, 69–71; public authorization in, 77; union fight to stave off poverty, 173; union working for public interest in, 144

Rae, Bob, 34

rationalization legitimation: described, 14–15, 188, 191–2; relationship with moralization, 15–16. *See also* instrumental-rationalization legitimation; theoretical-rationalization legitimation

Redford, Alison, 33

Reid, Marion L., 180

respect for working people, 146–7

responsibility/prudence, 131–3

Roberge, Carole, 176

Romanow, Roy: acts on behalf of people, 77; and back-to-work legislation, 101, 102, 106; cuts provincial debt, 54; leadership of, 125–6, 127, 131; on taking the right path, 121, 162. *See also* Saskatchewan, government of

Russell, Ronald, 102, 122, 130

Ryan, Marlene, 110, 140, 145

Saskatchewan, government of: economic situation of, 54–5; on making tough choices, 160–1, 163; on reaching prosperity, 164–5, 166

Saskatchewan nurses' strike (1998): back-to-work legislation, 44, 55, 101, 102, 106, 115–16, 128, 134–5, 139, 170; collective bargaining in, 134–5, 139; government leadership during, 125–6, 127–8, 131; government working in public interest, 121; and instrumental rationalization, 101–2, 104, 106, 112; overview of, 44, 55; public authorization in, 77–8, 81–2, 84–5; theoretical rationalization in, 114; union rationale for defying back-to-work

legislation, 170; union working for public interest in, 142, 173
The Seven Basic Plots (Booker), 18
Simard, Louise, 113–14, 137
Sinclair, Jim, 116
social construction of reality, 9–10
Sorbara, Greg, 37
speaker is one of the group in public authorization, 83–7
staying quiet on parts of dispute, 122, 149–50, 154, 200
Steele, Graham, 91
Stelmach, Ed, 183
stewardship, 77, 79
storytelling, 16–17, 18, 88, 148–9, 178. *See also* mythopoesis
strikes, history of, 4–5. *See also* specific strikes
Sullivan, Loyola, 59, 74, 132
Supreme Court 2007 decision on collective bargaining, 22–3, 185

Tchorzewski, Ed, 54–5, 84–5, 160–1, 163, 166
Thatcher, Margaret, 28, 29
theoretical-rationalization legitimation: defined, 99, 188, 192; by government, 113–16; strengths and weaknesses of, 118; by unions, 116–18; used with instrumental, 192
third-party authorization, 75, 190. *See also* impersonal-authorization legitimation
The Thirty Six Dramatic Situations (Polti), 18
Tweddell, Brent, 109, 173

unions: context of instrumental rationalization by, 111–13, 188, 192; emphasis on power inequality with government, 169–72; fight against B.C. government, 38–42; fight against Ontario government, 34–5; fight to save democracy, 73, 109, 111, 145, 172–4; instrumental rationalization by, 94, 99–100, 108–10; making government focus of their fight, 174–7; moralization legitimation by, 139–41; need of legitimacy, 12–13; overview of legitimation strategies, 97–8; pattern of government intervention in industrial relations, 20–6; The "Princess in the Castle" as framework story of, 154, 167–8, 177–8, 189; public authorization by, 76–7, 81–4, 92, 190; reaction to Klein Revolution, 31, 32; reaction to wage rollbacks in P.E.I. in 1994, 181–2; speaking for public interest, 76–7, 142–5, 147–8, 172–4; theoretical rationalization by, 116–18; thoughts on use of mythopoesis by, 197–8; unilateral actions against, 3–4; use of lack-of-respect strategy, 146–7; use of low wages as strike strategy, 109–10, 112, 144, 145–6; use of narrative by, 149; view of collective bargaining, 66, 139–41. *See also* specific strikes

values: in legitimation strategy, 15, 16; and moralization legitimation, 119–20; of public interest, 120–5; and theoretical rationalization, 115
victimization, 172

Wachowich, Allan, 67
wage-rollback legislation in P.E.I., 181–2

wages as focus of union demands, 109–10, 112, 144, 145–6
Walkerton tragedy, 36
White, Bob, 117–18
Williams, Danny: on being blindsided by previous government, 157; on dire financial situation, 58–9, 75, 161; and instrumental rationalization, 102; leadership of, 127, 130, 132, 162; and moralization legitimation, 122–3; on reaching prosperity, 165, 166; union view of, 171; use of narrative by, 73, 85–6, 148; view of collective bargaining, 135–6. *See also* Newfoundland and Labrador, government of
Wilson, David, 90
Wodak, Ruth, 10

York University strike (2008), 23, 184–5